Human Resource and Contract Management in the Public School

A Legal Perspective

Bernadette Marczely
David W. Marczely

A SCARECROWEDUCATION BOOK

The Scarecrow Press, Inc.
Lanham, Maryland, and Oxford
2002

A SCARECROWEDUCATION BOOK

Published in the United States of America
by Scarecrow Press, Inc.
A Member of the Rowman & Littlefield Publishing Group
4720 Boston Way, Lanham, Maryland 20706
www.scarecroweducation.com

4 Pleydell Gardens, Folkestone
Kent CT20 2DN, England

British Library Cataloguing in Publication Information Available

Library of Congress Cataloging-in-Publication Data

Marczely, Bernadette.
  Human resource and contract management in the public school : a legal
perspective / Bernadette Marczely, David W. Marczely.
        p. cm.
"A Scarecrow education book."
Includes index.
  ISBN 0-8108-4379-X (cloth : alk. paper)—ISBN 0-8108-4378-1 (pbk. :
alk. paper)
  1. School employees—Legal status, laws, etc.—United States. 2.
Labor laws and legislation—United States. 3. School personnel
management—United States. I. Marczely, David W. (David William), 1943–
II. Title.
  KF3409.S3 M37 2002
  371.2'01'0973—dc21   2002003893

⊗™ The paper used in this publication meets the minimum requirements of
American National Standard for Information Sciences—Permanence of Paper for
Printed Library Materials, ANSI/NISO Z39.48-1992.
Manufactured in the United States of America.

Contents

Preface

Law has been defined as an ordinance of reason for the common good, made by one who has care of the community (Summa Theologica, 1273). The human resource manager is, in many respects, the custodian of the educational community, caring for the minds, bodies, and souls of school employees. As such, the human resource manager is responsible for infusing that community with the ordinance of reason imposed on it by the laws, contracts, and policies that have been designed for the common good. This text explores all the many and complex facets of human resource management from the perspective of those laws designed to impose reason and order on these essential functions.

Chapter One

Human Resource and Contract Management in the Public School

DEFINING PUBLIC SCHOOL HUMAN RESOURCE MANAGEMENT

Human resource management is that unique part of public school administration dedicated to making the workplace comfortable and professionally nurturing for the adults employed in the school and district. Employees are every organization's most vital assets, each personally responsible for helping to bring some part of the organization's mission to fruition and thus maximizing potential for growth and achievement. This perspective, casting school employees at all levels as human resources, is particularly significant in today's public school environment in which the school's mission itself often eclipses employee value.

Organizational research, however, has never lost sight of how important it is to create conditions that will foster individual employee dedication, potential, and achievement. The Western Electric Company, beginning in 1924 and ending ten years later, conducted one of the earliest studies of motivation at work.[1] This study recorded the famous Hawthorne Effect showing a direct relationship between work productivity and such psychological factors as the expectations of others and being the focus of attention. While the intent of the experiment was to measure productivity as light intensity was increased, it became obvious that changing the lightbulbs in this experiment resulted in some increase in worker output regardless of the level of illumination provided. Workers were responding to the attention they were receiving and to their perception of what they were expected to do. Later research continued to document the effect of psychological factors on workplace productivity. Subsequent Western Electric studies showed that the women participating in these studies were made to feel they were an important part

1

of the company . . . , they had become participatory members of a congenial cohesive work group that shared feelings of affiliation, competence, and achievement . . . , and they worked harder and more efficiently than they had previously.[2]

Abraham Maslow, in a similar vein, suggested that the driving force that causes people to join an organization, stay in it, and work toward its goals is actually a *hierarchy of real and psychological needs.*[3] Maslow's hierarchy of needs is illustrated in figure 1.1 and provides a virtual motivational road map.

Maslow's work is important to the field of Human Resources in that successful human resource management entails a focus on the key issues that must be addressed before employees can reach Maslow's promised *self-actualization.* Employees worried about basic job security issues, such as salary, equitable treatment, overall benefits, and a sense of belonging, are unlikely to strive for Maslow's higher-workplace objectives of autonomy and self-actualization. Maslow's research showed that only once a lower need is satisfied could another higher-order need arise to take its place as a motivator.[4] Thus, it becomes incumbent on programs of human resource management to address and to satisfy basic lower-order needs, such as safety, equity, and financial security, and thereby pave the way for pursuit of higher-order goals and objectives to be met.

Maslow's research was echoed in Herzberg's identification of hygiene factors that must be addressed as a prerequisite to true motivating factors.[5] Although hygiene factors such as salary, fringe benefits, supervision style, working conditions, workplace climate, and policies are not, in themselves, motivators leading to job satisfaction, they are a prerequisite to motivational factors that do lead to job satisfaction and achievement. Motivational factors ultimately leading to job satisfaction include such elements as achievement, recognition, responsibility, promotion, and personal growth. Hygiene factors that are prerequisites are important in that they have a preventive effect if they are managed well. That is, they create an environment in which achievement, recognition, responsibility, promotion, and personal growth are not blocked by trivial concerns about Herzberg's hygiene factors. Left unattended, however, hygiene factors can create so much workplace dissatisfaction that motivational factors will not be able to have their desired effect.

The central difference between Maslow and Herzberg is that Maslow thought of every need as a potential motivator, with the range of human needs in a prepotent hierarchical order, whereas Herzberg argued only the higher-order needs are truly motivating, with lower-order needs being simply maintenance factors.[6] Modern management theory has come to recognize that both sets of factors play a role in ultimate organizational effectiveness.

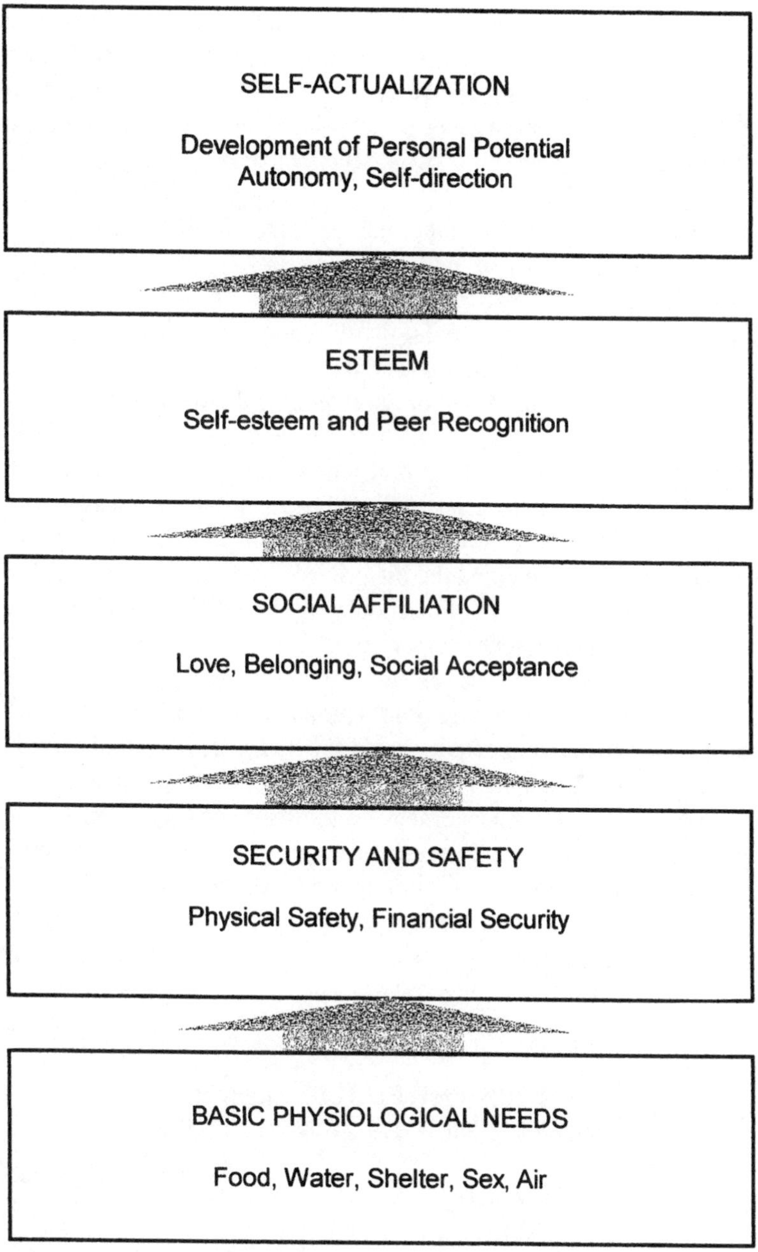

Figure 1.1   Maslow's Theory of Motivation and Hierarchy of Needs

Human resource management in public schools, however, has also retained the earmarks of an objective organizational bureaucracy defined by such theorists as Weber, who felt organizations should be impersonal, minimizing irrational personal and emotional factors in order to provide a workplace with minimum friction and confusion.[7] Weber's bureaucratic model had these elements:

1. A division of labor based on functional specialization
2. A well-defined hierarchy of authority
3. A system of rules covering the rights and duties of employees
4. A system of procedures for dealing with work situations
5. Impersonality of interpersonal relations
6. Selection and promotion based only on technical competence[8]

The labor contracts and district policies that frame human resource management in public schools have been negotiated to ensure the fairness, impartiality, and predictability proposed by Weber.

These theorists have provided the historical underpinnings of present human resource management in the public schools, and the definition of public school human resource management adopts some elements of each organizational model. Maslow's lower-order needs and Herzberg's hygiene factors have come to be equated with extrinsic job motivation made fair, impartial, and predictable through bureaucratic management. In contrast, Maslow's higher-order needs and Herzberg's motivators are cast as intrinsic catalysts for achievement, often at odds with bureaucratic management. In the final analysis, public school human resource management is the task of creating a work environment that is fair, impartial, and predictable by implementing the laws, regulations, policies, protocols, and contracts that govern the workplace, and in this context of equity and predictability, fostering the individual employee's opportunities for esteem, autonomy, and self-actualization.

WHO IS THE PUBLIC SCHOOL
HUMAN RESOURCE MANAGER?

The public school human resource manager is best identified by the many and varied functions linked to that position:

Record Keeping—The human resource manager creates a qualitative and quantitative history of all factors affecting human resource management in a given district, that is, enrollment, certification, class size, seniority, and retention.

Planning—The human resource manager uses past and present records, studies, and legal and contractual requirements to project personnel needs.

Job Description Development—The human resource manager studies district hiring needs and drafts documents describing those needs in terms of qualifications and job responsibilities.

Recruitment—The human resource manager advertises employment openings within a district with a view to securing the most qualified pool of candidates for each position.

Applicant Screening—The human resource manager reviews applications and written documents supporting each candidacy with a view to securing the most qualified pool of candidates for each advertised position.

Interviewing and Selection—The human resource manager coordinates the creation of an interview team to meet with and question qualified candidates regarding their ability to carry out the responsibilities of the advertised position.

Hiring—The human resource manager recommends qualified candidates to the school board for hiring, and once the board has voted to hire the candidate, the human resource manager presents the candidate with a contract describing employee rights and responsibilities, including salary placement.

Induction—The human resource manager provides the new employee with all the means, materials, and instructions needed to carry out the responsibilities of the given position as prescribed by law, contract, and board policy and to become acclimated to the school, district, and community.

Supervision—The human resource manager monitors employee performance and assists and assesses as provided for by law and contract.

Benefit Management—The human resource manager monitors the availability and use of benefits prescribed by law and contract, that is, life and health insurance, workers compensation, unemployment compensation, and retirement plans.

Negotiations—The human resource manager monitors existing contracts, providing data and information to assist the district's administration in developing future collectively bargained agreements for all employee groups.

Grievance Administration—The human resource manager represents the administration in carrying out the grievance process prescribed by the collectively bargained agreement or district policy.

Policy Development—The human resource manager advises the administration regarding the development of workplace policies and procedures that will enhance performance.

Policy Evaluation—The human resource manager provides quantitative and qualitative studies assessing the effectiveness of district employment policies and procedures.

Education—The human resource manager develops educational programs to keep line and staff employees informed regarding laws and regulations affecting the workplace.

In light of this extensive and varied list of responsibilities, the human resource manager obviously can be one or many different administrators within a school district. Superintendents, assistant superintendents, principals, assistant principals, and supervisors all perform one or more of the human resource functions listed. Some smaller districts, in fact, have no one central human resource manager, preferring to designate individual building administrators to manage human resources within their own schools. In larger school districts, it has become beneficial to have one central office administrator coordinate the human resources function for the district as a whole, ensuring consistent and predictable management.

Training and experience are pivotal to effective human resource management. Every administrator in charge of any aspect of human resource management must be schooled in the laws, regulations, policies, and procedures that provide the context for the decisions they will make and the actions they will take. No other aspect of public school administration demands a greater deference to organizational history, field experience, and job-specific training. The human resource manager should minimally have completed course work and training in *public school administration, school law, collective bargaining and contract management, school finance, and clinical supervision.* In addition, actual experience as a building-level administrator is essential for district-level human resource managers. Human resource management requires familiarity with the "big picture," that is, an understanding of how law, finance, collective bargaining, and policy interact in the school environment. Figures 1.2 and 1.3 give two examples of job descriptions for human resource managers/specialists.

The primary difference between these job descriptions is that figure 1.2 describes the human resource manager as a *line* position in which the manager has the power to make decisions. In contrast, figure 1.3 describes the human resource specialist as a *staff position*, an informational resource for building principals who will ultimately make decisions regarding human resource management in their buildings. In districts where building administrators will be responsible for human resource administration, the human resource educational and experience requirements noted should also be part of the administrative job description.

HUMAN RESOURCE MANAGER
SILVER LAKE BOARD OF EDUCATION

The applicant for this central office position will coordinate the following human resource functions districtwide:

Employee Record Management

Human Resource Planning

Recruitment & Screening

Interviewing & Selection

Hiring & Induction

Benefit & Salary Management

Negotiations & Grievance Administration

All Other Areas Affecting Human Resource Management |
| QUALIFICATIONS

A Master's Degree in School Administration

Five Years Successful Building-Level Administration Experience

Three Years Successful Teaching Experience

Familiarity with:

School Law
School Finance
Collective Bargaining |

Figure 1.2   Job Description: Human Resource Manager

HUMAN RESOURCE SPECIALIST
SILVER LAKE BOARD OF EDUCATION
The Human Resource Specialist will work directly with district principals assisting them in addressing their human resource needs. The Human Resource Specialist will provide principals with data and records needed to plan for building staffing and program management. The Human Resource Specialist will provide the logistical support district administrators need to make informed decisions regarding human resources, contract management, and negotiations.
QUALIFICATIONS
A Master's Degree in Educational Administration
3–5 Years Experience as a Building or Central Office Administrator
Good Communication Skills
Good Organizational Skills
Experience in Negotiations

Figure 1.3   Job Description: Human Resource Specialist

FACTORS INFLUENCING PUBLIC SCHOOL HUMAN RESOURCE MANAGEMENT

A wide range of national, state, and local factors directly affect human resource management (see figure 1.4). In addition to the obvious influence of federal and state laws regarding school and workplace behavior, human resource management must also be responsive to local goals and expectations. Local boards of education are the essence of representative government, and their policies and budgets reflect the will of their constituents. Every school district is unique. One district may struggle to have all students achieve the basics, while another may focus on broadening its advanced placement offerings. Districts with limited resources will limit the programs they offer, while well-funded districts will support programs that give students a wide range of academic options. Ultimately, district goals and resources will directly affect class size and staffing as well as local response to federal and state mandates for programs and procedures to ensure the education of all students. Human resource management does not occur in a vacuum, and, as illustrated, the factors affecting its implementation come from four sectors: federal, state, local, and contractual.

Federal Influences

In recent years Congress has passed a plethora of legislation aimed at protecting the rights of employees in the workplace. The Americans with Disabilities Act, the Fair Labor Standards Act, the Family and Medical Leave Act, Title VII, Title IX, and the Civil Rights Act of 1991 are just a few of Congress's more well-known efforts to legislate equity and fairness in the workplace. These laws, and the regulations subsequently developed to implement them, have a direct impact on public school human resource

FEDERAL	STATE	LOCAL	CONTRACTUAL
		▼	
▼	▼	Local School Boards	▼
Federal Laws & Regulations	State Laws & Regulations	▼	Wages
▼	▼	Local Funding	▼
Federal Court Decisions	State Board of Education	▼	Hours
▼	▼	Local Policies	▼
Political Trends	State Court Decisions	▼	Terms & Conditions of Employment
▼	▼	Local History	▼
Federal Funding	State Funding	▼	Negotiation History
▼	▼	Local Demographics	▼
		▼	
	HUMAN RESOURCE MANAGEMENT		

Figure 1.4   Factors Affecting Human Resource Management

management. Neither state laws nor collectively bargained agreements can overrule such federal protections. State laws and local contracts can give more protections in the workplace, but they cannot give fewer protections than those provided by the Constitution and federal laws, and the federal courts are a ready forum for enforcing the equity and fairness this federal legislation seeks to achieve. Thus, administrators charged with any aspect of human resource management must be familiar with the federal laws and regulations in place and with the legal precedents set by recent federal court decisions addressing these laws and regulations.

Federal politics will also influence human resource management in that political trends have a direct effect on public expectations. As views change regarding educational issues such as teacher testing and certification, class size, accountability, special education, curriculum, and program design, districts will change their own goals and expectations, thus requiring human resource managers to respond in kind. Public school human resource management is an area of school administration in the forefront with respect to the reactive response to political pressure.

Federal funding, although not the major method for financing public education, is also a prime consideration in human resource management. Many of the bills passed by Congress to protect employees tie federal funding to compliance with these laws. For example, public schools that violate the proscriptions of Title IX against gender-based discrimination risk losing any federal funding they presently enjoy. School districts cannot ignore the value of the federal contribution in times of lean budgets and increased fiscal demands.

State Influences

The federal Constitution contains no provision for public education. Thus, by virtue of the Tenth Amendment, which states that "the powers not delegated to the United States by the Constitution, nor prohibited by it to the States, are reserved to the States respectively, or to the people," responsibility for public education has come to rest with individual state governments. With this in mind, state constitutions, laws, regulations, and policies have an even more direct effect on every aspect of school administration. State laws, as noted, can give more protections to students and employees than federal laws, but never less, and to this end, many state laws have been drafted to simply reflect federal employment legislation, while others increase the protections afforded staff and students. State courts enforce state education and employment legislation and give injured employees a choice between judicial forums when asserting their rights. They may sue invoking the state constitution or specific state statutes, and state courts stand ready to rule in these suits based on state legislation, or they may sue in federal court if the issue addressed arises out of a federal law or a constitutional right.

The state boards of education also influence human resource management in that they are directly responsible for running a given state's schools. They promulgate the rules and regulations that will be used to implement state legislation addressing educational and employment issues. State boards of education help define, clarify, and implement the laws and procedures that schools must follow regarding education and employment practices by providing districts with the information and guidelines required for compliance.

Finally, state funding will be a primary influence in human resource management. The states provide the bulk of educational funding for public schools, and with control of the purse strings comes obvious control of the process. School districts cannot ignore state mandates with respect to any element of their programs if they hope to retain endorsement and funding for their programs.

Local Influences

The states have delegated their control of public education to individual school districts, and individual school boards exert the most direct and immediate effect on human resource management. School boards represent those living in their districts and, ideally, develop goals, objectives, and policies for local schools that reflect the wishes of the community. The school board, in its role as employer, is directly responsible for preparing and disseminating all local human resource policies and procedures. Boards are also held legally responsible for following the policies and procedures they adopt regarding human resource management. No teacher can be hired, disciplined, fired, or awarded tenure without official board action. In addition, local school boards have ultimate control over school budgets, and they participate, directly or indirectly, in collective bargaining where state law provides for it.

In most states, boards have broad discretion in managing public schools, and courts are not warranted to interfere with that discretion unless there is evidence of fraud, arbitrariness, unreasonableness, or other abuse of discretion.[9] Courts cannot substitute their own judgment for that of a board of education if the board adopts reasonable rules and regulations for the governance of employees, pupils, and others involved in the educational process. In the final analysis, local school boards exercise the most direct and significant influence on human resource management.

A school district's history will also influence the way the human resource function is conducted. Large urban districts cited for discriminatory practices are under pressure to make up for past wrongs with aggressive affirmative action policies. Their litigious histories and strong teachers' unions make them more sensitive to the letter of both employment and labor law. In contrast, suburban and rural districts may feel less pressure to avoid litigation and adopt policies and procedures that ignore the letter of the law as long as no one complains. Human resource administrators must get to know the communities they serve in order to put out potential fires where appropriate, but not create tempests in time-tested teapots.

Actually, all of a district's historical concerns will in one way or another come to bear on the human resource function. Districts with low academic achievement will seek better teachers, smaller classes, and ways to get more classroom time for failing students, while achieving districts may want to expand their extracurricular programs or increase class size. Districts that have been successfully sued for one reason or another will act on the memory of that experience for decades. Similarly, districts that have struggled to fund their programs can be expected to cut costs wherever possible and routinely question all expenditures. A school district, like an individual, inevitably comes with a past that must be explored to fully comprehend the district's needs and plan for its future.

Contractual Influences

The final, and often most important influence on human resource administration is the contract. Not all states have laws allowing teachers to collectively bargain, although other school employee groups may bargain. However, where employees do collectively bargain, the contract that is negotiated becomes a veritable bible for human resource management. In some states, in fact, the collectively bargained agreement overrides many state laws.[10] That is, parties to the agreement can forfeit rights given under state law in negotiations. The contract will address all issues related to wages, hours, terms, and conditions of employment and will establish a protocol for addressing future workplace issues through a grievance process.

LABOR LAW VERSUS EMPLOYMENT LAW

A unique difference exists between the legal status of employees who collectively bargain and those who do not. The workplace rights of employees who collectively bargain are determined primarily by the negotiated contract and the tenets of labor law. Labor law is that branch of law dealing with statutes and legal precedents affecting the employer–employee union relationship. Labor law concerns itself with the rights and responsibilities of employees covered by negotiated union contracts that define workers' rights and responsibilities for large groups of similarly situated employees.

Employment law, on the other hand, deals with the legal rights and responsibilities of employees who are not members of unions and who are not covered by negotiated contracts. The rights of these nonunionized employees emanate primarily from state and federal legislation. Employment law is that branch of law dealing with statutes and legal precedents affecting the rights and responsibilities of individuals in the workplace, the employer–employee relationship. These employees have no union to represent them and essentially rely on existing laws and related legal precedents to define their rights and responsibilities in the workplace.

In all human resource management forums there are both unionized and nonunionized employees. Therefore, human resource administrators must be familiar with both employment and labor law. The workplace rights of unionized employees will be defined primarily by the negotiated agreement. Their individual contracts, statutes, and legal precedents addressing the workplace issues of nonunionized individuals will define the workplace rights of the nonunionized employee. Unionized employees who feel their contract rights may have been breached can grieve for redress. Nonunionized employees who feel their rights may have been violated can sue in either state or federal court for redress. Later chapters will discuss both procedures in greater detail.

MINISTERIAL VERSUS DISCRETIONARY POWER

The individual states exercise all power and control over public education. But, as discussed earlier, they delegate the governance of public education to local boards of education. This delegated power and control takes two forms: ministerial and discretionary. Discretionary power exists where the law vests the exercise of judgment and discretion in a board of education or other officers in a school district and that exercise of judgment and discretion cannot be delegated to any other person or body.[11] In contrast to this discretionary power, a board of education or other officers in a school district may delegate the execution of law or contract, that is, ministerial power. Ministerial power merely refers to the delegated authority to follow existing laws and policies.

Administrators holding line positions have the authority to make discretionary decisions, and they will not be legally liable for those discretionary decisions, even if a court disagrees with them. On the other hand, administrators holding line positions who fail to properly exercise their ministerial power do risk legal liability. The courts will hold administrators legally liable for making employment decisions based on race, color, creed, gender, or national origin because Title VII clearly proscribes such behavior. However, the courts will not overrule the decision of a human resource administrator to hire one applicant over another based on impressions made during an interview. Human resource management involves the exercise of both discretionary and ministerial power and requires sensitivity to both aspects of the job. Human resource administrators are agents of the local board of education. Their discretionary decisions will ultimately be attributed to the board, and their failure to properly exercise the ministerial aspects of the job will make the local board of education vulnerable to lawsuits.

CONCLUSION

The thorough understanding of what human resource management entails and of the context in which it takes place is important. Human resource management is a complex function defined by both subjective and objective factors, individual concerns, and institutional goals. The human resource manager must relate to the big picture in order to be able to successfully address the unique singular aspects of that picture and the job. Human resource management is the vital underpinning of public school administration that creates an environment in which the educational mission can be pursued without the distraction of workplace concerns.

THEORY INTO PRACTICE

1. Using Maslow's Hierarchy of Needs as presented in figure 1.1, evaluate your own job satisfaction at each level, and discuss the validity of Maslow's theory of motivation.
2. Maslow maintained that every need, even those at the bottom of the hierarchy, serves as a motivator and that one cannot progress to the next level until lower-order needs are addressed. Herzberg, on the other hand, viewed lower-level needs as mere hygiene factors that maintain a work environment in which truly motivating higher-order needs can be pursued. Discuss the validity of each theory in light of your own personal experience.
3. Evaluate your own school's effectiveness in addressing Maslow's lower-order needs and Herzberg's hygiene factors.

4. Investigate how your school district handles the human resource functions identified in this chapter, that is, Record Keeping, Planning, Job Description Development, Recruitment, Applicant Screening, Interviewing and Selection, Hiring, Induction, Supervision, Benefit Management, Negotiations, Grievance Administration, Policy Development, Policy Evaluation, and Education. Who is responsible for each function?

5. Review the job description for the human resource manager in your school district. How does it compare with the job descriptions appearing in figures 1.1 and 1.3?

6. Does your state license human resource managers? If so what are the educational requirements for this license?

7. Interview a human resource manager and discuss the manager's perception of federal, state, and local influences on the functions of the position.

8. Describe the community in which your school is located with respect to housing costs, average income, business and industry, and educational goals.

9. Identify employees in your school who are not covered by collective bargaining agreements.

10. Discuss the perceived importance and effectiveness of collective bargaining for teachers in your district if collective bargaining is permitted under state law.

NOTES

1. See G. C. Homans, "The Western Electric Researches," in *Human Factors in Management,* ed. Schuyler Dean Hoslett (New York: Harper & Brothers Publishers, 1951), 211.

2. Homans, "The Western Electric Researches," 217.

3. A. A. Maslow, *Motivation and Personality,* 2d ed. (New York: Harper & Row Publishers, 1970), 35–46.

4. Maslow, *Motivation and Personality*, 46.

5. F. Herzberg, *Work and the Nature of Man* (Cleveland: World Publishing, 1966), 56.

6. R. G. Owens, *Organizational Behavior in Education* (Englewood Cliffs, N.J.: Prentice Hall, 1991), 118.

7. J. P. Mayer, *Max Weber and German Politics* (London: Faber & Faber, 1943), 128.

8. R. H. Hall, "The Concept of Bureaucracy: An Empirical Assessment," *The American Journal of Sociology* 69, no. 1 (July 1963): 33.

9. *See, e.g.,* OHIO REVISED CODE § 3313.47, and Russell v. Gallia County Local Bd. of Educ., 80 Ohio App. 3d 797, 610 N.E.2d 1130 (1992) (board may eliminate high

school busing for financial reasons); Holroyd v. Eibling, 116 Ohio App. 440, 188 N.E.2d 797 (1962) (rule prohibiting social clubs).

10. *See, e.g.,* OHIO REVISED CODE ANN. § 4117.10(A), State Dep't. of Admin. v. Pub. Employees Relation Bd., 894 P.2d 777 (Kan. 1995) (holding that contract takes precedence over conflicting civil service regulations).

11. *See, e.g.,* 15 Ohio Jur. 3d, Civil Servants § 230 (Lawyers' Coop. 2000).

Chapter Two

Collective Bargaining

Since negotiated agreements determine the wages, hours, and terms and conditions of most public school employees, it is essential that administrators responsible for any part of the human resources function understand how these agreements are developed and implemented. Of the factors influencing human resource management, negotiated contracts, where they exist, exercise the most direct and powerful impact on human resource management, serving as the legal parameters for day-to-day decisions regarding employee rights and responsibilities. Also important is that human resource managers in states that do not officially endorse collective bargaining, or in states that outright prohibit public sector bargaining, understand the political, economic, and philosophical motivations for the state's position on bargaining and the effect that decision has on human resource management and employee relations.

Collective bargaining, or negotiations, is a process by which groups of employees with similar backgrounds, assignments, and needs organize for the purpose of meeting with their employers and bargaining, as a group, for discussion of wages, hours, and terms and conditions of employment. The concept of negotiations is premised on the belief that there is strength in numbers, that is, that employee groups have more power to compel employers to hear and respond to their concerns than an individual employee would have. Where individual employees would be virtually powerless to exert any demonstrative pressure, an employee group's dissatisfaction has the potential for jeopardizing the success of any business venture dependent on their loyalty and cooperation.

THE HISTORICAL PERSPECTIVE

The right to collectively bargain did not come easily in either the private or the public sector. Employees who work for local, state, or federal government or for agencies funded by the government are public sector employees, while employees who work for businesses or industries that are not funded by the government are private sector employees. Neither private sector nor public sector employers, however, were eager to share decision-making control of their enterprises with employee groups. The private sector labor movement began in the middle of the nineteenth century, but it was not until the passage of the National Labor Relations Act (NLRA), also known as the Wagner Act, in 1935, that private sector employees won the right to join unions and collectively bargain.[1] Public sector collective bargaining rights came even later. President Kennedy's Executive Order 10988 in 1962 opened the door to granting federal employees the right to join labor unions and bargain collectively. In 1968, President Nixon's Executive Order 11491 superseded Kennedy's efforts and established actual bargaining procedures and protocols that mirrored those found in the private sector.

However, while federal employees were granted the right to collectively bargain by these executive orders, state and local government employees, including teachers, were not. Although the union movement in education began as early as 1857,[2] teachers did not collectively bargain until the 1940s when a Norwalk, Connecticut, teachers' association achieved formal recognition as a bargaining agent, and a Pawtucket, Rhode Island, teachers' union used a strike to force the board of education to negotiate proposed salary increases.[3] In 1959, Wisconsin became the first state to actually pass a law mandating compulsory collective bargaining for state public employees.[4] Connecticut, Massachusetts, and Michigan in 1965 and Rhode Island in 1966 were the first states to follow Wisconsin's lead in legislating mandatory compulsory collective bargaining for state public employees.[5]

STATE LAWS AND COLLECTIVE BARGAINING

Not all states have passed laws allowing public sector collective bargaining. Presently, the District of Columbia and thirty-six states have laws allowing and governing collective bargaining for at least some public employees.[6] While these thirty-seven jurisdictions have bargaining for some public sector employees, two, Kentucky and Wyoming, do not include teachers; thus, only the District of Columbia and thirty-four states have statutorily authorized collective bargaining for teachers.[7] Basically, states have the option of granting public employees the right to bargain, and they have the added option of deciding to exclude specific groups of public employees, such as teachers and administrators, from the right to collectively bargain.

By the mid-1980s, 86 percent of the nation's public school teachers did collectively bargain with almost two million teachers belonging to either the National Education Association or the American Federation of Teachers, the two major teachers' unions.[8]

As noted, private sector collective bargaining was mandated at the federal level by the NLRA of 1935, however, this law and the decisions of its administrative arm, the National Labor Relations Board, do not apply to public sector employees such as teachers.[9] The collective bargaining rights of public sector state employees, including teachers, are determined solely by state laws, state agencies, and state courts, and as figures 2.1, 2.2, and 2.3 indicate, those rights can and do vary from state to state. Nevertheless, states that have legislated collective bargaining rights for their public employees have based their laws on the NLRA, requiring bargaining for wages, hours, and other terms and conditions of employment,[10] and mirroring procedures prescribed by the NLRA for the private sector.

As figure 2.1 indicates, Georgia, Missouri, North Carolina, Texas, and Virginia specifically prohibit collective bargaining for teachers. States that prohibit collective bargaining for teachers view the prospect of public sector collective bargaining, particularly with teachers, as an unbalanced power struggle between the bargaining unit and the public sector employer. These states cite three significant differences between the private and public sectors that support legislation prohibiting public sector collective bargaining:

1. The public sector is politically and economically different from the private sector.
2. There is a direct public interest in public sector collective bargaining.
3. The means for funding public and private sector agreements differs notably.[11]

Unlike private sector businesses, public sector employment is not subject to market forces. Market pressures that would normally curb extravagant bargaining settlements are absent in the public sector. Private sector employers must take stands in negotiations that will allow them to remain competitive and in business. Public sector employers, with school districts as a case in point, have no competition. They are a virtual monopoly holding the public hostage to financing their decisions. When a labor dispute or protracted negotiation jeopardizes delivery of government services, the government employer, such as a school district, can either refuse to deliver their services to the public, possibly creating pressure to settle with the union, or concede to the union's demands.[12] In either case, states prohibiting collective bargaining for teachers believe that

State	Citations
Alaska	ALASKA STAT. § 23.40.070 *et seq.*
California	CAL. GOV'T CODE ANN. § 3500 *et seq.*
Connecticut	CONN. GEN. STAT. § 10-153a *et seq.*
Delaware	DEL. CODE ANN. tit. 14 § 4001 *et seq.*
District of Columbia	D.C. CODE ANN. § 618
Florida	FLA. STAT. ANN. § 447.201 *et seq.*
Hawaii	HAW. REV. STAT. § 89
Idaho	IDAHO CODE § 33-1271 *et seq.*
Illinois	115 ILL. COMP. STAT. ANN. ¶ 5
Indiana	IND. CODE ANN. § 20-7.5 *et seq.*
Iowa	IOWA CODE ANN. § 20
Kansas	KAN. STAT. ANN. § 72.5413 *et seq.*
Maine	ME. REV. STAT. ANN. tit. 26 § 961
Maryland	MD. EDUC. CODE ANN. § 6-401 *et seq.*
Massachusetts	MASS. GEN. LAWS. ANN. ch. 150E
Michigan	MICH. COMP. LAWS ANN. § 423
Minnesota	MINN. STAT. § 179A
Montana	MONT. CODE ANN. § 39-31
Nebraska	NEB. REV. STAT. § 81-1373
Nevada	NEV. REV. STAT. ANN. § 288.150
New Hampshire	N.H. REV. STAT. ANN. § 273-A
New Jersey	N.J. STAT. ANN. § 34:13A
New York	N.Y. CIV. SERV. LAW § 200
North Dakota	N.D. CENT. CODE § 15-38.1
Ohio	OHIO REV. CODE ANN. § 4117
Oklahoma	OKLA. STAT. ANN. tit. 70 § 509
Oregon	OR. REV. STAT. § 243 *et seq.*
Pennsylvania	PA. STAT. ANN. tit. 23 § 1101
Rhode Island	R.I. GEN. LAWS § 28-9.3
South Dakota	S.D. CODIFIED LAWS § 3-18
Tennessee	TENN. CODE ANN. § 49-5-601 *et seq.*
Vermont	VT. STAT. ANN. tit. 16 § 1981 *et seq.*
Washington	WASH. REV. CODE ANN. § 41.59
Wisconsin	WIS. STAT. ANN. § 111.70 *et seq.*

Figure 2.1   States with Collective Bargaining Law Including Teachers

State	Citations
Georgia	GA. CODE ANN. § 20-2-989.10
Missouri	MO. REV. STAT. § 105.510
North Carolina	N.C. GEN. STAT. § 95-98
Texas	TEX. GOV'T CODE ANN. § 617.002
Virginia	VA. CODE ANN. § 40.1-57.2

Figure 2.2   States Prohibiting Collective Bargaining for Teachers

Alabama	Mississippi
Arizona	New Mexico
Arkansas	South Carolina
Colorado	Utah
Kentucky	West Virginia
Louisiana	Wyoming

Figure 2.3   States Neither Prohibiting nor Authorizing Collective Bargaining for Teachers

allowing collective bargaining amounts to an illegal delegation of discretionary governing power to the teachers' union. The union, a private interest group, becomes a participant in the school board's legislative process, a public activity,[13] in that the end effect of collective bargaining requires the public served to fund the contract developed through taxation and essentially gives the union an element of control over the fiscal resources of a community.

If states neither require nor forbid bargaining for teachers, school boards are at liberty to bargain collectively or individually with employees, and there are no legislated procedures and timelines to guide the process. On the other hand, if states have collective bargaining laws for public employees, including teachers, in place, school boards and teachers' unions are required to comply with the laws' procedures. While specific regulations and timelines may vary from state to state, most collective bargaining laws share similar procedural formats, prescriptions, and definitions. For example, most collective bargaining laws discuss:

1. Management rights and responsibilities
2. Employee rights and responsibilities
3. Bargaining unit definition
4. Scope of bargaining
5. The bargaining process and timelines
6. Impasse procedures
7. Unfair labor practices
8. Grievance procedures
9. Agency oversight, penalties, and enforcement procedures

States with public sector collective bargaining laws have usually authorized the development of labor relation boards to oversee and monitor the implementation of these laws. These employment relations boards, like the laws themselves, mirror the structure and procedures of the National Labor Relations Board,[14] adjudicating disputes between public employers and employees such as teachers and school boards, mayors and police unions, and bus drivers and transit authorities. In an effort to settle employment disputes without resorting to formal litigation, these labor relations boards have been given great quasi-judicial power at the state level, with their decisions rarely being overturned by the state courts that help them to enforce their judgments and penalties.

State employment relations boards assist and monitor the implementation of the state's collective bargaining law by

1. determining bargaining units,
2. conducting recognition elections,

3. investigating unfair labor practices,
4. monitoring collective bargaining progress,
5. assigning mediators, fact finders, and arbitrators as needed.

Some boards also adopt an educational program; this provides training for both sides of the bargaining table as well as for prospective mediators, fact finders, and arbitrators. In summary, for all intents and purposes, the state employment relations boards created in the image and likeness of the National Labor Relations Board are the final arbiters in matters regarding the implementation of a given state's public sector collective bargaining law. Their purpose is to maintain labor peace in the public sector and to keep public sector employers and employees out of the courtroom.

DETERMINING THE BARGAINING UNIT

The size and makeup of any union obviously will play a significant role in determining the balance of power in collective bargaining. Collective bargaining can be analyzed in terms of the power relationship that exists between management and the union or unions with which management must deal under contract or legal duty.[15] All-inclusive unions could literally hold management hostage to their demands, while too many small splinter groups could exhaust management's time and resources in the very process of collective bargaining. Thus, the question of defining the bargaining unit becomes very important. State employment relations boards decide appropriate unit membership, and their decisions are final and unappealable.[16] Workers in a given collective bargaining unit should hold positions that have comparable wages, hours, and other working conditions and should share an overall community of interests. In determining community of interests in the private sector, the National Labor Relations Board considered such facts as differences in employee benefits, separate supervision, degree of dissimilar qualifications, training, skills, differences in job functions, time away from employment, frequency of contact with other employees, integration of work functions, and collective bargaining history.[17] Bearing in mind that public sector collective bargaining laws and the boards that enforce them take their cues from the NLRA and the National Labor Relations Board, it is informative to note that a Michigan Court, for example, determined that a public university's bargaining unit could not include lecturers, academic advisors, counselors, and residence hall advisors, since these employees were auxiliary to actual classroom teaching and did not share a policy-making function.[18] Also, an Illinois appellate court upheld the Illinois

Educational Labor Relations Board's ruling that Chicago assistant principals without full-time teaching duties are managerial employees ineligible for membership in the teachers' union.[19]

Those seeking to unionize will be required to identify the groups of employees they hope to represent and to prove by factual statistics that these groups do indeed share a community of interests. Evidence of sharing a community of interests is one factual method that employment relation boards and courts will use to ultimately determine and justify the makeup of the bargaining units they recognize.

DETERMINING THE BARGAINING AGENT

Once the bargaining unit is defined, the union seeking representation rights will request recognition. However, recognition is usually based on a show of support from the prospective membership identified. Members of the proposed unit must be polled to determine which union, if any, they want to represent their interests in the collective bargaining process. Public employers, when confronted with a union's request for recognition, may request a formal election in order to determine the actual number of proposed bargaining unit members favoring union representation, or the employer may simply post notice of the union's request for recognition giving prospective members and rival factions an opportunity to challenge the organizational effort. If a majority of members in the proposed bargaining unit decline representation, the union's bid to collectively bargain will fail. The union may also encounter competition from a rival union forcing an election that is no longer a sure thing under the percentages set by state law for recognition.

Recognition elections essentially give prospective bargaining unit members the opportunity to choose between rival organizations or to choose no union at all to represent them. However, should a majority select a given union to represent them in collective bargaining, the employer will be bound under state law to bargain all matters regarding wages, hours, and terms and conditions of employment with the chosen representative. The union will represent all members of a given bargaining unit, and the public employer will be obliged to deal exclusively with the recognized union.

Exclusivity

The concept of exclusivity was developed in the interest of labor peace. Once a union has been officially recognized as representing an employee group, employers such as school districts must deal solely with the designated union on all matters affecting wages, hours, and terms and conditions of employment. The Supreme Court has concluded that a law requiring employers to "meet and confer" only with the designated bargaining representative did not violate other employees' speech or associational rights since these sessions were not public forums, and the Constitution does not grant to members of the general public a right to be heard by public bodies making decisions of policy.[20] However, the concept of exclusivity is often more challenging in practice than it is in theory as evidenced by the legal cases dealing with the doctrine.

The somewhat ambiguous catchall "terms and conditions of employment" can mask a wide range of exclusivity pitfalls for even the most vigilant employer or human resource manager. While it may seem obvious that the concept of exclusivity precludes discussion of wages, hours, and terms and conditions of employment with a rival union, the concept also precludes such discussion with individual employees as well. Discussing employment matters with individuals is considered "direct dealing," a violation of exclusivity and a recognized unfair labor practice that is sure to draw the scrutiny of the state's employment relations board.

Nevertheless, the temptation to direct deal is always present for the school administrator, and the following examples illustrate how easy it is to fall into the trap of direct dealing. There is a need for a teacher to supervise the after-school detention room, and an easy solution to the problem appears to be allowing a willing teacher to start school an hour later in return for the extra hour spent supervising detention at the end of the day [an obvious change in contractual hours]. The contract contains a clause limiting class size to twenty-five students, and a budget-conscious administrator urges a teacher to accept a twenty-sixth student without grieving [a direct violation of the class-size clause]. The contract assures every teacher a duty-free lunch period for thirty minutes, but the administration asks a teacher who does not eat lunch to help supervise the cafeteria [a direct violation of the contractual assurance of a duty-free lunch]. Each of these examples illustrates how easy it is to let immediate administrative need become an excuse for ignoring the contract and the duty to bargain only with the union on terms and conditions of employment.

Note that even when individual teachers may be willing to strike deals or honor the wishes of the administration, any union worth its weight will object to such direct dealing because this practice violates the contract and the concept of exclusive collective bargaining. To allow management to deal directly with individuals is to defeat the purpose of collective bargaining and to replace the term "collective" with the term "individual." Neither individuals nor rival groups can bargain with management throughout the life of the contract. As noted, the overriding reason for honoring exclusivity is the preservation of labor peace. Unions rivaling for control, or individuals seeking to override group contracts, will inevitably defeat the purpose of collective bargaining. They will create separate agreements ignoring collective needs.

Exclusivity, however, relates only to the act of negotiating. Individual employees and employee groups retain the right to speak out on issues of public concern and to criticize the contract or the way in which the recognized union represents them. The contract and the way in which a union functions are matters of public concern, and teachers are not "compelled to relinquish the First Amendment rights they would otherwise enjoy as citizens to comment on matters of public concern in connection with the operation of the public schools in which they work."[21] That is, teachers and teacher groups, outside of officially recognized bargaining units, retain the right to voice their individual or collective opinions regarding issues of public concern affecting public education including collective bargaining. While school administrators and human relations managers are prohibited from negotiating wages, hours, and terms and conditions of employment with individuals or groups not recognized as the official bargaining agent, neither they nor the designated union have the right or authority to silence individual or collective opinion on matters of public concern that may impinge on bargaining. The wise human resource administrator silences none, but negotiates with one.

At the same time, note that while individuals and rival groups retain their free speech rights, the concept of exclusivity can limit their channels of communication regarding labor issues. Although the recognized union may have access to the school's mailboxes, as long as other channels of communication are available, school districts are not constitutionally obligated to grant rival unions access to school mailboxes because a school's internal mail system is not a public forum.[22] A school can, however, create a public forum by allowing the general public and all employee organizations to use its mailboxes. The Supreme Court has said that schools may reserve a forum for its intended purposes, communicative or otherwise, as long as the regulation on speech is reasonable and not an effort to suppress expression merely because public officials oppose the speaker's view.[23] Once a public forum is created, the school will then have to justify its reasons for allowing one group to use the forum while at the same time denying access to another.

Agency Shop

Union membership and the fiscal support of union goals and objectives are yet another central concern in human resource management and collective bargaining. It is against the law to require employers to hire only union members. This practice, referred to as a *closed shop* is forbidden in the private sector by both the NLRA and the Taft-Hartley Amendments. In the private sector some private employers do sometimes agree to maintain *union shops,* that is, to require employees to join the designated union *after* they are employed. However, in the public sector, *agency shop* or *fair share* agreements prevail.[24] Agency shop and fair share agreements are union security provisions found in public sector negotiations requiring all members of a given bargaining unit to fiscally support the union's efforts on their behalf and pay a fee reflecting the employee's fair share of the expenses incurred. An agency shop clause in a contract requires every employee to pay the union an amount equal to the union's customary initiation fee and monthly dues, but it does not require any employee to become a formal member of the union, to take any oath of obligation, or to observe the internal rules and regulations of the union.[25] Teachers, for example, can choose not to join the union that represents them, but if there is an agency shop or fair share clause in the district's contract with the union, nonmembers can nevertheless be required to pay the designated fair share fee. Such a mandatory payment of fair share fees was upheld by the Supreme Court in *Abood v. Detroit Board of Education*, a 1977 case eliminating free riders and rejecting free speech and association claims presented by teachers objecting to fair share assessments.[26] The Court reasoned that even employees who choose not to belong to the recognized union must pay their fair share of the funds needed to subsidize union representation including the costs of bargaining and contract administration. However, an employee who does not officially join a union cannot be forced to contribute support for an ideological cause the employee opposes.[27] Employees who are not members of the union can request a rebate of the portion of their fair share fees used to advance political activities or causes having no direct bearing on collective bargaining or contract administration. Expenditures for union publications, conventions, strike preparations, and chargeable state and national affiliation assessments have been upheld by the Supreme Court, while lobbying, public relations campaigns, and other political efforts having no direct bearing on negotiations or contract management have not been upheld.[28] Teachers, for example, may object to union financial support for a political candidate whose views do not accord with their own. In order to protect nonmember constitutional rights in this regard, unions must provide an adequate explanation of the basis for the fee charged, a reasonably prompt opportunity to challenge the amount of the fee before an impartial decision maker, and an escrow for the amounts reasonably in dispute while such challenges are pending.[29] In other words, unions must provide enough information to allow nonmembers to make informed decisions regarding the propriety of the union's fee.[30] Unions must also develop procedures for expediently and fairly address-ing requests for rebates by nonmembers.

Employees may also object to fair share payments to unions on religious grounds. Any public employee who is a member of, and adheres to estab-lished and traditional tenets or teachings of, a bona fide religion or religious body that has historically held conscientious objections to joining or finan-cially supporting an employee organization, and which is exempt from taxa-tion under the provisions of the Internal Revenue Code, can claim this ex-emption.[31] The burden of proof for qualifying for this exemption rests with the objecting employee, and even if the employee succeeds in showing ac-tive membership in a recognized religious body that forbids union member-ship and financial support, the employee is nevertheless responsible for do-nating an amount equal to the fair share fee to a mutually agreed upon nonreligious charity. In states where this exemption exists, it is not an easy one to claim. If it were an easy option, or one in which the fair share fee could simply be avoided entirely, it could easily undercut union strength and the purpose of collective bargaining legislation.

Union membership and financial strength have had an enormous impact on public education. Since 1961, National Education Association membership has increased from 766,000 to 2.2 million, and American Federation of Teachers membership has grown from 70,821 in 1961 to 947,000 in 1997.[32] In a survey of six hundred superintendents and professors conducted by the Horace Mann League in 1996, the power of teacher and other school employee unions was cited among the top eleven challenges facing public schools.[33] That power most directly affects all aspects of human resource management.

BARGAINING UNIT MEMBER
RIGHTS AND RESPONSIBILITIES

All members of a given bargaining unit, whether they join the union or not, have the right to be represented by the union in collective bargaining and all matters pertaining to contract administration. Bargaining unit members who choose not to belong to the union and pay only the fair share fee required by the contract are entitled to the same level of representation as union members pay-ing for full participation in union activities. In addition, bargaining unit mem-bers who pay no fair share fee because the contract does not have an agency shop clause are also entitled to the same level of union representation as union members paying for full participation in union activities. Unions cannot pick and choose which bargaining unit members they will represent. Once officially designated the bargaining unit representative, the union must represent *all* members recognized by a community of interests as part of the bargaining unit.

The individual employee's right to union representation becomes particularly significant when the employee is faced with disciplinary action or management behavior that appears to breach the contract, affecting the individual employee's working conditions. The courts have based their support for representational exclusivity on the union's legitimate interest in presenting a united front and in not seeing its strength dissipated and its stature denigrated by subgroups within the unit separately pursuing what they see as separate interests.[34] Thus, it becomes important that the union be aware of all issues that have an impact on contract administration, including those affecting only individual employees. Section 7 of the NLRA guarantees an employee's right to the presence of a union representative at an investigatory interview in which the risk of discipline exists.[35] The National Labor Relations Board has found that it is a serious violation of the employee's individual right to engage in concerted activity by seeking the assistance of the statutory representative if the employer denies the employee's request for representation and compels the employee to appear unassisted at an interview that may put job security in jeopardy.[36] Section 7 of the NLRA, on which public sector collective bargaining laws are patterned, guarantees the right of employees to act in concert for mutual aid and protection. The denial of this right to representation has a reasonable tendency to interfere with, restrain, and coerce employees in violation of § 8(a)(1) of the NLRA.[37] The union representative safeguards not only the particular employee's interest but also the interests of the entire bargaining unit by exercising vigilance to make certain that the employer does not initiate or continue a practice of imposing punishment unjustly.[38] A single employee confronted by an employer investigating whether certain conduct deserves discipline may be too fearful or inarticulate to relate accurately the incident being investigated or too ignorant to raise extenuating factors.[39] The union representative is present to assist the employee and may attempt to clarify the facts or suggest other employees who may have knowledge of them.[40]

While individual bargaining unit members have the right to be represented by the union in all situations affecting contract administration or job security, the question arises as to whether they *must* be represented, that is, Does the union have an absolute right to be present? The National Labor Relations Board has maintained that the right to union representation arises only in situations in which the employee requests representation. In other words, the employee may forgo this guaranteed right and, if preferred, participate in an interview unaccompanied by a union representative.[41] Collective bargaining agreements and the union representation they entail represent compromise between the rights of the individual employee and the rights of the group, and the complete satisfaction of all who are represented is hardly to be expected.[42] The NLRA provides that an individual employee or group of employees shall have the right at any time to present grievances to their employer and to have such grievances adjusted, without the intervention of the bargaining representative, as long as the adjustment is not inconsistent with the terms of a collective bargaining contract or agreement then in effect, and if the bargaining representative has been given the opportunity to be present.[43] Therefore, it is incumbent on human resource managers to make individual employees aware of their right to union representation at conferences where contract or job security is at issue and to encourage union representation in order to avoid later misunderstandings and charges of direct dealing from the excluded union.

Employees who join the union will also have the right to fully participate in the union's decision-making processes. They will vote on the adoption or rejection of union initiatives, contract proposals, and on the decision to strike. They will also have the opportunity to monitor and perhaps participate in the selection of the union's negotiating team and in the way the union allots its funding. Nonmembers, even those compelled to pay fair share fees, will not have a direct say in the way the union conducts its business.

All employees, members and nonmembers alike, however, will be responsible for complying with the negotiated contract. They will have a right to the wages and benefits set forth in the agreement, but they will also be responsible for adhering to the hours and terms and conditions of employment set forth in the agreement. Management can reprimand or discipline employees who do not fulfill their contractual responsibilities. On the other hand, employees may grieve management actions that appear to violate the contract. Every negotiated contract must contain a grievance procedure for dealing with employee complaints regarding contract violations.

Employees have essentially two categories of rights: those created by the contract and those created by local, state, and federal law. Federal laws creating employee rights include such statutes as the Americans with Disabilities Act, the Family and Medical Leave Act, Title VII, Title IX, the Age Discrimination in Employment Act, and the Equal Pay Act, as well as a host of other laws affecting the workplace. States frequently have their own versions of laws creating employee rights that mirror those passed at the federal level. State laws can give *more* rights than those accorded by federal legislation, but they cannot give *fewer* rights or take away rights promised under federal laws. Federal laws create the floor, not the ceiling for civil rights in the workplace. Where no collective bargaining agreement exists or where an agreement makes no mention of a matter, the employer and employees are subject to all applicable state laws and local ordinances pertinent to wages, hours, and terms and conditions of employment.[44] Where a collective bargaining contract exists or develops, the contract may prevail, depending on the state, over existing provisions of law except laws pertaining to (1) civil rights, (2) affirmative action, (3) unemployment compensation, (4) workers' compensation, (5) retirement of public employees, (6) residency requirements, (7) minimum education requirements, and (8) minimum standards promulgated by a state board of education.[45]

EMPLOYER RIGHTS AND RESPONSIBILITIES

If a state has a law giving public employees the right to collectively bargain, public employers such as school districts are obligated to meet in good faith with the union in order to discuss and bargain wages, hours, and terms and conditions of employment. The NLRA on which states with bargaining laws pattern their legislation does not compel either party to agree to a proposal or to require the making of a concession,[46] but it does require that both parties meet at reasonable times and try to reach a mutual agreement without compulsion on either side to agree.[47] However, unless the public employer agrees otherwise in a collective bargaining agreement, it cannot be required to bargain on any matter that impairs the right and responsibility of the employer to determine matters of inherent managerial policy that include, but are not limited to, areas of discretion or policy such as the functions and programs of the public employer: standards of services, its overall budget, utilization of technology, and organizational structure.[48] Public employers such as school districts retain the right *not* to bargain regarding their responsibilities to direct, supervise, evaluate, or hire employees, as well as their right to suspend, discipline, demote, or discharge employees for just cause, and the right to lay off, transfer, assign, schedule, promote, or retain employees.[49] They also retain their right to maintain and improve the efficiency and effectiveness of governmental operations; to determine overall methods, means, or personnel by which to conduct their business; and to determine the adequacy of the workforce and the overall mission of the district.[50] In other words, school districts are not obligated to include areas of managerial discretion in collective bargaining.

That being said, however, many areas reserved for managerial discretion have worked their way into the collective bargaining process because those areas have a direct impact on the terms and conditions of employment that are the subject matter of collective bargaining. In some state laws, while the decisions left to managerial discretion are not themselves bargainable, the *effect* of these decisions on the terms and conditions of employment is bargainable.[51] For example, a school district has the right to decide to close a school, but the effect of that decision on displaced employees will be a bargainable issue. Class size would also appear to be a managerial prerogative affecting a bargainable term and condition of employment, in that teachers with larger classes would have greater demands placed on them. However, the Nevada state legislature specifically excludes class size from a detailed list of permissible items for negotiation.[52] In the final analysis, the state legislatures and state labor relations boards are called on to decide whether an issue in dispute is a management right or a bargainable term and condition of employment. Therefore, management rights and their susceptibility to bargaining will vary from state to state.

Theoretically, management rights should never be mandatory subjects for collective bargaining, but often, in an effort to win a concession from the union during the give and take of negotiations, management itself will sometimes make a management right it feels can be sacrificed a permissible subject of bargaining. For example, management may negotiate class size with a union in return for monetary concessions regarding the negotiated pay scale. This explains the growing number of teacher contracts that prescribe procedures and limitations for such managerial prerogatives as transfer, assignment, discharge, and evaluation. It should also be noted, however, that once a management right becomes part of a negotiated agreement, the conceded issue will attain mandatory bargaining status in the next round of negotiations.

Many contracts actually contain *Management Rights Clauses* such as the one that follows:

> The Board and the ECEA agree that the Board retains all of the management rights vested in public bodies as set forth in Section 4117.08(C) of the Ohio Revised Code. In addition, except as may be expressly limited by law or by some express provision of this agreement, it is understood and agreed that the Board and those empowered to act for and under the Board retain the authority with regard to all matters relating to the operation, management, planning and direction of the school system, and of the schools and of personnel employed therein including, but not limited to, finances, staffing, standards and employment.[53]

Such clauses make it clear that the board will retain all management rights accorded it by law unless expressly limited by a provision of the negotiated contract that it has signed.

Once a contract has been negotiated and ratified, the school board and its agents are also responsible for abiding by its terms and honoring the procedural commitments it prescribes. This means that building administrators and human resource managers must read the contract and make management decisions that reflect both the spirit and letter of the agreement. The collectively bargained agreement takes on the force of law, but the negotiating process provides the context, the legislative history, so to speak, for the contract. All administrators, particularly those charged with any element of human resource management, should take responsibility for participating either directly or indirectly in the negotiating process itself. They should be aware of which issues were particularly sensitive to either side during negotiations and of what concessions went into reaching ultimate agreement. Labor peace will depend on informed and responsive human resource management throughout the life of the contract.

SCOPE OF BARGAINING

In paralleling the NLRA, most states have public sector collective bargaining laws that say that the scope of negotiations should include wages, hours, and other terms and conditions of employment.[54] There is, however, no universal agreement among states with collective bargaining laws as to what should be negotiated beyond wages, hours, and fringe benefits. The definition of terms and conditions of employment can be narrow or wide ranging. Iowa and Nevada, for example, identify specific items that must be negotiated,[55] and Michigan's collective bargaining law identifies subjects that cannot be bargained.[56] In contrast, Ohio's collective bargaining law provides for bargaining wages, hours, and terms and conditions of employment and for the continuation, modification, or deletion of an existing provision of a collective bargaining agreement,[57] and the law has been interpreted to require boards of education to bargain even management decisions as to their *effects* on the bargaining unit.[58] The bright line of demarcation between nondelegable management rights and negotiable terms and conditions of employment has blurred in recent years, and courts have repeatedly been called on to decide issues of negotiability. Virtually every managerial decision in some way relates to "salaries, wages, hours, and other working conditions," and is therefore arguably negotiable: yet at the same time, virtually every such decision also *involves* educational policy considerations and is therefore arguably nonnegotiable.[59] Human resource managers responsible for any aspect of collective bargaining must not only be familiar with the law itself but also with the Employment Relations Board and state court decisions that have interpreted the law's scope of bargaining.

Basically, items for negotiation can be mandatory, permissive, or forbidden. Mandatory items, wages, hours, and terms and conditions of employment, *must be negotiated*, and can be bargained to impasse. In other words, failure to reach agreement on mandatory items can lead to a strike if the state's law permits

public employees to strike. Permissive items *can be negotiated* if both parties
agree to bring them to the table, but neither side has a legal duty to do so, and
failure to reach agreement on permissive items cannot be a reason to strike. If
agreement on permissive items cannot be reached, boards of education retain
the management right to act unilaterally on these matters. However, if a board
of education brings a permissive item to the table as a bargaining chip and negotiates the item into the contract, the item will become a mandatory subject of
bargaining in future negotiations.[60] Prohibited items are those beyond a board's
power to negotiate. These include nondelegable management rights and civil
rights protected by state and federal statutes. For example, the U.S. Supreme
Court overturned a collectively bargained agreement that violated the equal
protection rights of nonminority teachers by protecting members of certain minority groups from layoffs.[61]

A LEGAL PERSPECTIVE

Collectively bargained agreements, where they exist, have the force of law in
prescribing and limiting both employee and management rights and responsibilities. Thus, it is important to understand what collective bargaining entails
and the legislative context in which the right to collectively bargain has been either granted or denied. There has been no national adoption of the right to collectively bargain in the public schools, nor has there been any uniform definition of what such bargaining should entail. With this in mind, it is important for
human resource managers to understand the historical and legislative perspective that determines whether teachers, in a given state, may or may not collectively bargain, and how that perspective applies to a given district's human
resource management.

THEORY INTO PRACTICE

1. Does your state have a public sector collective bargaining law that includes
   teachers? Why or why not?
2. If your state has a collective bargaining law that includes teachers, interview a member of the negotiating team to find out how your district conducts collective bargaining?
3. If your district collectively bargains, read the contract and note any parts of the
   contract that surprise you. If your district does not collectively bargain, how
   are your wages, hours, and terms and conditions of employment determined?

4. If your district collectively bargains, how are employee relations problems resolved [see grievance clause]? If your district does not collectively bargain, how are employee relations problems resolved?
5. If your district does not collectively bargain, are there limits set on management rights? If your district does collectively bargain, is there a management rights clause in your contract? Why or why not?
6. Is there an agency shop clause in your contract? How many teachers are actually members of the union, and how many are not members of the union?
7. Who do you feel is stronger, union or management, in your district? What evidence supports your position?
8. Compare fair share fees and union membership fees in districts with collectively bargained contracts.
9. Are you personally an advocate of collective bargaining? Why or why not?
10. Discuss a clause of your contract that has presented problems for either the union or administration.

NOTES

1. Wagner Act, NLRB § 7, 29 U.S.C. § 157, 29 Stat. § 452 (1935).

2. C. Perry and W. Wildman, *The Impact of Negotiations in Public Education: The Evidence from the Schools* (Worthington, Ohio: C. A. Jones Publishing, 1970), 3.

3. Perry and Wildman, *The Impact of Negotiations in Public Education*, 9.

4. WISC. STAT. §§ 111.70, 111.71 (2001).

5. W. L. Sharp, "Collective Negotiations: An Historical Perspective," *Journal of Collective Negotiations in the Public Sector* 21 (1992): 235.

6. See K. D. Magnusen and P. A. Renovitch, "Dispute Resolution in Florida's Public Sector: Insight into Impasse," in *Strategies for Impasse Resolution,* ed. H. Kershen and C. Meirowitz (Amityville, N.Y.: Baywood Publishing, 1992), 29, 30 (providing a table of states with collective bargaining legislation for public employees).

7. See K. Schneider, ed., *Public Employees Bargain for Excellence: A Compendium of State Public Sector Labor Relations Laws* (Washington, D.C.: Public Education, 1993), 23–24, 54.

8. C. T. Kerchner and D. E. Mitchell, *The Changing Idea of a Teachers' Union* (New York, N.Y.: Falmer Press, 1988), 46–50.

9. *See* NLRA § 2(2), 29 U.S.C.S. 152(2) (2002).

10. NLRA § 8(d), 29 U.S.C.S. 158(d) (2002).

11. T. L. Leap, *Collective Bargaining and Labor Relations* (New York, N.Y.: Macmillan, 1991), 646–649.

12. R. G. Neal, "It's Time to Cut Back on Collective Bargaining for Teachers and Other Public Employees," *Journal of Collective Negotiations in the Public Sector,* no. 14 (1985): 91–93.

13. G. M. Smit, "The Effect of Collective Bargaining on Governance in Education," *Government Union Review* (Winter 1984): 28, 32.

14. 29 U.S.C. § 153; *See, e.g.,* PA. CONS. STAT. ANN. tit. 43 § 1101.501 (1976), and OHIO REV. CODE ANN. § 4117.02 (Anderson 2001).

15. D. P. Rothschild et al., *Collective Bargaining and Labor Arbitration*, 3d ed. (Charlottesville, Va.: The Michie Company, 1988), 3.

16. *See, e.g.,* OHIO REV. CODE ANN. § 4117.06(A) (Anderson 2001).

17. Kalamazoo Paperbox Corp., 136 NLRB 134 (1962).

18. Michigan University v. Eastern Michigan University Chapter American Assn. of University Professors, 2 PBC ¶ 20,014 (Mich. Ct. App. 1973).

19. Chicago Teachers Union, IFT/AFT v. IELRB, 695 N.E.2d 1332 (Ill. App. Ct. 1998).

20. Minnesota State Bd. for Cmty. Colls. v. Knight, 465 U.S. 271, 283 (1984).

21. Pickering v. Bd. of Educ., 391 U.S. 563, 568 (1968).

22. Perry Educ. Ass'n v. Perry Local Educators' Ass'n, 460 U.S. 37, 46 (1983).

23. Perry Educ. Ass'n v. Perry Local Educators' Ass'n, 460 U.S. 37, 46 (1983).

24. See C. Russo et al., "Agency Shop Fees and the Supreme Court: Union Control and Academic Freedom," in *Education Law Reporter,* vol. 73 (1992): 609–615.

25. D. L. Leslie, *Cases and Materials on Labor Law: Process and Policy,* 2d ed. (Boston, Mass.: Little, Brown and Company, 1985), 120.

26. Abood v. Detroit Bd. of Educ., 431 U.S. 209 (1977).

27. *Abood,* at 209, 235.

28. Lehnert v. Ferris Faculty Ass'n, 500 U.S. 507 (1991).

29. Chicago Teachers' Union, Local No. 1 v. Hudson, 475 U.S. 292, 310 (1986).

30. Chicago Teachers' Union, Local No. 1 at 292, 306.

31. *See, e.g.,* OHIO REV. CODE ANN. § 4117.09 (C) (Anderson 2001).

32. M. Lieberman, *The Teacher Unions* (New York, N.Y.: The Free Press, 1997), 1–2.

33. Horace Mann League, "Survey of Six Hundred Superintendents and Professors," *Education Daily,* 15 March 1996, 4.

34. Emporium Capwell Co. v. Western Addition Cmty. Org., 420 U.S. 50 (1975).

35. NLRB v. Hearst Publ'n, Inc., 322 U.S. 111, 124 (1944).

36. Mobil Oil Corp., 196 NLRB 1052 (May 12, 1972).

37. Mobil Oil Corp., 196 NLRB 1052 (May 12, 1972).

38. NLRB v. J. Weingarten, Inc., 420 U.S. 251 (1975).

39. *J. Weingarten, Inc.,* at 251.

40. *J. Weingarten, Inc.,* at 251, Brief for Petitioner 22.

41. *J. Weingarten, Inc.,* at 251 (1975).

42. Ford Motor Co. v. Huffmann, 345 U.S. 330, 338 (1953).

43. 29 U.S.C.S. § 159(a) (2002).

44. J. F. Lewis and S. Spirn, *Ohio Collective Bargaining Law: The Regulation of Public Employer–Employee Labor Relations* (Cleveland, Ohio: Banks-Baldwin Law Publishing Company, 1983), 70.

45. Lewis and Spirn, *Ohio Collective Bargaining Law,* 70.

46. 29 U.S.C.S. § 158(d) (2002).

47. Belfield Educ. Ass'n v. Belfield Pub. Sch. Dist. No. 13, 496 N.W.2d 12 (N.D. 1993).

48. *See, e.g.,* OHIO REV. CODE ANN. § 4117.08(C)(1) (Anderson 2001).

49. *See, e.g.,* § 4117.08(C)(2)(5).

50. *See, e.g.,* § 4117.08 (C)(3)(4)(6)(7).

51. *See, e.g.,* § 4117.08(C).

52. NEV. REV. STAT. ANN. § 288.150 (MB 2001).

53. *Agreement between East Cleveland Board of Education and East Cleveland Education Association,* effective April 4, 1999 to April 3, 2002, 6.

54. 29 U.S.C.S. § 158(d) (2002).

55. IOWA CODE § 20.9 (2002); NEV. REV. STAT. ANN. § 288.150 (2001).

56. MICH. COMP. LAWS § 423.215(3) (2001) (4).

57. OHIO REV. CODE ANN. § 4117.08(C) (Anderson 2001).

58. *See, e.g.,* SERB v. Findlay City Sch. Dist. Bd. of Educ., Case No. 88-2-M (Hancock Co. CP, 1988) (board required to negotiate impact of drug/alcohol policy); Beaver Local Sch. Dist. Bd. of Educ. v. SERB, Case No. 87-CIV-298 (Columbiana Co. CP, Oct. 10, 1987) (board required to negotiate effect of implementing competency-based education program).

59. Montgomery County Educ. Ass'n v. Bd. of Educ. of Montgomery County, 534 A.2d 980, 986 (Md. 1987).

60. *See, e.g.,* DiPiazza v. Bd. of Educ. of Comsewogue Union Free Sch. Dist., 625 N.Y.S.2d 298 (App. Div. 1995).

61. Wygant v. Jackson Bd. of Educ., 476 U.S. 267.

Chapter Three

The Collective Bargaining Process

Many different approaches to the collective bargaining process have evolved, but whether the approach is traditional or nontraditional, adversarial or collaborative, certain basic elements exist. Good bargaining requires preparation at every step. Successful bargaining requires careful planning in the composition of the bargaining team, the development of proposals, the review of opposing proposals, the crafting of contract language, and the ultimate acceptance or rejection of the final product. Even where the human resource director is not specifically a member of the negotiating team, the process affects human resource management. This chapter will discuss the process of collective bargaining.

THE NEGOTIATING TEAM

Probably no decision is as central to the success or failure of negotiations as the selection of negotiating team members. Figure 3.1 lists prospective members of the union team and evaluates the relative positive and negative aspects of their participation in bargaining.

The teachers' union will usually be represented by its president, select teachers representing different grade levels and interests within the union, and either a lawyer or field representative hired by the state affiliate. On the one hand, both the National Education Association and the American Federation of Teachers have a vested interest in monitoring the collective bargaining process on a district-by-district basis. In this way they can ensure planned and steady progress in teachers' pay, benefits, and terms and conditions of employment in regions across a given state. The state organizations' field representatives and attorneys are familiar with the contracts negotiated within a region, and they are skilled in helping local unions develop and present proposals backed by supporting data and tried arguments from comparable districts. Each union main-

Prospective Member	Pros	Cons
Association President	Recognized Leader Internal Expertise Ultimately Responsible	Can Take Political Position Time Requirement
State/National Consultant	Knows Law Knows Trends Negotiation Expertise	No Vested Interest in Local Settlement No Knowledge of Local Need/History
Association Attorney	Legal Expertise Expert in Contract Language	No Vested Interest in Local Settlement Conflict of Interest [Money to Be Made from Contract Disputes]
Teacher(s) Representatives	Can Facilitate Teacher Understanding and Adoption of Contract Can Provide Input Regarding Feasibility of Implementation	May Not See "Big" Picture Time Requirement

Figure 3.1   Participation in Bargaining: Union Negotiation Team

tains a database of contracts, state employment relation board decisions, and court rulings addressing the issues and practices most likely to be addressed during collective bargaining. On the other hand, association attorneys and state consultants bring no personal interest to the bargaining table, and they will not have to live with the contract they help develop. Teacher representatives, in contrast, bring their personal history and interests to the table and lend the process a sense of credibility it would not otherwise have, but they rarely have the time or training required to grasp the fiscal and philosophical impact of collective bargaining.

Boards of education, for their part, have more of a quandary to face in deciding who will represent them in negotiations. Board teams could potentially include one or more board of education members, the superintendent, the school district's attorney, the human resource director, and one or more district administrators. That being said, there are pros and cons to the presence of each of these parties on the bargaining team. Figure 3.2 summarizes the positive and negative consequences board team membership might pose for each of these parties.

The superintendent would seem the most likely candidate for leading the board's team in negotiations, but there are pitfalls to including the superintendent on the team. While the superintendent is the recognized head of the district's educational program, presumably chosen based on expertise and ability

Prospective Member	Pros	Cons
Superintendent	Recognized Leader Expertise Ultimately Responsible	Can Be Viewed as an Adversary after Negotiations Time Requirement
Board Member(s)	Can Facilitate Contract Ratification Can Promote Community Support Will Understand Contract Implications	Can Take Political Positions May Not Be Knowledgeable Time Requirement
Human Resource Director	Knowledge of Negotiations Knowledge of Law Information Source Insight into "Big" Picture	Time Requirement
District's Attorney	Legal Expertise Expert in Contract Language	No Direct Interest in Outcome Cost and Time Requirement Conflict of Interest [Money to Be Made from Contract Disputes]
Select Administrators	Firsthand Knowledge of Need and Problems	Can Be Viewed as an Adversary after Negotiations Time Requirement

Figure 3.2   Participation in Bargaining: Board of Education Negotiation Team

to lead, the superintendent's leadership ability rests on the concomitant ability to unite and inspire staff to work together for a common cause. Collective bargaining, particularly in a traditional adversarial format, tends to divide faculty and administration. Good adversarial bargaining often requires an aggressive, argumentative posture and can lead to open confrontation. The memory of such open aggression can outlast the bargaining itself and make it difficult for a superintendent to regain the neutrality needed for effective leadership after the contract is ratified.

Even when the mode of bargaining is win-win and collaborative, a superintendent can become a victim of the process. In this case, the board and the community can view the superintendent as selling out to the union. In the end, someone must pay the bill for concessions made, even in the spirit of collaboration, and superintendents who participate in collaborative bargaining that results in increased taxes chance the loss of public trust. There will always be members of the board and the community who equate leadership with opposition rather than collaboration.

In addition to these political considerations, the superintendent must also be concerned with the time commitment required by members of the bargaining team. There will be meetings to prepare, to discuss, to negotiate, to revise, and to finally ratify. Marathon sessions are a common practice as timelines approach and tempers flare. Collective bargaining can be truly time consuming, and the question of who will run the district while the superintendent negotiates is a significant one.

Similarly, there are pluses and minuses to the presence of board members on the negotiating team. A primary benefit of board participation in negotiations is that board members who play a role in the development of the contract are more likely to facilitate its ratification. Participating board members are also more likely to promote community support for the contract, including the adopted pay scale. In addition, board members who participate in the negotiations process will have a better understanding of administrative and teacher concerns and will provide the kind of informed leadership so rare but necessary in representational government at the local level.

Time considerations must again be a negative consideration. Most board members hold other jobs that may not allow them the option of participating fully in the negotiations process, and limited participation can undermine the process itself. Another serious drawback to board member participation in negotiations is a lack of knowledge and experience regarding the process and the issues at stake. Generally, board members are not ex-teachers or ex-administrators, nor are they usually education lawyers or negotiators. As a result, they come to the bargaining table with serious gaps in knowledge and experience. Finally, the political nature of board membership can prove a detriment to effective negotiations. Board members are elected and therefore may have personal political pressures that will directly influence their roles on the bargaining team.

The inclusion of the school district's attorney on the negotiating team would seem a safe and positive choice, but here, too, there could be negative consequences. On the positive side of the ledger, the district's attorney brings obvious legal expertise to the bargaining table and a show of external power. The contract will be a legal and binding document, and the district's attorney can play a vital role in ensuring that contract language is unambiguous and enforceable. However, a school district must pay for the attorney's participation in negotiations, and the cost of representation at the bargaining table should be a consideration. Districts should also recognize that there could be a conflict of interest for their attorneys in that unclear contract language and oversights at the bargaining table will inevitably lead to more billable attorney hours after ratification as district administrators seek legal counsel in attempting to implement the contract.

One final and very important concern for districts that include attorneys on their negotiating teams should be the attorney's lack of personal investment in the outcome of the process. Money considerations aside, the attorney works for the school district, not in it. Attorneys, like union consultants, are disinterested third-party professionals, hired guns if you will, who can leave when their job is done, sometimes with a field of victims in their dust. Attorneys, like outside consultants, can be formidable opponents and freely antagonistic during the bargaining process. They can be caustic, cold, and challenging, and often that is the very reason they were hired to negotiate. However, the bitterness they engender seldom disappears after a settlement is reached. Hired guns tend to leave the stench of battle in their wake long after the contract is signed.

Select administrators can also be named to the board's bargaining team. Supervisors and administrators, those who hire, fire, and discipline, cannot themselves collectively bargain in most states, but as former teachers, they do understand the process and the issues that are brought to the table and do have a stake in the outcomes. They also have firsthand knowledge of the district's needs and problems at the various grade levels. Unfortunately, like the superintendent, administrators, too, risk sacrificing their ability to lead to the perception of being a lifetime adversary because of what is said and done at the bargaining table. In addition, like the superintendent, there must be concern for the time demands that negotiations will place on participating administrators. Who will run the buildings and programs they are responsible for during the long and tedious process of contract development?

The human resource director is probably the only obvious choice for appointment to the district's bargaining team. The contract that is developed during collective bargaining will affect every aspect of human resource management, and the director is an essential resource for informing the process. The job of human resource director or specialist presumes knowledge of law, contract, bargaining, and relevant state and district data. The human resource director is the curator of facts and figures pertinent to the negotiations process, including, but not limited to, pay scale histories, sick leave data, benefit plan comparisons, enrollment studies, and all the other sundry details at the core of day-to-day school district personnel management. If the needed data is not in hand, it is presumed that the human resource manager will know how to get it. The human resource director is in the enviable position of seeing the "big picture" in terms of the array of details that create it and, as such, is invaluable to the negotiations team. Only the required time commitment weighs in against the human resource director's participation, and, on balance, the time required is justified.

In the final analysis, a district preparing for negotiations must consider the pros and cons of each appointment to the negotiating team and must also consider the individual personalities of the proposed players. How will each team member relate to other team members as well as to opposing team members? What history does each team member bring to the table? Are there personal agendas that could interfere with the process? The selection of the district's bargaining team is a task that should never be taken lightly. Even if the superintendent does not personally lead the negotiations process, the superintendent should actively guide the selection process and must take the time and effort to make considered and informed membership choices.

There is no set magic number of ideal participants on either negotiations team. While a small team can be informal and may reach agreement more easily, a team that is too small is prone to make serious mistakes and foster misunderstanding.[1] Meanwhile teams that are too large can be difficult to manage and can undermine efforts to find consensus. Costs in time and money also rule against large teams. If negotiating teams meet during working hours, the cost of substitute coverage and the disruption to the program can be a real concern when large numbers of employees participate. With this in mind, some contracts actually specify the number of negotiators each team can have.

Once the team is in place, members must decide what roles they will individually play on the team and establish their individual and group authority to make and react to proposals. Negotiators on either team must have the authority to revise proposals as needed in caucus and to bargain concessions without having to seek permission to do so. Inevitably, a team leader will emerge for each side, and it must be decided whether the leader will act as the sole voice for the team on all issues or whether leadership will shift with member expertise on a particular issue. Each team should also appoint a member responsible for recording what happens during each negotiating session, that is, noting the issues and language discussed and the positions taken for later team discussion and planning. Essentially the bargaining teams must set their own performance ground rules to develop a united front and to avoid public stumbling and disagreement.

PREPARING FOR NEGOTIATIONS

A number of factors will have a direct impact on collective bargaining. Negotiating teams must do their homework in order to become successful bargainers. They must gather information from a variety of sources to develop proposals that respond to state and local pressures and address district needs. Figure 3.3 describes the factors that will most directly inform and influence preparation for bargaining for the board of education. Figure 3.4 describes the factors likely to influence teacher union preparation.

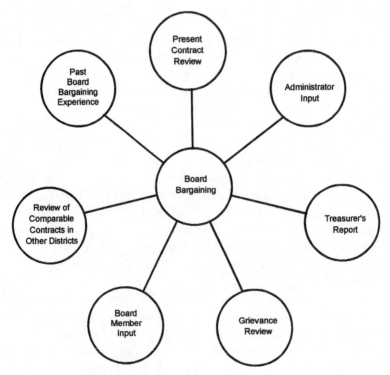

Figure 3.3   Factors Affecting Board Bargaining

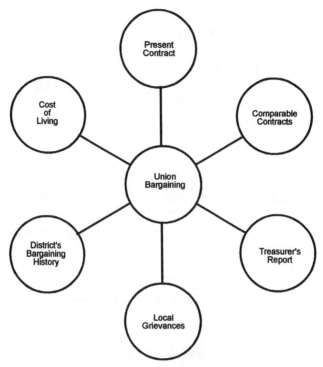

Figure 3.4   Factors Affecting Union Bargaining

Board and union preparation should begin with a thorough review of the existing contract. Specifically, what parts of the contract have caused problems, and what language has engendered grievances throughout the life of the expiring contract? Special attention should be given to grievances that repeatedly arise from specific contract clauses. Grievance review can red flag contract language that is perceived as ambiguous, and cleaning up such clauses should be a focus of impending negotiations. Administrators can help the board's team with this phase of preparatory research and should be polled concerning perceived problems, as well as program changes, new legal mandates, and personnel concerns unique to their buildings. Building representatives can provide similar input for the union's team. In addition, negotiators on both sides should have a clear understanding of where the school district stands financially before negotiations begin. Inasmuch as the board will be ultimately responsible for ratifying and funding the contract, the district's chief financial officer, usually the treasurer, should provide this information before negotiations begin. Negotiators must realize that bargaining never occurs in a vacuum. Negotiators on both sides will inevitably point to wages, hours, and terms and conditions in comparable districts to support the proposals they make. Similarly, negotiators will defend their own positions either by pointing to comparable contracts in other districts or by presenting reasons to distinguish those districts from their own. Good bargaining is always founded on sound preparation, and good bargainers have researched reasons for the positions they take. Should bargaining end in impasse, the mediators, fact finders, and arbitrators sent to assist districts and unions in resolving their differences will also rely on the research each side has garnered to make their own recommendations regarding the settlement. Thus, each side must do their homework well in anticipation of disinterested third-party review.

Disclosure

The union, in doing its own preparation for collective bargaining, will in-evitably be forced to turn to the district for information. Under the National Labor Relations Act (NLRA),[2] the prototype for most public sector collective bargaining laws, employers have a duty to provide a union with relevant infor-mation needed for the proper performance of its duties as the bargaining repre-sentative. Thus, districts in states with collective bargaining laws patterned on the NLRA will be expected to respond to union requests for such information as financial statements, enrollment reports, sick leave usage reports, and bene-fit plan comparisons that can be used to formulate and support union bargain-ing. And even in states that make no legal provision for collective bargaining, The Freedom of Information Act and comparable state public records acts pro-vide for public disclosure of information contained in agency files,[3] written re-ports, records, and budget accounts that unions will find helpful in preparing for the possibility of bargaining. Boards that deny the union access to information needed to bargain will be guilty of an unfair labor practice in states with col-lective bargaining statutes and a violation of state freedom of information acts in states that neither provide for nor prohibit bargaining.

PROPOSAL AND STRATEGY DEVELOPMENT

This preliminary research helps each side formulate a bargaining plan that begins with the development of a "wish list." The wish list should include all items team members consider worthy of bargaining time. As noted, wages, hours, terms and conditions of employment, and items already included in an existing collective bargaining agreement are mandatory subjects of bargaining. However, each side should also prepare a list of permissive subjects, items that while not mandatory warrant bargaining consideration, perhaps simply as bargaining chips.

An essential part of preparation is prioritizing the items on the bargaining agenda: which items are most important to each side, and what modifications or sacrifices is each side prepared to make in order to win on high-priority issues? Figure 3.5 presents a five-step plan for analyzing and setting bargaining priorities.

The first step in this process is to know what is desired and to put that objective in clear and unequivocal contract language. This initial wish should express the ideal, that is, the contract clause formulated should reflect the *best* possible language and outcome. Next, the team should consider alternatives that will modify the ideal but still be acceptable. In effective bargaining it is unlikely that either side will get everything it wants. Compromise is the essence of good bargaining, and so good preparation entails looking at what might be an acceptable compromise on each issue. Third, it is equally important, to identify a compromise that would be found unacceptable and to articulate why it will be unacceptable before it is on the table. An example of how these three steps work in reviewing a board's pay-scale proposals follows:

The Ideal

The board proposes to give the teachers a 1 percent raise in each of the three years of the contract because this would be the most economically expedient proposal. A 1 percent raise would save the district money while preserving educational services.

The Acceptable

The board has the resources to give the teachers a 3 percent cost-of-living raise in each of the three years of the contract. Research shows that teachers

Step 1	Set bargaining goals and develop contract language to achieve those goals. *The Ideal Proposal*
Step 2	Prepare alternative proposals adjusting controversial languages. *The Acceptable Proposal*
Step 3	Articulate language and conditions that would not be acceptable. *The Unacceptable Proposal*
Step 4	Provide documented research to support the decision to label a proposal as ideal, acceptable, or unacceptable.
Step 5	Look for ways to make proposals acceptable or ideal.

Figure 3.5 Developing a Plan for Negotiating

in comparable districts are receiving 3 percent annual raises during the life of the contract.

The Unacceptable

A raise of more than 3 percent annually without a cut in either the district's retirement contribution or benefit plan funding would be unacceptable because the district does not have the money to fund this proposal.

Step 4 requires negotiators to justify their judgment as to what is *ideal, acceptable, and unacceptable* by providing documented evidence. In other words, negotiators would be required to find the cost of a 1 percent proposal and to compare it with the cost of a 3 or 4 percent proposal and to identify and compare funding resources to the amounts needed for each proposal. Required documentation will discourage rash assumptions that may, in the end, prove more costly to the bargaining process itself. Finally, Step 5 gets to the heart of the bargaining process, by requiring that negotiators actually search for ways to make ideal and acceptable proposals possible and palatable to both sides. Step 5 can actually provide a bridge between the adversarial and collaborative approaches to collective bargaining.

As a case in point, are there ways to modify other parts of the contract to save money or get important concessions that would make raises of 3 percent or more a viable option? There are two bargaining scenarios. In one, the negotiating teams bargain item by item. In the other, items are fungible, that is, concessions in one area of the contract can be exchanged for concessions in another area. In the first scenario, there is always the danger of deadlock on a given issue such as salary. However, in the second scenario there may be concessions in other areas of the contract that would warrant reconsideration of a union's salary proposal. For example, a higher medical deductible that lowers a district's insurance premium could generate money for pay raises. Step 5 requires negotiators to consider the contract as a whole and to balance the worth of concessions in one area against the worth of concessions in other areas.

TYPES OF BARGAINING

There are basically two approaches to public school collective bargaining: the traditional or adversarial approach and collaborative bargaining. Collaborative bargaining is sometimes called win-win, best practice, mutual gain, principled, or integrative bargaining.[4] These two types of bargaining differ in their goals, methods, and outcomes. In adversarial bargaining, the goal is ideally partisan satisfaction, a win for one side or the other. In interest-based bargaining, the goal is mutual satisfaction. Collective bargaining adversaries plan for bargaining by defining partisan interests, while win-win bargainers define mutual interests and concerns. Adversarial bargaining begins with the partisan definition of issues and the development of partisan proposals for resolving those issues. In adversarial bargaining, there is a series of give-and-take exchanges with each side yielding on some demands in return for concessions from the other side.[5] Win-win bargaining begins with the identification of mutual concerns, or mutual ground in resolving partisan interests. Adversaries bluff, bargain, and eventually win a partisan victory or resolve themselves to an acceptable compromise. Win-win bargainers brainstorm solutions that will bring both sides victory. Figure 3.6 gives a summary comparison of the adversarial and win-win bargaining procedures.

There are positive and negative aspects to each bargaining approach. Adversarial bargaining, as its name implies, pits one side against another and can lead to impasse and eventual strike if no room for compromise is found. On the other hand, adversarial bargaining sets the stage for an exchange of feelings and interests that often need to be vented. In effective adversarial bargaining, neither side gets everything it wants, but both sides get a better understanding of what it will take to maintain labor peace in the midst of constituent interests. The final agreement will reflect the relative strength of each representative.

In contrast, win-win or collaborative bargaining, while it may never lead to impasse, may also never lead to real labor peace. Parties to win-win bargaining must trust each other before, during, and after agreement is reached. In addition, the constituents they represent must trust that the solutions mutually reached by the win-win bargainers are effective, not simply expedient, solutions. Collaborative bargaining is still not the norm.[6] There has been no rush to win-win bargaining, and adversarial bargaining, even with the risk of impasse is still common in states that collectively bargain.

Adversarial Bargaining	*Collaborative Bargaining*
1) Partisan Positions Identified by Each Side	1) Common Concerns and Interests identified
2) Emphasis on Winning	2) Emphasis on Compromise
3) Sides Meet Separately to Plan	3) Sides Meet Together to Collaborate
4) Sides Can Be Flexible	4) Flexibility Stressed
5) Power Is Paramount	5) Trust Is Paramount
6) One Side Wins; One Side Loses	6) Both Sides Win Something

Figure 3.6   Adversarial and Collaborative Bargaining: A Comparison

Win-win bargaining is a process that must be learned. It focuses on issues, not personalities; interests not positions; and mutual gain.[7] Those who participate in win-win bargaining must assume that

1. Bargaining enhances the parties' relationship;
2. Both parties can win;
3. Parties will help each other win;
4. Open and frank discussion and information sharing expands opportunities for mutual interests, and this in turn expands the options available to the parties;
5. Mutually developed standards for evaluating options can move decision making away from reliance on power.[8]

Power and the perception of power are central factors in adversarial bargaining. Trust and the perception of mutual benefit are central factors in win-win bargaining.

Perhaps the best way to illustrate the difference between adversarial and win-win bargaining is to show how each approach would work in resolving an actual contract issue.

The Adversarial Approach

The Issue

Each teacher, under state law, is entitled to fifteen sick days. At present, teachers who do not use all fifteen days of sick leave in a given year simply lose the remaining days. As a result, many teachers use all fifteen days of sick leave each year. The board has proposed a contract clause to curb unwarranted use of sick leave. The union has proposed a clause to reward teachers for not using sick leave unless truly needed.

Board's Interests

1. Discourage unwarranted use of sick leave
2. Cut substitute coverage costs
3. Maintain program continuity in the face of a shortage of substitutes

Union's Interests

1. Preserve fifteen sick days as a teacher benefit
2. Preserve teachers' right to use sick days without permission or written doctor's note
3. Maintain program continuity in the face of a shortage of substitutes

Board Proposal

Teachers who use sick days must provide a doctor's note indicating that the absences were medically justified. This note must be filed with the district's human resource manager within five days of return to work. Teachers who do not supply this note will lose pay for each day's unexcused absence.

Union Proposal

Teachers will continue to receive the fifteen days of sick leave guaranteed them each year under state law. Teachers who do not use all fifteen days of sick leave in a given year will receive half of their per diem pay for each unused day. This reimbursement for unused sick days will appear as a bonus in the teacher's last yearly pay check.

Board's Arguments

1. Sick leave exists should the need arise. Teachers have no right to use sick leave unless they are sick.
2. Teachers should not be rewarded for simply being honest.
3. The board has a right and a duty to ask teachers to justify absence from work necessitating the payment of both the teacher and a substitute.
4. The board must take whatever action is needed to preserve both the integrity and continuity of the educational program.

Union's Arguments

1. Teachers are entitled to fifteen days of sick leave under state law.
2. Teachers have a right to privacy regarding health issues.
3. A teacher may be too sick to report for work, but not sick enough to go to a doctor.
4. The board's plan would require payment to a doctor each time a teacher used sick leave.
5. Teachers have no incentive for preserving sick leave.
6. The use of sick leave when needed is a right, not a privilege.

The Collaborative Approach

The Issue

Each teacher, under state law, is entitled to fifteen sick days. At present, teachers who do not use all fifteen days of sick leave in a given year simply lose the remaining days. As a result, many teachers use all fifteen days of sick leave each year.

Mutual Interests

1. Teachers who are ill will have the right to fifteen sick days.
2. Teachers who are not ill do not have the right to use sick days.
3. Teachers who are ill should not be discouraged from using sick leave.
4. Teachers who are not ill should be discouraged from using sick leave.
5. It is difficult to get substitute teachers if too many teachers are absent.
6. The integrity and continuity of the educational program are adversely affected by teacher absence.

Brainstormed Solutions

Team members from both sides proposed the following ideas, without criticism or comment:

1. Pay teachers full per diem for unused sick leave at end of each year.
2. Allow teachers to accumulate sick leave from year to year. Sick leave in excess of fifteen days can be used in case of a lengthy health emergency. Teachers will receive 50 percent of their per diem pay at time of retirement or separation for each day of unused sick leave in excess of fifteen days.
3. Teachers will receive a set bonus at the end of each year based on the number of days of sick leave they have not used.
4. Teachers must arrange their own substitute coverage.
5. Teachers must provide a doctor's statement justifying use of sick leave.

Consensus Decision Making

Team members will discuss, revise, and ultimately reach consensus regarding the development of a workable and equitable contract clause that will discourage the unwarranted use of sick leave. Brainstorming is used to get every possible solution on the table for group consideration. The final solution will be one benefiting both sides, hence the title win-win bargaining.

Probably the most significant difference between interest-based, collaborative bargaining and traditional or adversarial bargaining is that opposing sides are not allowed to take and maintain partisan positions. Both sides identify issues of mutual concern and then randomly brainstorm proposals that may address these identified mutual concerns. Brainstorming cannot be either critical or partisan. Brainstorming is simply a way to get all possible solutions on the table for a consensus-building discussion. As noted earlier, participants must be trained to bargain this way, and they must trust each other or this method will not work.

THE LOGISTICS OF BARGAINING

In order to bargain effectively, ground rules and procedures should be developed before the process begins. A primary initial decision for the negotiating team is whether bargaining will be adversarial or collaborative. In addition to the time, place, and manner of bargaining, the number of bargainers on each side should be established. The length of bargaining sessions and procedures for calling time for separate group discussion, or caucusing, should also be determined. Although each side may keep its own notes on what is said and done at each meeting, it may be wise to reach agreement on having an independent stenographer present to record specific contract language as agreement is reached or to agree to use a tape recorder. The recorder could then generate a written record of the proposed settlement language for each side to review, discuss, or modify in the next session. Procedures for team replacements, canceling sessions, calling breaks in bargaining, and postponements should also be clarified before formal bargaining begins to avoid unnecessary misunderstandings and interruptions. Figure 3.7 serves as a guide to some of the procedural issues that should be addressed in setting ground rules for bargaining.

CONFIDENTIALITY

Confidentiality, an issue listed in figure 3.7, is so important it merits separate discussion. Procedures for communicating with constituents and the public at large should also be established before the need arises. A board of education must be wary of communicating directly with teachers while negotiations are in progress. Employer communications to employees during negotiations about items of tentative agreement or proposals and counterproposals are held suspect by state employee relations boards regardless of the employer's intent.[9] Such direct communication risks being found to be "direct dealing," an unfair labor practice, particularly if the union maintains that such communications have in some way undermined its representative role in the negotiations process or generated labor unrest. Ideally, the parties should establish a mutually agreed on protocol for communicating with constituents and the press before negotiations begin, a part of the ground rules. Some alternatives for dealing with this sensitive issue are

- Type of Bargaining: Adversarial or Collaborative

- Time of Meetings: Before, After, or During Workday

- Frequency of Meetings

- Length of Meetings

- Place of Meetings

- Procedure for Postponement

- Procedure for Breaks in Bargaining

- Number of Negotiators on Each Team

- Procedure for Caucusing During Bargaining

- Procedure for Recording Bargaining Session Minutes

- Procedure for Developing Final Draft of Contract Language

- Procedure for Declaring Impasse

- Procedure for Resolving Impasse

- Procedure for Communicating with Press, Public, or Constituents

- Confidentiality Issues

- Procedure for Communicating with State Employment Relations Board

- Discovery Procedure, i.e., Request for Information Relevant to Bargaining

Figure 3.7   Bargaining Logistics

1. neither side shall issue progress reports on negotiations until the negotiations process is completed,
2. neither side shall issue progress reports on negotiations without the prior review and consent of the other party,
3. parties shall issue joint reports clarifying positions taken during negotiations,
4. press releases must be approved by both parties.

A LEGAL PERSPECTIVE

In states that collectively bargain, the contract that evolves from the negotiation's process will become a virtual bible for the union and the human resource manager. Most negotiated contracts touch on every aspect of human resource management by virtue of the requirement that all terms and conditions of employment be negotiated. Management's right to act unilaterally is limited by the negotiated contract, and failure to comply with both the letter and the spirit of the contract will inevitably lead to grieving, a continuation of negotiations.

The union's goal is to include all aspects of human resource management in the contract, thus legally creating a total waiver of legislated management rights. The board's goal is to incorporate as few aspects of human resource management as possible in the contract and thereby preserve the board's legislated right to determine district employment policy.

THEORY INTO PRACTICE

1. Identify the members of the board's team that negotiated your district's last contract. What positions do they hold, and what expertise did they bring to the bargaining table?
2. Identify the members of the union's bargaining team that negotiated your district's last contract. How were team members chosen?
3. Which clauses in your current contract have generated grievances? Discuss the reasons you believe these contract clauses are controversial.
4. Which comparable school district contracts would you review in preparing for negotiations? Why do you consider these districts comparable to your own school district?
5. Compare your salary scale with that of three comparable school districts identified in activity 4. Discuss your findings.
6. Compare your contract's policy regarding sick leave with that of the three comparable school districts in activity 4. Discuss your findings.
7. Develop a contract clause addressing the length of the school year from the standpoint of the union. Use state law, educational research, and comparable contracts as data to support the position you take in your clause.
8. Develop a contract clause addressing the length of the school year from the standpoint of the board. Use school law, educational research, and comparable contracts as data to support the position you take in your clause.
9. Conduct an adversarial bargaining session with a colleague to negotiate the clause developed in questions 7 and 8. One of you should argue the board's position; the other should argue the union's position.
10. Conduct a collaborative bargaining session with the same colleague to negotiate the clause addressing the length of the school year.

NOTES

1. M. Lieberman, "Forming Your Negotiations Team," *School Management* 13, no. 12 (1969): 30.

2. 29 U.S.C.S. §§ 151 to 169 (2002).

3. 5 U.S.C.S. § 552(a)(3) (2002).

4. J. T. Barrett, *A Successful Model for Interest-Based Collective Bargaining and Partnering in the Public Sector* (Danvers, Mass.: LRP Publications, 1996), 1:9.

5. D. E. Mitchell et al., "The Impact of Collective Bargaining on School Management and Policy," *American Journal of Education* 89 (1981): 147–188.

6. Public Employee Relations Library, PERL No. 63, 1995.

7. J. T. Barrett, *A Successful Model for Interest-Based Collective Bargaining and Partnering in the Public Sector* (Danvers, Mass.: LRP Publications, 1996), 4:2.

8. Barrett, *A Successful Model for Interest-Based Collective Bargaining,* 4:3.

9. *See, e.g.,* SERB v. Mentor Exempted Vill. Sch. Dist. Bd. of Educ., Case No. 84-UR-12-2548 (SERB 89-011) (May 12, 1989).

Chapter Four

Collective Bargaining and Controversy

GOOD FAITH BARGAINING

The state courts have defined the concepts of negotiations and good faith bargaining because they have been asked to rule on whether one party or another was truly negotiating in good faith. To negotiate simply means to present proposals and offer counter proposals, to discuss proposals, to carry on a dialogue, and to exchange ideas, all for the purpose of persuading or being persuaded by logic and reasoning.[1] This entails parties being willing to listen and not only talk and to engage in the art of friendly persuasion. Neither side is required by law to surrender or abrogate any of its duties and responsibilities nor to engage in formal or binding arbitration.[2] Good faith bargaining consists simply of an honest intention to engage in the bargaining process with an open mind and a sincere desire to reach agreement.[3]

The Supreme Court of Michigan has said:

> The primary obligation placed upon the parties in a collective bargaining setting is to meet and confer in good faith. The exact meaning of the duty to bargain in good faith has not been rigidly defined in the case law. Rather, the courts look to the overall conduct of a party to determine if it has actively engaged in the bargaining process with an open mind and a sincere desire to reach an agreement. The law does not mandate that the parties ultimately reach agreement, nor does it dictate the substance of the terms on which the parties must bargain. In essence the requirements of good faith bargaining are simply that the parties manifest such an attitude and conduct that will be conducive to reaching an agreement.[4]

The question of good faith bargaining usually arises when a board of education refuses to bargain issues that the union perceives as wages, hours, or terms and conditions of employment. As discussed earlier, boards are under no obligation to bargain policy and managerial issues. Unless the public employer agrees otherwise, it cannot be required to bargain on any matter that impairs the right and responsibility of the employer to determine matters of inherent managerial policy; to direct, supervise, evaluate, or hire employees; to maintain and improve the efficiency and effectiveness of governmental operations; to determine the overall methods, process, means, or personnel by which governmental operations are to be conducted; to suspend, discipline, demote, or discharge, lay off, transfer, reassign, schedule, promote, or retain employees; to determine the adequacy of the work force; to determine the overall mission of the employer; to effectively manage the workforce; or to take action to carry out the mission of the public employer.[5] However, relatively few management or policy issues will not deal in one way or another with wages, hours, or terms and conditions of employment. Boards that refuse to bargain with the teachers' unions on issues they perceive as management prerogatives can therefore expect to be accused of not bargaining in good faith, and the courts will be called on to determine the validity of each side's position.

In *Clark County School District v. Local Government Employee Management Relations Board* and *Washoe County Teachers Ass'n v. Washoe County School District,*[6] two cases were decided together, for example, and the question at issue was classroom preparation time. The board in the *Clark County* case maintained that classroom preparation time was a policy issue and not a mandatory subject of bargaining. The Supreme Court of Nevada disagreed, holding that anything that significantly related to wages, hours, and working conditions was negotiable, even though it might also be related to a management prerogative. In the Washoe County case, this court included in the negotiable category such issues as class size, professional improvement, student discipline, school calendar, teacher performance, differentiated staffing, teacher load, and instructional supplies.

The manner in which a board of education conducts negotiations can also give rise to charges of bad faith bargaining. For example, in *Belfield Education Ass'n v. Belfield Public School District No. 13,* the union asserted that the District exhibited bad faith by attempting to limit the negotiations to two, two-hour meetings and by twice describing its proposals as "final offers" when they were not. In assessing good faith, courts do not focus on isolated actions, but look to the overall conduct of a party to determine whether it has actively engaged in the bargaining process with an open mind and sincere desire to reach an agreement.[7] In the Belfield case, the Board of Education had historically reached agreement with the union in a few sessions and felt two sessions would therefore be adequate. In view of this explanation, the court in this case did not believe that the union had affirmatively demonstrated a lack of good faith bargaining on the board's part. Discussing reasonable ground rules for negotiations, as discussed in an earlier chapter, and sticking to those ground rules can go far in heading off a charge of bad faith bargaining.

IMPASSE IN COLLECTIVE BARGAINING

Impasse occurs when parties are no longer willing to communicate on unresolved issues. Agreement has not been reached, yet neither party is willing to compromise. Like a married couple in need of outside counseling to avoid divorce, union and management at the point of impasse need a disinterested third party to avoid a strike, if permitted, to help them get negotiations back on track. Such third-party intervention in the negotiations process is referred to as Alternative Dispute Resolution, and it can take many forms. Some state collective bargaining laws actually prescribe alternative dispute resolution procedures. In states without such statutory prescriptions, parties are free to decide for themselves how they will resolve impasses. The alternative dispute resolution procedures available may include mediation, fact-finding, and arbitration in various forms and combinations. In states where striking is prohibited, these procedures are a last resort in the effort to resume negotiations and arrive at a settlement. In states where teachers are allowed to strike, mediation, fact-finding, and arbitration are used to avoid that alternative. Figure 4.1 compares the procedures available under Pennsylvania, Illinois, Florida, and Ohio Public Sector Collective Bargaining Laws.

Mediation

It is always preferable for the parties engaged in negotiations to reach their own agreement, as opposed to having an outsider impose agreement on them. After all, the parties are the ones that must ultimately live with the agreement. With this in mind, mediation is the form of alternative dispute resolution best designed to achieve this end. The mediator's role is that of helping the parties themselves to resolve their differences and find solutions each side can accept. The mediator may be appointed by the State Employment Relations Board or may be requested by one or both parties from the board or a private agency such as the American Arbitration Association. State law and/or individual contracts will determine the method of appointment. The parties usually share the mediation fee. Mediators from either source come to the impasse trained to assist the parties in resolving the problems that have brought them to impasse.

Mediators do this by helping negotiators at impasse clarify the issues fueling their conflict. The first step in negotiating a constructive settlement is to confront the opposition.[8] A *confrontation* is the direct expression of one's views of the

Ohio	Ohio Rev. Code Ann. § 4114.14

- Allow any dispute settlement procedure mutually agreed to by the parties.
- Either party may request mediation by a State Employment Relations Board.
- Board appoints mediator.
- Board may appoint fact-finding panel.
- Panel's findings and recommendations are deemed agreed unless rejected by either three-fifths vote of the legislative body or three-fifths vote of the employee membership.
- Board may appoint an arbitrator.

Pennsylvania	Pa. Stat. Ann. tit. 43 § 1101.801.2

- Mandatory mediation with Pennsylvania Bureau of Mediation.
- Either party may request the Bureau to appoint fact-finding panel.
- Either party may reject the fact-finding panel's recommendations.
- Arbitration limited to final best-offer arbitration, but only if part of contract.
- Arbitration impasse procedure a required bargaining issue, but not a required contract provision.
- Final best-offer arbitration may be best package, issue-by-issue, or separate economic and noneconomic packages.
- Final best-offer arbitration allows arbitrator to accept fact-finding recommendation, if available, instead of best offer.

Illinois	115 Ill. Comp. Stat. Ann. § 5/12

- Either party or the Illinois Educational Labor Relations Board may initiate mediation.
- Board may appoint mediator or parties may agree to use American Arbitration Association or Federal Mediation and Conciliation Services.
- No formal fact-finding other than fact-finding conducted by mediator upon request by either party.
- Parties may agree to final and binding impartial arbitration over unresolved issues.
- Educational employees may not strike unless mediation has been used without success.

Florida	Fla. Stat. Ann. § § 447.403, .405, .603

- No arbitration procedures available.
- Employer alone or both parties jointly may secure a mediator.
- If there is no mediator, State Commission may appoint a Special Master.
- Special Master holds hearings on unresolved issues.
- Broad discretion to review comparisons with similar employees in state and comparable private employees in area, ability of employer to finance interests and welfare of the public.
- Special Master's recommendations are deemed approved unless specifically rejected by either party.
- Rejected Special Master's recommendation presented to legislative body.
- Legislative body's action on disputed issues becomes part of final contract for the remainder of the first fiscal year.
- Local legislative body may elect by ordinance, etc., to adopt own procedures in lieu of state provisions.

Figure 4.1   Comparing Approaches to Alternative Dispute Resolution Procedures

conflict and one's feelings about it, coupled with an invitation to the opposition to do the same.[9] The mediator's job is to structure this confrontation in such a way as to clearly inform each party of the other's concerns without creating further hostility. Ideally, the mediator helps the parties approach their conflict as a mutual problem to be solved. Often conflict arises because the parties do not really understand the needs and feelings fueling each party's position.

In the video series *Negotiate Like the Pros*,[10] John Patrick Dolan gives an interesting example to illustrate this point. Two sisters argue about who should get one remaining orange. The obvious solution to divide the orange, giving each one half, is met with heated opposition because each claims a need for the whole orange. However, the parent mediating the struggle for ownership of the orange begins by asking each sister why she so adamantly wants the whole orange for herself. The first sister says that she wants the whole orange because she is baking a cake that calls for her to use the rind of a whole orange. The second sister says that she needs the whole orange because she is making a fruit salad. When the sisters hear each other's reasons for wanting the whole orange, a solution to their disagreement becomes obvious. The first sister will remove the rind she needs for her cake and allow her sister to use the remainder of the fruit in her salad. As Dolan explains, conflicts in negotiating sometimes arise simply because the parties at impasse do not really understand the reasons for the positions taken by their opponents. The role of the mediator is to help parties clarify positions and seek mutually beneficial solutions. Mediators do not choose between the parties or impose their own solutions on the parties. Also, The role of the mediator is to help the parties find their own way around the impasse. A competent mediator can educate unsophisticated negotiators about the bargaining process and the give-and-take inherent in that process, while diffusing the emotions that gave rise to impasse.

Fact-Finding

If mediation fails to help the parties resolve their differences, law or contract may require fact-finding. The fact finder, like the mediator, is a neutral third party. The fact finder's mission, however, is to gather all relevant information pertinent to the issues in conflict and to actually propose a solution to the impasse based on this data. Some state laws allow fact finders to continue the mediation process, offering suggestions, but ultimately allowing the parties to fashion their own settlement. Other state laws define fact-finding as a separate stage of the alternative dispute resolution process in which the disinterested third party may independently fashion a resolution to the conflict based on the information each side has provided or choose between the solutions presented

Florida	FLA. STAT. ANN. § 447.405

- Comparison of annual income of similar work exhibiting similar skills under similar working conditions in the local operating area.
- Comparison of annual income of public employees in similar public employment in governmental bodies of comparable size within the state.
- Interest and welfare of the public.
- Comparison of peculiarities of employment in regard to other professions, specifically with respect to hazards of employment, physical qualifications, educational qualifications, intellectual qualifications, job training and skills, retirement plans, sick leave, and job security.
- Availability of funds.

Figure 4.2   Fact-Finding Criteria in Florida

by the sides. In either case, the fact finder's solution must be based on the data and oral arguments presented at the fact-finding hearing and must take into consideration certain legally delineated concerns. State law often prescribes the criteria fact finders are to use in developing their settlement suggestions. Most are expansive. Figure 4.2 examines the criteria to be used by fact finders in Florida, a representative example.

Fact-finding differs from mediation in two significant ways. First, the impasse resolution may be developed solely by the fact finder, and, second, the fact finder may be at liberty to release the suggested settlement to the public as well as to the parties. While the parties are free to reject the fact finder's solution, this public release of the proposed settlement is usually supported by factual data giving reasons for the fact finder's suggested solution. Such documented reasoning supporting the fact finder's proposal can go far in creating public pressure for the parties to settle. In addition, the fact finder's report, if rejected, sets the stage for arbitration, and the arbitrator will give significant weight to the information gathered by the fact finder and to the fact finder's suggestions for resolving impasse.

Arbitration

Arbitrators are like mediators and fact finders in that they are also neutral third parties trained to resolve impasse. Unlike mediators or fact finders, however, arbitrators are not at liberty to improvise and fashion their own solutions to the problems presented by the parties. Arbitrators choose between the solutions developed and proposed by the parties themselves. Arbitrators, like fact finders, are trained to base their decisions on criteria prescribed by the state's collective bargaining law. For example, the criteria to be considered in making an arbitration award in the state of Michigan include the authority of the public employer, the financial ability of the public employer, the interests of the public, consumer prices, and comparable wages.[11]

Arbitration of contract disputes is called "interest" arbitration and takes place only at impasse, usually only after mediation or fact-finding or both have been unsuccessfully tried. Arbitration can be advisory or binding. Advisory arbitration may be voluntary or prescribed by law, but in either case, the parties using advisory arbitration are under no obligation to accept the decision of the arbitrator. On the other hand, if arbitration is binding, the parties will be forced to accept the decision of the arbitrator as their final settlement and honor it for the life of the contract. The scope of arbitration may be limited to specific items remaining in dispute, or it may encompass the whole of the contract. The term *last best offer binding arbitration* refers to the specific form of arbitration in which the arbitrator chooses between the final and best offers each side is prepared to make. The advantage of this approach is that parties are unlikely to play games in making their proposals, and the proposals will be based on researched data and positions intended to persuade the arbitrator. Essentially, last best offer binding arbitration forces both sides to do their homework.

Twenty-seven states have legislation authorizing voluntary or compulsory arbitration for the resolution of some or all outstanding issues in certain public sector disputes. These states are Alaska, Connecticut, Delaware, Hawaii, Illinois, Indiana, Iowa, Maine, Massachusetts, Michigan, Minnesota, Montana, Nebraska, Nevada, New Hampshire, New Jersey, New York, Ohio, Oklahoma, Oregon, Pennsylvania, Rhode Island, Texas, Vermont, Washington, Wisconsin, and Wyoming.[12] While advisory arbitration is common, binding arbitration is often reserved for those public employees who do not have the right to strike. Police and firefighters, for example, are usually accorded binding arbitration under state law. Teachers in some states, such as Connecticut, also fall into this category, with the law according them last best offer binding arbitration in lieu of the right to strike. However, teachers in many other states retain the right to strike.

It has been suggested that the availability of binding arbitration undermines the collective bargaining process because it encourages parties to hold out and relies on the arbitrator as a substitute for meaningful negotiation.[13] Critics maintain that binding arbitration amounts to an inappropriate delegation of power to the arbitrator who has the ultimate authority to determine important employment matters that could profoundly affect the services being provided for the public and the manner in which finite governmental revenues are to be expended.[14] Boards of education can blame expensive settlements that raise taxes on the arbitrator, thereby politically distancing themselves from the repercussions of that decision. At the same time, unions have gone on record as opposing binding arbitration where it is used as a substitute for their right to strike but doing little to change the state laws mandating its use as a substitute for the right to strike.[15] In the final analysis, empirical data from jurisdictions using arbitration to resolve bargaining impasses show that the availability of this method of alternative dispute resolution actually diminishes strike activity.[16]

Strike

If mediation, fact-finding, and advisory arbitration fail and binding arbitration is not an option, teachers may strike in states that statutorily permit them to do so.[17] A strike is a willful and concerted work stoppage. No employee, public or private, has a constitutional right to strike in concert. State or federal law must give that right. Section 7 of the National Labor Relations Act gave private sector employees the right to engage in concerted activities for the purpose of collective bargaining, and striking is viewed as a form of such concerted activity. State public sector collective bargaining laws may, in a similar fashion, give some or all public sector employees the right to strike, but state public sector collective bargaining laws may also specifically forbid public employee strikes. States that prohibit public employee strikes do so because they feel that such strikes are a threat to public health, safety, and welfare.

In states that do allow teachers to strike, they must usually follow certain legislated procedures. Only after the contract has expired and the union has engaged in good faith bargaining, including the use of prescribed alternative dispute resolution procedures, does the strike become an option. Even then, teachers are required to notify both the board of education and the State Employee Relations Board of their planned work stoppage and to provide assurances that the strike will not endanger public health or safety. In Ohio, for example, teachers' unions must complete the form appearing in figure 4.3, serving notice of their intent to strike to both the State Employee Relations Board and the board of education ten days before striking so that the boards of education can prepare for impending work stoppages.[18] Failure to comply with legislated restrictions on the right to strike can make the work stoppage illegal, and teachers who participate in illegal strikes are subject to loss of pay and disciplinary action.

The goal of the school district is to keep schools open during a strike. Strikes that close schools result in lost learning time as well as lost funding for the district. In addition, since the length of the school year is prescribed legislatively, students must make up days lost during a strike. Schools that can stay open during a strike with substitute coverage actually save money since the pay to sub-

STATE OF OHIO
**STATE EMPLOYMENT
RELATIONS BOARD**
65 East State Street, 12th Floor
Columbus, Ohio 43215-4213
(614) 644-8573

ENTER MEDIATION CASE NUMBER IN THIS SPACE	DO NOT WRITE IN THIS SPACE
Case No.	

NOTICE OF INTENT
TO STRIKE OR PICKET

SERB Official Time Stamp

INSTRUCTIONS: File *one original and one copy* of this form with the State Employment Relations Board at the above address and serve *one copy* on the employer. See Ohio Revised Code Sections 4117.14(D)(2) and 4117.11(B)(8), Ohio Administrative Code Rule 4117-13-01, and related SERB unauthorized strike determinations.

1. NOTICE OF INTENT TO STRIKE ONLY ❑ | NOTICE OF INTENT TO PICKET ONLY ❑ | NOTICE OF INTENT TO STRIKE AND PICKET ❑

2. DATE AND TIME WHEN INTENDED STRIKE WILL COMMENCE: | **3.** DATE AND TIME WHEN INTENDED PICKETING WILL COMMENCE:

4. NAME OF EMPLOYER WHERE STRIKE OR PICKETING IS TO OCCUR: | Telephone:
( )
Address: | Fax:
( )
City, County, State, Zip: |

5. NAME OF EMPLOYER'S REPRESENTATIVE: | Telephone:
( )
Address: | Fax:
( )
City, State, Zip: |

6. NAME OF EMPLOYEE ORGANIZATION RECOGNIZED AS EXCLUSIVE REPRESENTATIVE OF EMPLOYEES WHO INTEND TO STRIKE OR PICKET: | Telephone:
( )
Address: | Fax:
( )
City, State, Zip: |

7. NAME OF EMPLOYEE ORGANIZATION'S REPRESENTATIVE: | Telephone:
( )
Address: | Fax:
( )
City, State, Zip: |

8. BARGAINING UNIT: (List classifications included in certification or collective bargaining agreement recognition clause, or attach copy of the agreement.)
   Included: | **9.** APPROXIMATE NUMBER OF EMPLOYEES IN UNIT:

Revised   ERB 1016   (7/99)

Figure 4.3a   Notice of Intent to Strike

10. COLLECTIVE BARGAINING AGREEMENT:

Are any of the employees who intend to strike or picket currently
covered by a collective bargaining agreement?   ❑ Yes   ❑ No

If yes, state expiration date   (1) of agreement   _____

                            (2) of extension   _____ *(if any)*

Are negotiations for a REOPENER of the bargaining agreement?   ❑ Yes   ❑ No

If yes, designate section of reopener provision: _____

11. DESCRIPTION OF EFFORTS MADE TO RESOLVE THE DISPUTE, INCLUDING STATUTORY OR ALTERNATE DISPUTE SETTLEMENT PROCEDURES:

THIS NOTICE OF INTENT TO STRIKE OR PICKET WILL NOT BE ACCEPTED FOR FILING IF THE PROOF
OF SERVICE IS NOT FULLY COMPLETED AND SIGNED BY A REPRESENTATIVE OF THE EMPLOYEE
ORGANIZATION.

DECLARATION

I declare that I have read the contents of this Notice of Intent to Strike or Picket and that the statements it contains are
true and correct to the best of my knowledge and belief.

To distinguish originals, please do not use black ink for signatures.

_____   _____

Signature of Person Attesting to Content of Form   Date

_____

Print or Type Name

PROOF OF SERVICE

I certify that an exact copy of the foregoing Notice of Intent to Strike or Picket has been sent or delivered to:

_____

(Name and complete address of employer.)

_____

by   ❑ Regular U.S. Mail   ❑ Certified U.S. Mail   ❑ Hand Delivery   ❑ Other _____

this _____ day of _____(month), _____(year).

_____   _____

Signature of Person Attesting to Service of Form   Print or Type Name

Figure 4.3b   Notice of Intent to Strike

stitutes is less than that to regular teachers, and the district continues to get its
average daily membership funding with no obligation to make up time lost during the strike. The board is also under no obligation to continue pay or benefits
to striking teachers.

For unions, striking, if it closes the district's schools, is a way to bring public pressure on boards of education to settle. If schools close, parents must make arrangements to have students supervised. Strikes that close schools result in lost work time for both parents and students. On the other hand, if the district can keep its schools open during a strike, each day is a day of lost wages for teachers who will not have the opportunity to make up the day, and while the district is required to honor the existing contract during negotiations, mediation, fact-finding, and arbitration, it is not required to continue benefits to striking employees. In states that do not legislatively give teachers the right to strike, the parties can agree to continue to use alternative dispute resolution procedures to help them come to a mutual agreement or the board can unilaterally implement its last best offer.[19]

Districts notified that a strike is imminent must decide whether they can safely keep the schools open and operating. They have four basic groups they can call on to supervise students and the program: teachers who are not members of the union, teachers who are members of the union but choose to cross picket lines, substitute teachers, and administrators. Building administrators must carefully assess the number of certified and qualified employees ready, willing, and able to provide classroom coverage. If adequate coverage cannot be provided, student safety might come into jeopardy and the school should be closed. Also, those covering classrooms during a strike should be provided with adequate protection, supervision, and continuing support for their efforts.

School strikes are extremely disruptive and demoralizing events. Individual schools and teachers rarely emerge from them unscathed, and sometimes the dissension they create goes on for years. Teachers who struck, no matter what the outcome of the action, feel alienated from those who chose to cross the picket lines. Teachers who philosophically disagree with the concept of striking will resent the social pressure used by the union as it seeks compliance. In summary, the strike is an impasse resolution alternative that should be avoided if at all possible.

CONTRACT ADMINISTRATION

Once the parties have ratified their settlement agreement by a vote of their respective memberships, it becomes the rule book for human resource management. That is why human resource managers at every level must be familiar with the agreement and understand how it came into being. Good human resource management requires an appreciation for the language of the contract and for the positions and feelings at the bargaining table that created the contract. For the negotiated term of the contract, both the union and the administration will be bound by it. The union and the administration will also be bound by the tenets of the state's collective bargaining law requiring them to negotiate wages, hours, and terms and conditions of employment. In order to avoid midterm bargaining, some contracts contain "zipper clauses" essentially ensuring that any matter not addressed in the contract remains a management right. A typical zipper clause would appear in the management rights section of the contract and might say:

> The Board of Education and those empowered to act for the Board retain the authority with regard to all matters relating to the operation, management, planning and direction of the school system, and of the schools, including, but not limited to staffing, standards, employment and finance, except as expressly limited by law or an express provision of this agreement.[20]

Zipper clauses give the board of education the right to act unilaterally during the life of the contract on matters that are not part of the negotiated agreement.

A grievance is the mechanism for addressing a perceived breach of the contract. Every negotiated contract must include a clause detailing the process for filing a grievance and resolving claims that the contract has been breached. In contrast, an unfair labor practice is the means for addressing a perceived violation of employee rights under the collective bargaining law, and the collective bargaining law outlines the procedures required for filing an unfair labor practice claim. An understanding of each process is essential to successful contract administration.

Unfair Labor Practices

An unfair labor practice is an act or a course of conduct by either the union or the administration that violates the existing rights accorded either party under the state's collective bargaining law. Unfair labor practice charges are filed with the State Employment Relations Boards by either the employer or the employee union against the other party. The standard of "unfairness" is difficult to define,[21] although a state's collective bargaining law usually makes some effort to define employee and employer practices deemed "unfair." These basic attempts to define the concept of the unfair labor practice, however, evolve case by case as State Employee Relations Boards rule on acts or courses of conduct, by boards of education and unions, perceived as violations of the states' collective bargaining laws.

Employer Unfair Labor Practices

While the term "unfair" may be difficult to define, collective bargaining laws frequently cite typical unfair labor practices on the part of both union and employer. In general, an unfair labor practice is any act or course of conduct that interferes with an employee's rights under the collective bargaining law. A list of behaviors likely to give rise to the charge of an unfair labor practice for either side follows.

Board of Education Unfair Labor Practices

It is an unfair labor practice for a board of education or its agents or representatives to

1. interfere with the selection of a union to represent teachers in collective bargaining;
2. initiate, create, dominate, or interfere with the formation or administration of a teachers' union;
3. contribute financially or otherwise support a union;
4. discriminate in hiring or employment practices on the basis of union membership and support;
5. discharge or discriminate against a teacher because he or she has filed charges or given testimony regarding a board's violation of the collective bargaining law;
6. refuse to bargain collectively and in good faith with the union selected;
7. fail to process grievances and requests for the arbitration of grievances;
8. lock out or otherwise prevent employees from performing their regularly assigned duties in an effort to force employees to accept the board's terms during a labor dispute;
9. communicate directly with employees rather than with the union representative on matters of wages, hours, and terms and conditions of employment;
10. refuse to provide the union with requested information pertinent to its representative duties.

This list is by no means exhaustive, but it does give a sense of the kinds of actions that can sustain a charge of an unfair labor practice against a board of education.

Teachers' unions can also be charged with committing unfair labor practices. Some samples of prohibited activities on the part of the union follow.

Teachers' Unions Unfair Labor Practices

It is an unfair labor practice for an employee organization, its agent, representatives, or public employees to

1. restrain or coerce employees in the exercise of their rights under the collective bargaining law;

2. cause or attempt to cause the board to ignore standards promulgated by the state board of education;
3. refuse to bargain collectively;
4. call, institute, or maintain, or conduct an illegal work stoppage;
5. induce or encourage employees to participate in an illegal work stoppage;
6. fail to fairly represent all public employees in a bargaining unit;
7. engage in picketing, striking, or other concerted actions without giving written notice to the public employer and to the State Employment Relations Board as prescribed by the collective bargaining law;
8. encourage secondary boycotts;
9. cause an employer to commit an unfair labor practice;
10. cause an employer to ignore existing laws regarding workplace practices.

This list, too, gives a sense of the kinds of union activity that would give rise to the charge of an unfair labor practice against a union. It should be noted that unfair labor practice charges may be brought against a union by the board of education and by bargaining unit members who feel they have not been fairly represented by the union.

Unfair labor practice charges are filed with the State Employment Relations Board, and a representative of the board will investigate the complaint. If there is a showing of probable cause, a hearing will be held, if not, the charge will be dismissed. If the hearing officer determines that an unfair labor practice has been committed, the offending party will be ordered to cease and desist, and if need be, to take affirmative action to right the wrong done. The State Employment Relations Board may use the courts to enforce its orders.

Grievances

While unfair labor practices are based on violations of the collective bargaining law, grievances are based on violations of the collective bargaining agreement. Grievances must connect to specific contract clauses. Grievance arbitration is referred to as "rights" arbitration because the arbitrator is limited to interpreting rights accorded employees under the contract. An essential element of every collective bargaining agreement is the clause outlining the procedure for resolving grievances. Figure 4.4 is an example of a typical grievance procedure clause in a negotiated agreement.[22]

As with the "interest" arbitration used to resolve impasse in bargaining, "rights" arbitration can be used to resolve grievances arising out of the contract if it is part of the grievance procedure. Rights arbitration can be either advisory

A. Definition of Grievance

A Grievance is a claim by an employee, group of employees, or the ECEA that there has been a violation, misinterpretation, or misapplication of the specific term or terms of this Agreement.

B. Procedure

The purpose of the grievance procedure is to reach an equitable solution consistent with the terms of this Agreement in the shortest time at the lowest administrative level possible. If the grievance involves more than one work location or a group or class of employees and the Immediate Supervisor is without authority to grant the relief sought, or arises from the action or inaction of an administrator above the level of the Immediate Supervisor, it may be filed initially with the Personnel Director at Step 3 of the grievance procedure, and the informal discussion may be waived by either party.

Step 1. Informal Discussion

An employee or the ECEA with a claim that the basis exists for a grievance shall discuss the grievance with the Immediate Supervisor informally.

Step 2. Immediate Supervisor

If the informal discussion in Step 1 does not provide a satisfactory disposition of the grievance, ECEA may submit the grievance in writing to the Immediate Supervisor on the Grievance Form found in Appendix A within twenty (20) workdays after the grievant had knowledge, or reasonably could have had knowledge, of the event or condition giving rise to the grievance. A written decision is to be rendered by the Immediate Supervisor to the ECEA within five (5) workdays of presentation of the grievance form.

Step 3. Personnel Director

If the grievance is not resolved at Step 2, the grievance may be presented by ECEA to the Personnel Director within five (5) workdays after receipt of the decision of the Immediate Supervisor under Step 2. The Personnel Director will render a written decision to the ECEA within five (5) workdays of presentation of the grievance.

Step 4. Arbitration

If the grievance is not resolved at Step 3, ECEA may submit the grievance to arbitration by giving written notice to the Superintendent of its intent to do so within twenty (20) workdays of failure of resolution at Step 3. ECEA shall then request the American Arbitration Association to administer the proceedings under the Voluntary Labor Arbitration Rules of that Association. The arbitrator shall be chosen from a list of seven (7) names furnished by the American Arbitration Association. Either party shall have the right to reject one list of arbitrators and to direct the AAA to submit a new list.

The arbitrator's decision shall be binding on all parties including, but not limited to, the board, the grievant, and the ECEA. The cost of arbitration shall be borne equally between the board and the ECEA.

Figure 4.4a   Grievance Procedure

C. Stipulations

1. The fact that an employee files a grievance shall not be recorded in his personnel file or in any file used in the transfer, assignment, or promotion process; nor shall such fact be used in any recommendation for re-employment or recommendation for other employment; nor shall the grievant, the ECEA, or its officers be placed in jeopardy or be the subject of reprisal or discrimination for having followed the grievance procedure.

2. The grievant shall be entitled to be accompanied by a representative designated by the ECEA President or Grievance Chairperson at any stage of this procedure.

3. A grievance may be withdrawn at any level without prejudice.

4. The parties agree that grievance proceedings shall be kept as informal and confidential as may be appropriate at the level of the procedure. Further, it is agreed that the investigating and processing of any grievance shall be conducted in a professional manner at such time and in such ways as not to cause interruption or interference with established teaching schedules and duties and are consistent with past practices. There shall be no releases regarding the grievance to the news media during the processing of a grievance.

5. The Administration will cooperate with the Grievance Committee in its investigation of any grievance.

6. Since it is important that grievances be processed as expeditiously as possible, the number of days stipulated shall be considered maximum. However, the time limit may be extended for just cause by mutual agreement. The absence of a party-in-interest shall constitute just cause for time limit extensions of up to five (5) days.

7. The time limitations set forth hereinafter for the submission of a grievance at any step shall be deemed of essence, and the failure by the ECEA to submit a grievance within the time specified shall be deemed an abandonment of that grievance.

8. A grievance may be submitted within the timeline but shall not be processed until it is assigned a grievance number by the ECEA President/designee.

9. Settlements between the parties at any stage short of arbitration shall bind the immediate parties and the ECEA to the settlement and shall be deemed binding precedent in any later grievance proceeding unless the board and the ECEA agree otherwise.

Figure 4.4b   Grievance Procedure

or binding. However, employees bringing grievances must first follow the steps in the bargained process, including arbitration, if it is part of the process, before they will be allowed a day in court.

Arbitrators hearing grievances have two questions to decide: (1) is the grievance arbitrable, and (2) who wins? Both questions are inextricably tied to the language of the contract. Arbitrators can only decide issues that arise from the language of a contract that specifically empowers an arbitrator to hear the issue, and arbitrators are required to render their decisions based solely on their interpretation of the language of the contract.

GRIEVANCE NO. _____

Date of Filing: _____

NAME OF GRIEVANT _____

SCHOOL BUILDING _____

DATE GRIEVANCE OCCURRED _____

SECTION(S) OF AGREEMENT ALLEGEDLY VIOLATED, MISINTERPRETED, OR MISAPPLIED

_____

_____

DATE OF STEP 1 FORMAL DISCUSSION: _____

A. Facts upon which this grievance is based:

B. Relief sought:

_____   _____
Signature of Grievant   Signature of Person Receiving Grievance
                                            at Initial Filing

_____   _____
Date   Date Received

Figure 4.5   Form for Filing Grievance

Arbitrators, like judges, will have both sides present evidence and arguments supporting their positions on these questions. Administrators involved in the grievance process should frame both the issue and their proposed resolution of the grievance in terms of their interpretation of the contract. The arbitrator is confined to the four corners of the contract, therefore, to win, the administrator must convince the arbitrator that actions taken were based on a valid interpretation of the contract clause in question.

Figure 4.5 is an example of a form used to process a grievance. Note that the grievant is required to cite the section of the agreement breached, to describe how this clause has been violated by the administration, and, finally, to describe the relief sought.

Administrative responses to grievances must relate to the administration's interpretation of the contract. Evidence supporting this interpretation might include past practice and similar grievances decided in favor of the administration's interpretation. If external law has an impact on the way the contract is to be interpreted, the side offering this argument must introduce the law in question to support their position. Arbitrators have no authority to introduce external law, that is, they are not authorized to advance arguments for either side, or to go beyond the language of the contract. They must rely on each party to prepare arguments that introduce all relevant factors.

In preparing for a grievance hearing, administrators must do their homework as they would in interest, that is, contract impasse arbitration. Specifically, they must frame the issue in contractual terms and support their positions with factual data based on past practice, relevant external law, and previously decided arbitrations and interpretations of the contract. With this in mind, it becomes an important part of human resource management to keep accurate records regarding past practice and grievance resolutions. Past practice may serve to clarify, implement, and even amend contract language, and, in some cases, an established practice is regarded as a distinct and binding condition of employment, one that cannot be changed without the mutual consent of the parties.[23]

Examples

The American Arbitration Association publishes a monthly summary of *Arbitration Awards in the Schools*. The two abbreviated examples cited from this publication give some insight into how arbitrators make decisions regarding the arbitrability and resolution of grievances:

Stillwater Central School District (NY) and Stillwater Teachers Association:[24] This issue pertains to the assignment of jobs—the assignment of a regular teacher as a substitute. The grievant, a tenured remedial teacher serving as an instructional support teacher, protested assignment as a substitute for a teacher attending a meeting. The Association argued that the language of the contract was clear and unambiguous and stated that members of the regular teaching staff could not be used as substitutes without their consent. The Association also asserted a long-standing past practice supporting its position. The District argued that there was a distinction between a "teacher" and a "regular classroom teacher." The District maintained that a "regular classroom teacher" was any faculty member "whose schedule is solely defined by the administrator in the building and one who is committed to a student or group of students according to the schedule created by someone other than that regular teacher, usually the building administrator." The District also asserted that it was not unusual in her position as an instructional support teacher to be asked to cover a class by her regular teaching colleagues or to team teach with them.

The arbitrator in this case found that the Agreement "makes no distinction between classroom teachers, remedial teachers and instructional support teachers. The operative contract language regulating District use of teachers in the 'substitute process' refers only to 'members of the regular teaching staff.'" Thus, the arbitrator ruled that the District violated the Agreement when it used a regular classroom teacher as a substitute without her consent.

Marysville Public Schools and St. Clair County Education Association:[25] This dispute arose when the grievant, a music teacher, was questioned in the hall by the superintendent about her use of a "without review" leave day. The superintendent said that if she did not explain her absence within a week, she would lose a day's pay, and if she lied, the superintendent would be forced to consider issuing discipline. The Association viewed this encounter as a disciplinary meeting and argued that the District failed to follow the disciplinary protocol outlined in the Agreement. Specifically, the grievant's immediate supervisor did not contact her and discuss the issue in private, the grievant was not allowed representation during this disciplinary meeting with the superintendent, and the Association was not supplied with information regarding the charges against the grievant. The District called the encounter "a mere correction of the leave situation."

The Arbitrator agreed with the union that this encounter with the superintendent did amount to a disciplinary meeting. The superintendent's actions reflected a decision that leave had been improperly used and that pay, which was not voluntarily relinquished, had to be deducted. The District in this case failed to comply with the contractual disciplinary process when the superintendent did not meet with the grievant in private or give her the opportunity to secure union representation.

A LEGAL PERSPECTIVE

In states with collective bargaining laws, the parties to a contract will be expected to follow the procedures and timelines prescribed by the law in negotiating wages, hours, and terms and conditions of employment. The State Employment Relations Board will oversee compliance with the process and will assist the parties in overcoming impasse should it occur. Once the contract has been ratified, it has the force of law, but in a sense, negotiations continue through the filing of grievances and unfair labor practices. Grievances are used to clarify contract language that is ambiguous and to modify or amend the contract by way of past practice. Unfair labor practices address conduct on the part of either the district or the union that appears to violate the collective bargaining law itself.

THEORY INTO PRACTICE

1. What impasse provisions are provided for in your state's collective bargaining law?
2. Investigate how states with no collective bargaining laws determine wages, hours, and terms and conditions of employment? Who makes this determination?
3. Investigate how teacher grievances are handled in a school district with a collective bargaining agreement.
4. Private schools seldom have negotiated contracts. Interview a private school teacher regarding wages, hours, and terms and conditions of employment and how problems with wages, hours, or terms and conditions of employment are addressed in private schools. What recourse do dissatisfied teachers have?
5. Discuss terms and conditions of employment that are perceived as problems in your school district.
6. Interview a school principal regarding the number of grievances filed in a given school year and how they were resolved.
7. Compare teacher salaries in a school with a negotiated agreement to teacher salaries in a comparable school without a negotiated agreement.
8. Interview the head of a teachers' union regarding the nature of any unfair labor practices they have filed.
9. How were the unfair labor practice claims in problem 8 resolved?
10. Discuss the pros and cons of last best offer binding arbitration as opposed to the right to strike.

NOTES

1. Belfield Educ. Ass'n v. Belfield Pub. Sch. Dist. No. 13, 496 N.W.2d 12 (N.D. 1993).

2. Belfield Educ. Ass'n at 12.

3. Edgeley Educ. Ass'n v. Edgeley Pub. Sch. Dist. No. 3, 256 N.W.2d 348, 352 (N.D. 1977).

4. Detroit Police Officers Ass'n v. City of Detroit, 391 Mich. 44, 214 N.W.2d 803, 808 (1974).

5. *See, e.g.,* OHIO REV. CODE ANN. § 4117.08(C) (Anderson 2001), and SERB v. Brookfield Local Sch. Dist. Bd. of Educ., 4 Ohio Pub. Employee Rep. ¶ 4044 (1987) (no duty to bargain creation of new position); SERB v. Morgan Local Sch. Dist. Bd. of Educ., Case Nos. 87-ULP-6-0253 and 87-ULP-7-0284 (1989) (no duty to bargain reassignment of music teachers).

6. Clark County Sch. Dist. v. Local Gov't Employee Mgmt. Relations Bd., and Washoe County Teachers Ass'n v. Washoe County Sch. Dist., 90 Nev. 442, 530 P.2d 114 (Nev. 1974).

7. Edgeley Educ. Ass'n at 348, 352; Fargo Educ. Ass'n v. Paulsen, 239 N.W.2d 842, 847 (N.D. 1976).

8. C. Argyris, *Intervention Theory and Method* (Reading, Mass.: Addison-Wesley, 1970).

9. D. W. Johnson and F. P. Johnson, *Joining Together: Group Theory and Group Skills,* 3d ed. (Englewood Cliffs, N.J.: Prentice-Hall, 1987), 289.

10. J. P. Dolan, *Negotiate Like the Pros* (Boulder, Colo.: CareerTrack Publications, 1994).

11. MICH. COMP. LAWS § 423.239 (2001).

12. D. P. Rothschild et al., *Collective Bargaining and Labor Arbitration,* 3d ed. (Charlottesville, Va.: The Michie Company, 1979), 801.

13. Rothschild, *Collective Bargaining and Labor Arbitration,* 798–799.

14. Rothschild, *Collective Bargaining and Labor Arbitration,* 799.

15. B. Marczely, "Binding Arbitration Stops Teacher Strikes," *The American School Board Journal* 170, no. 11 (1983): 31–32, 54.

16. Rothschild, *Collective Bargaining and Labor Arbitration,* 799.

17. Alaska, Colorado, Hawaii, Illinois, Minnesota, Montana, Ohio, Oregon, Pennsylvania, Vermont, and Wisconsin grant public employees a limited right to strike.

18. State of Ohio State Employment Relations Board, *Form ERB 1016* (7/99).

19. *See, e.g.,* Mountain Valley Educ. Ass'n v. Maine Sch. Admin. Dist. No. 43, 655 A.2d 348 (Me. 1995).

20. East Cleveland Board of Education and East Cleveland Education Association, *Agreement,* Effective April 4, 1999 to April 3, 2002, Article III, 6.

21. *See,* annotations to 29 U.S.C.S. § 158 (2002) interpreting "unfairness."

22. East Cleveland Board of Education and East Cleveland Education Association, *Agreement,* Effective April 4, 1999 to April 3, 2002, Article III, 4.

23. R. Mittenthal, "Past Practice and the Administration of Collective Bargaining Agreements," 59 Mich. L. Rev. 1017, 1026-40 (1961).

24. D. E. Eischen, Arbitrator, *Arbitration in the Schools,* 363-1 (Horsham, Pa.: LRP Publications, May 2000), 2.

25. S. Sperka, Marysville Public Schools (MI) and St. Clair County Education Association, 364-7, *Arbitration in the Schools* (Horsham, Pa.: LRP Publications, June 2000), 6.

Chapter Five

Laws Affecting
Human Resource Management

While collectively bargained agreements have a direct and localized effect on wages, hours, and terms and conditions of employment, there are also federal and state laws that will have an equally important effect on employee rights and human resource management. Employees who collectively bargain are protected by the contract and by federal and state laws prescribing specific rights in the workplace. Employees who do not collectively bargain, for example, administrators and teachers in some states, however, must rely solely on federal and state laws to prescribe and protect their workplace rights. These laws deal with such civil rights as protection from discrimination, freedom of expression and association, job safety, employee privacy, workers' compensation, and job security. The protections such federal and state laws provide cannot be overridden or ignored by local contracts or management rights.

The list of federal laws affecting employment is formidable. This chapter will review and discuss those federal laws and constitutional provisions that are most likely to have a direct effect on human resource management in the public schools. Where they exist, state statutes addressing these issues mirror these federal laws. It must be remembered, however, that federal laws provide a floor, not a ceiling, for state legislation affecting employee rights. That is, state laws can give employees more rights than those granted by federal law, but they cannot give employees fewer rights than those accorded under federal statutes. Figure 5.1 provides a summary of the major federal legislation that will have an impact on public school human resource management.

TITLE VII

Discrimination has always been a problem in the workplace. Title VII of the Civil Rights Act of 1964[1] prohibits employment discrimination on the basis of race,

Law	Citation	Purpose
Title VII	42 U.S.C. § 2000e *et seq.*, Pub. L. 88-352 (1964)	Eliminates discrimination based on race, color, creed, gender, and national origin.
Equal Employment Opportunity Act of 1972	42 U.S.C. § 2000e *et seq.*, Pub. L. 92-261 (1972)	Extends Title VII coverage to all private employers with fifteen or more employees, state and local governments, public and private employment agencies, and labor unions.
Pregnancy Amendment to Title VII	42 U.S.C. § 2000e *et seq.*, Pub. L. 95-555 (1978)	Eliminates unequal treatment for pregnant women in employment.
Title IX	20 U.S.C. § 1681 *et seq.* Pub. L. 92-318 (1972)	Eliminates gender discrimination in funded education programs and activities.
Equal Pay Act of 1963	29 U.S.C. § 206(d), Pub. L. 88-38 (1963)	Eliminates discriminatory pay practices based on sex.
Section 504 of the Rehabilitation Act of 1973	29 U.S.C. § 701 *et seq.*, Pub. L. 93-112 (1973)	Protects rights of the disabled in the workplace.
Americans with Disabilities Act of 1990	42 U.S.C. § 12101 *et seq.*, Pub. L. 101-336 (1990)	Protects and extends rights of the disabled.
Age Discrimination in Employment Act	29 U.S.C. § 621 *et seq.* Pub. L. 90-202 (1967)	Eliminates age discrimination in employment.
Age Discrimination in Federally Assisted Programs Act	42 U.S.C. § 61101 *et seq.*, Pub. L. 94-135 (1975)	Withholds federal funding for age discrimination in employment.
Family and Medical Leave Act	29 U.S.C. § 2601 *et seq.*, Pub. L. 103-3 (1993)	Allows employees leave for family emergencies.
Teacher Tenure Laws	See individual state statutes.	Protects teachers' right to continued employment.
COBRA	42 U.S.C. § 300bb-1 *et seq.*, Pub. L. 99-272 (1986)	Continuation of group health plan coverage.
The Fourteenth Amendment	U. S. CONST. amend. XIV	Accords equal protection of the laws, ensures due process, protects life, liberty, and property interests.

Figure 5.1a   Federal Laws Affecting Human Resource Management in Public Schools

| Workmen's Compensation | 5 U.S.C. § 8101 et seq. See individual state statutes. | Protects employees hurt in the course of employment. |
| Unemployment Compensation | 5 U.S.C. § 8501 et seq. See individual state statutes. | Protects employees who lose their jobs through no fault of their own. |

Figure 5.1b   Federal Laws Affecting Human Resource Management in Public Schools

color, religion, sex, or national origin and is applicable to public school districts as part of the Equal Employment Opportunity Act of 1972.[2] Hiring, firing, promotion, demotion, and similar employment decisions cannot be based on race, color, religion, sex, or national origin. Specifically, the law says that a public school, or any other publicly funded institution, cannot discriminate against an individual with respect to compensation, terms, conditions, or privileges of employment because of the individual's race, color, religion, sex, or national origin.[3] In practical terms, this means public schools cannot limit, segregate, or classify employees in any way that would affect an employee's job status or cause the employee to lose job opportunities.[4] Employment decisions must be made without consideration of these protected categories.

Employees who believe they have been the victims of workplace discrimination can register a charge of discrimination with the Equal Employment Opportunity Commission (EEOC), the federal agency responsible for ensuring compliance with Title VII. The EEOC will investigate the employee's claim, and if it finds reasonable cause to believe that the charge has validity, the agency will try to eliminate the discriminatory practice initially by informal conferencing, conciliating, and persuading. If these methods prove unsuccessful, the EEOC may then bring a civil action against the employer. The U.S. Attorney General has exclusive authority to initiate litigation against political subdivisions such as school districts.[5] The EEOC itself, however, does not routinely become embroiled in court action unless a case has wide-ranging implications. Instead, where it has reason to believe there has been a Title VII violation, the EEOC is more likely to issue the complaining employee a "right to sue" letter, essentially authorizing the complaining employee to go to court and request a jury trial.[6] It should be noted, however, that before employees are accorded a day in court, they must first show that they have exhausted all administrative remedies available to them. That is, if they collectively bargain and the contract addresses the issue in dispute, they must first file a grievance regarding their complaint and proceed through the grievance process. Practically speaking, this means that the human resource administrator must process the grievance in a timely fashion or risk having failure to meet contractual timelines become part of the employee's EEOC complaint. Thus, only when the complaint has not been resolved by grievance procedures or by administrative protocols in place to deal with such problems will the EEOC and the courts become involved.

In order to prove a charge of employment discrimination, plaintiff employees must show that they are members of one of the classes protected by Title VII, that they applied for and were qualified for a position, that they were denied the position, and that the employer continued to seek applicants with the plaintiff's qualifications.[7] This same approach, the development of a prima facie case of Title VII discrimination, will be required when employees dispute promotions, tenure, nonrenewal and discipline, termination, or other terms and conditions of employment they perceive to be discriminatory.

Potential remedies available under Title VII include orders to hire or reinstate with back pay. In addition, as a result of the Civil Rights Act of 1991,[8] victims of employment discrimination may also be awarded compensatory and punitive damages if they prove that the discrimination was intentional. Compensatory damages include amounts awarded for "future pecuniary losses, emotional pain, suffering, inconvenience, mental anguish, and loss and enjoyment of life."[9] These damages can range from $50,000 to $300,000, depending on the size of the employer's workforce as described below:

14–100 employees	$50,000
101–200 employees	$100,000
201–500 employees	$200,000
over 500 employees	$300,000[10]

Also, note two areas of discrimination that are not subject to these limitations. If age discrimination, prohibited by the Age Discrimination in Employment Act,[11] is proven, the victim will be entitled to twice the amount of lost pay and benefits as well as reinstatement or promotion.[12] If race discrimination, prohibited by Title VII, is proven, there will be no limit to the victim's damages.[13]

Although school districts themselves, because they are government agencies, cannot be sued for punitive damages, district agents such as superintendents, assistant superintendents, and school board members, named as codefendants in a discrimination case, can be assessed for punitive damages. Title VII and the Civil Rights Act of 1991 were passed to ensure equality of opportunity in employment and to eliminate practices that discriminate on the basis of race, color, religion, sex, or national origin, and public school officials have the responsibility of complying with the letter and spirit of these laws. Together Title VII and the Civil Rights Act of 1991 prohibit not only conscious and overt discrimination in employment practices but also employment practices that, while fair in form, have a "disparate impact" on any group protected by Title VII.[14] Even if an employer is unaware of the disparate impact an employment practice may be having, the employer will be liable under Title VII, and good faith will be no defense.[15] In school districts, employment practices having a disparate impact might include locally developed employee tests that appear to eliminate African American applicants or include job descriptions with requirements that unnecessarily limit the number of qualified female applicants.

The potential impact of these laws on human resource management is obvious. They affect the way positions are developed and advertised, as well as application review, interviewing, and ultimate selection. However, they also affect the ongoing treatment of present employees. Employees in the protected categories who feel discriminated against can be expected to challenge their perceived violations of Title VII as well. In keeping with the old football adage that the best defense is a good offense, employees who are reprimanded, disciplined, or dismissed are also likely to claim some form of discrimination as a defense. In either case, however, the employer in a Title VII discrimination action can prevail if there is documented proof that the disputed employment practice was warranted.

Employees charging discrimination based on race, color, creed, gender, or national origin have the burden of proving their claim. A defending employer must merely produce a nondiscriminatory reason for the employment decision in dispute, but the employer is not obligated to prove that the reason offered is legitimate and nondiscriminatory.[16] The burden is on the complaining employee to show that the reason the employer has given is false and that the reason for the lie is intentional discrimination.[17] Furthermore, even if the employee succeeds in proving that discrimination played a role in the disputed employment decision, an employer can still avoid liability by showing that it had other valid reasons for the decision even if discrimination had not played a role in the decision-making process.[18]

In cases such as these, where the employer has mixed motives for its employment decisions, the courts may grant declaratory or injunctive relief, essentially telling the employer to stop the discrimination, and may grant the employee attorney's fees and court costs, but they will not award damages or issue an order requiring any admission, reinstatement, hiring, promotion, or payment.[19] Congress enacted Title VII to eliminate discrimination in the workplace, but at the same time, the legislative history of Title VII shows that Congress wanted to preserve the right of employers with nondiscriminatory reasons for their actions to act as they deemed necessary.[20]

Affirmative Action

Affirmative Action is the policy of hiring, promoting, and enhancing the employment opportunities of protected classes such as women and minorities. Title VII prohibits discrimination in employment, but it does not mandate that employers act affirmatively to hire applicants in the protected categories. Affirmative action programs are detailed, result-oriented programs, which, when carried out in good faith result in compliance with the equal opportunity clauses found in most legislative and executive orders.[21] The concept of affirmative action first appeared in a 1965 executive order issued by President Lyndon Johnson in which he gave the Secretary of Labor and the Office of Federal Contract Compliance enforcement powers and said that federal contractors must agree in writing to take affirmative action measures in hiring. Earlier executive orders issued by Franklin Roosevelt and John Kennedy had merely prohibited discrimination by federal contractors. Thus, affirmative action initiatives were initially tied solely to federal contracts. However, when public schools were found to have violated Title VII by discriminating in the hiring of teachers and administrators, the concept of affirmative action was extended to public schools as a means of remediating past employment discrimination where it existed and as a means of proving compliance with the equal opportunity provisions of other laws for schools with no history of discriminatory employment practices. Essentially, all antidiscrimination laws and executive orders call for equal employment opportunities, and affirmative action policies serve to prove that employers have provided such opportunities.

The EEOC has disseminated the following guidance for employers who wish to establish affirmative action programs:

1. Develop and disseminate a written policy ensuring that there will be no discrimination in employment practices.
2. Appoint a director to oversee administration of this policy.
3. Analyze staffing with respect to the number of females and minorities employed.
4. In light of this analysis, develop measurable remedial goals for hiring and a timetable for achieving these goals.
5. Develop and implement specific programs to eliminate discrimination in employment.
6. Review employment selection processes with respect to their direct and disparate impact on protected classes.
7. Conduct internal audits to monitor employment practices.
8. Develop district and community programs that support affirmative action goals.[22]

Districts that follow the EEOC's affirmative action guidelines will be able to document their attempts to comply with laws requiring equal employment opportunities in public school human resource management.

Reverse Discrimination

Note once again that Title VII protects the very general categories of race, religion, gender, and national origin. No specific races, religions, genders, or national origins are cited, and although historically African Americans and women have been the primary targets of employment discrimination, they have not been the exclusive plaintiffs filing charges of Title VII discrimination. In recent years, there have been a number of significant reverse discrimination suits brought by Caucasians and men.

In *United Steelworkers, Etc. v. Weber,*[23] a union and an employer entered into a collective bargaining agreement that included an affirmative action plan designed to increase African American participation in a craft training program. When junior black employees were chosen over senior white employees, the white employees brought a reverse discrimination lawsuit. In this case, the Supreme Court upheld the affirmative action plan because it was a temporary plan designed to eliminate a *manifest racial imbalance* in the workforce. Essentially, the Court upheld affirmative action plans that result in reverse discrimination if the plans are temporary and the employer is attempting to correct a history of past discrimination.

In contrast, in *Wygant v. Jackson Board of Education,*[24] the Supreme Court rejected a school board's argument that race-based layoffs of more senior White teachers were necessary to remedy the effects of societal discrimination. There was no clear and convincing evidence in this case that the board itself had engaged in past racial discrimination. The Supreme Court also rejected the argument that minority students needed African American role models, saying that "carried to its logical extreme, the idea that black students are better off with black teachers could lead to the very system the Court rejected in *Brown v. Board of Education.*" The Court found that the proposed layoffs were impermissible because "denial of future employment is not as intrusive as loss of an existing job." Essentially this case stands for the proposition that there must be a history of discrimination to justify racially discriminatory affirmative action plans, and even if there is a history of discrimination, earned seniority rights should not be sacrificed to an affirmative action plan addressing past wrongs.

Human resource managers must learn to anticipate both claims of discrimination and reverse discrimination. Unless a school district has a history of past discrimination in employment, affirmative action plans and hiring practices based on race or gender considerations violate Title VII. To consider race, gender, religion, or national origin in a hiring decision or an employment practice is to discriminate on the basis of race, gender, religion, or national origin. Employment decisions should be based on training, experience, and potential ability to do the job as described. Hiring decisions and employment practices should not be based on the factors protected by Title VII, nor should employment practices have a disparate impact on members of these protected classes.

TITLE IX

Title IX of the Education Amendments of 1972 prohibits gender discrimination in education programs and activities that receive federal financial assistance.[25] Under Title IX, individuals who feel they have been the victims of gender discrimination can bring lawsuits, and federal funding will be withdrawn from the noncomplying institutions.[26] Title IX is implemented through regulations issued by the U.S. Department of Education in 1975 and has affected school district employment practices in several ways. Although initially thought to protect only students from discriminatory school practices, the Supreme Court found no reason to limit Title IX coverage to students alone, noting that the statute clearly states:

> No person in the United States shall, on the basis of sex, be excluded from participation in, be denied the benefits of, or be subjected to discrimination under any education program or activity receiving Federal financial assistance.[27]

The Court found that the legislative history of the law brought employment practices within its purview. In light of this background, Title IX has been invoked to challenge discriminatory school employment practices such as job classifications, work assignments, and pregnancy leave.[28]

Sexual Harassment

In 1992, the Supreme Court used Title IX to make compensatory and punitive damages available for victims of sexual harassment.[29] Sexual harassment in the workplace is any unwelcome sexual advance, request for sexual favors, or other verbal or physical conduct of a sexual nature. There are essentially two kinds of sexual harassment. The first is referred to as *quid pro quo,* and it occurs when submission or rejection of unwelcome sexual conduct is used as the basis for employment decisions. An example of *quid pro quo* harassment in the school environment might be a principal who offers a teacher a lighter teaching schedule in return for sex, or a rejected principal who retaliates by giving the teacher an unsatisfactory evaluation. With this type of harassment, the employee is injured in that they are forced to submit or become the victim of an adverse employment decision. The second type of harassment, on the other hand, may not result in an actual loss or injury, but rather subjects the victim employee to a *hostile environment.* A hostile environment is created when an employee is subjected to unwelcome sexual conduct, and the harassment is sufficiently severe or pervasive as to alter the terms or conditions of employment and create an abusive working environment. The Supreme Court has said that the standard for determining whether a hostile environment exists requires only an objectively hostile environment—one that a reasonable person would find hostile—as well as the victim's subjective perception that the environment was abusive, based on whether there was frequency, whether there was severity, whether the conduct was humiliating, whether it unreasonably interfered with the employee's performance, and whether the victim incurred psychological harm.[30] Hostile environments often result in *constructive discharge,* that is, the victim resigns in an effort to flee the harassment.

Under Title VII, employers have always been liable for tangible losses sustained as the result of *quid pro quo* harassment. Employees who could show that they had lost promotions, benefits, or jobs because they would not submit to a supervisor's advances have been able to hold the employer liable for the acts of its agent. The courts have consistently held employers liable for the discriminatory treatment of employees by supervisory personnel, whether or not the employer knew, or should have known, or approved of the supervisor's actions.[31] Such strict liability is perceived to be a legitimate cost of properly conducting business. However, in 1998, the Supreme Court ruled that an employer is also subject to vicarious liability for an actionable hostile environment created by a supervisor with immediate authority over an employee,[32] that is, an employer is liable for the acts of its harassing employee. Therefore, in light of Title VII, Title IX, and the Supreme Court's recent rulings, school districts that do nothing to discourage *quid pro quo* and *hostile environment* sexual harassment will be liable for punitive and compensatory damages.

At the same time that it extended employer liability for sexual harassment in the workplace to include hostile environment claims, the Supreme Court offered employers liable for charges of hostile environment harassment an affirmative defense. Employers could avoid liability by showing that

1. the employer exercised reasonable care to prevent and promptly correct any sexually harassing behavior,
2. the plaintiff employee unreasonably failed to take advantage of any preventive or corrective opportunities provided by the employer or to otherwise avoid harm.[33]

Thus, school districts wishing to avoid liability for sexually harassing hostile environments must show that they had a sexual harassment policy in place, disseminated that policy to all employees, and trained employees to recognize harassing behavior. The policy should not be cumbersome and should provide alternative options for reporting offensive behavior to circumvent potential offending supervisors. Once these measures are in place, it then becomes the responsibility of harassed school employees to take advantage of the preventive and corrective opportunities the district policy provides. An example of a sexual harassment policy is provided in figure 5.2.

As this sample sexual harassment policy indicates, simply defining sexual harassment and saying that the district is opposed to it is not enough to take advantage of the Supreme Court's affirmative defense. The administrator receiving a report of harassment is duty bound to investigate the charge, being ever mindful of the confidentiality of the parties, and to document the results of the investigation. Needless to say, the investigation should be prompt and thorough, and a decision regarding the investigator's findings and recommendations for discipline should be documented and shared with all parties involved. If the charge is found to be valid, then the harasser should be warned or disciplined as prescribed by contract, policy, and severity of the offense. If the charge is not found to be valid, the alleged harasser and the plaintiff should receive a clear explanation for this finding, and both parties should be warned to avoid further contact. Finally, if the results of the investigation prove inconclusive, the parties should also be given a written explanation for this finding and once again warned to avoid further contact. In short, no complaint should ever be ignored or given short shrift. Every complaint must be processed, investigated, and resolved in one way or another if the school district is to avoid a charge of deliberate indifference and liability for an escalating situation.

In a closing note to this section dealing with sexual harassment, it must be emphasized that the Supreme Court has extended Title VII and Title IX protections against gender discrimination to cover same-sex harassment.[34] Sexual harassment can be male to female, female to male, male to male, and female to female. In addition, harassing colleagues as well as supervisors can create a hostile environment. Sexual harassment in the school environment has many faces, and each places an indifferent school system in legal jeopardy.

THE PREGNANCY DISCRIMINATION ACT OF 1978

In 1978, Congress amended section 701 of the Civil Rights Act of 1964 (Title VII) to specifically protect the rights of pregnant women.[35] This law

Definition:

Sexual harassment is any unwelcome sexual advance, request for sexual favors, or other verbal or physical conduct of a sexual nature when (1) submission to such conduct is made either explicitly a term or condition of an individual's employment; (2) submission to or rejection of such conduct by an individual is used as the basis for employment decisions affecting the individual; or (3) such conduct has the purpose or effect of unreasonably interfering with an individual's work performance or creating an intimidating, hostile, or offensive work environment [Equal Employment Opportunity Commission].

Reporting Sexual Harassment:

Employees must report sexual harassment either to their immediate supervisor or building administrator, or to the assistant superintendent if the harasser is the employee's supervisor or building administrator.

Process for Addressing Complaints:

The administrator receiving the harassment complaint will be responsible for investigating all reported allegations. This investigation will maintain the confidentiality of all parties, and a written summary of the results of the investigation will be given to all parties named in the complaint and to the superintendent.

The Investigation:

A. The party registering a complaint of harassment will be asked to complete a written report describing the offensive behavior, noting dates and times of incidents, and including the names of any available witnesses to the incidents.

B. All parties named as alleged harassers in a complaint will be asked to respond in writing to the victim's charges and to name any witnesses prepared to verify their accounts of the incidents.

C. All witnesses named by the victim and the alleged harasser will be interviewed, and a transcript of these interviews will be made and signed by the witnesses. These transcripts will become part of the investigative record.

D. Based on the results of the investigation, the administrator will make one of the following findings:
    1. There was harassment meriting disciplinary action.
    2. There was no harassment meriting disciplinary action.
    3. The investigation proved inconclusive.

E. The investigative report will cite one of these options and will include specific evidence supporting that position.

Disciplinary Action:

The Superintendent will take disciplinary action commensurate with the severity of the sexual harassment reported. Discipline may include, but is not limited to, written reprimands and warnings placed in the harasser's personnel file, suspensions with or without pay, and dismissal. Where appropriate, the police will be notified.

Figure 5.2 A Sample School District Sexual Harassment Policy

provided that "women affected by pregnancy, childbirth, or related medical conditions shall be treated the same for all employment-related purposes, including the receipt of benefits under fringe benefit programs, as other persons not so affected but similar in their ability or inability to work." Before the passage of this amendment, boards commonly treated disabilities related to pregnancy in arbitrary ways unrelated to their policies for other disabilities. Pregnancy and maternity leave policies were the subject of repeated litigation. Passage of the Pregnancy Discrimination Act made pregnancy a basis for Title VII sex discrimination and required that women affected by pregnancy, childbirth, or related medical conditions be treated the same for all employment-related purposes, including eligibility for fringe benefits, as persons disabled by sickness, accident, or other physical conditions. Essentially, pregnancy leave was to be equated with sick leave for all intents and purposes.

This amendment legislated two earlier Supreme Court decisions that found school district rules for when a teacher must take pregnancy leave and when she may return to be arbitrary irrebuttable presumptions.[36] The Court viewed the district's rules as discriminatory and didn't accept the board's arguments that they were based on a need for continuity of instruction, the physical inability of the returning teacher to teach, and a concern for the health of the teacher and unborn child. The Court left the determination of parting and returning dates to the discretion of the woman.

Later Supreme Court rulings prohibited similar discriminatory practices related to leave and benefits extended to those expecting a child. In a case with elements of reverse discrimination, the Court held that pregnancy benefits provided for spouses of male employees must be the same as those provided for female employees.[37] Leave for childbirth and pregnancy has also been challenged by male employees as discriminatory, however, the Family and Medical Leave Act of 1993, appears to have eliminated this problem by providing nondiscriminatory leave to *men* and women to care for a newborn or adopted child.

In summary, the Pregnancy Act and the Supreme Court cases reviewing school policies on this issue make it clear that human resource plans must treat pregnancy as any other disability or medical condition. Attempts to influence or to legislate when a pregnant teacher may take leave or when she may return are illegal, a violation of the Due Process Clause of the Fourteenth Amendment. The school district can, however, require a teacher to have a physical examination before returning to work.[38]

THE EQUAL PAY ACT OF 1963

The Equal Pay Act,[39] passed in 1963, was extended to state and local government employees in 1974.[40] The Act makes it unlawful to pay employees of one sex more than employees of another sex where the jobs performed require equal skill, effort, and responsibility and are performed at the same site under the same or similar working conditions. The Act will not be relevant to teachers' pay where contracts are collectively bargained and contain negotiated pay scales. However, the Act may be used to dispute pay provisions under individually negotiated agreements such as supplemental contracts to coach or perform nonteaching assignments. For example, a school district can be guilty of violating the Equal Pay Act if it pays the female coach of a girls' softball team less than it pays the male coach of a boys' softball team although they have the same recruiting, supervising, and instructing duties, and both travel with the teams, handling equipment, uniforms, schedules, and transportation under similar working conditions.[41]

One may wonder why there is a need for the Equal Pay Act since it appears to cover the same discriminatory ground addressed by Title VII discrimination. However, in an effort to discourage this once prevalent discriminatory practice, Congress made the remedies available under the Equal Pay Act potentially better than those available under Title VII. Successful plaintiffs under the Equal Pay Act may obtain damages equal to twice the amount of any unpaid wages.[42]

SECTION 504 OF THE REHABILITATION ACT

Section 504 of the Rehabilitation Act of 1973[43] states that "no otherwise qualified handicapped individual . . . shall, solely by reason of handicap, be excluded from the participation in, be denied the benefits of, or be subjected to discrimination under any program or activity receiving Federal financial assistance." School personnel at all levels are keenly aware of how Section 504 affects students, but it is equally important to recognize its impact on school employees. The law prohibits recipients of federal funding from discriminating against qualified disabled individuals with respect to recruitment, hiring, compensation, job assignment, and fringe benefits and requires employers to provide reasonable work environment accommodations for qualified disabled applicants or employees unless these accommodations result in undue hardship for the employer.

In essence, Section 504 protects the rights of the disabled employee and prohibits discrimination against the disabled. In discussing discrimination under

Title VII, the emphasis was placed on turning a blind eye to race, color, creed, gender, and national origin in making employment decisions. In contrast, Section 504 states that disabled persons may actually require differential treatment in order to be afforded equal access, and identical treatment, may, in fact, be discriminatory.[44]

THE AMERICANS WITH DISABILITIES ACT

In 1990, seventeen years after the passage of Section 504, it became obvious that disabled adults were still not part of mainstream American life, and in an effort to draw them in, Congress passed the Americans with Disabilities Act (ADA),[45] extending, clarifying, and enhancing the protections of Section 504. The ADA is designed to eliminate the barriers the disabled encounter, particularly in the work environment. It differs from Section 504 in that it applies to both public and private sector employees and includes provisions regarding public accommodations, public transportation, telecommunications, and the receipt of government services for the disabled. It is a far-reaching piece of legislation that has been compared to Title VII, a virtual civil rights law for the disabled.

Employment protections under the ADA are extended to *qualified* individuals with a *disability*. The word disability is defined as a physical or mental impairment substantially limiting one or more of the major life activities of an individual, having a record of such impairment or being regarded as having such an impairment.[46] In light of this definition, a person with a bad case of the flu or a broken arm would not be protected by the law, but a person with a history of mental illness and a person with a cancer that is in remission would both be protected by the law, as would a recovered alcoholic. It should also be noted that the ADA specifically excludes homosexuality, bisexuality, transvestism, transsexualism, pedophilia, exhibitionism, voyeurism, gender identity disorders not resulting from physical impairments, and other sexual behavior disorders, compulsive gambling, kleptomania, pyromania, and psychoactive substance abuse disorders resulting from the current use of illegal drugs. It does extend protection to individuals who are HIV positive.[47] A *qualified* disabled person is an individual with a disability who, with or without reasonable accommodation, can perform the essential functions of the employment position that such individual holds or desires to hold.[48]

The ADA prohibits discrimination against any qualified disabled individual because of the individual's disability with respect to job application procedures, hiring, advancement, discharge, compensation, job training, and other terms, conditions, and privileges of employment.[49] In actual practice, this means that an employer cannot ask if a potential employee has a disability or the nature or severity of an obvious disability. An employer may only ask if an applicant can perform a particular job function as described,[50] and any qualification standard or selection criteria used must be job-related and consistent with business necessity.[51] For example, while sight may be a legitimate job requirement for a swimming instructor charged with monitoring student safety during a lesson, it would not necessarily be a valid requirement for an English teacher.

Medical examinations are also not a preemployment option for ferreting out information about an applicant's disability. An offer of employment may be made conditional upon a subsequent medical examination, but only if such medical examinations are required for all other entering employees.[52] Reasonable drug testing, however, is permitted to confirm that an individual is not using drugs,[53] because current drug use is not protected by the ADA.

The ADA requires more extensive accommodations for disabled employees than Section 504 and has specifically listed the kinds of accommodations that are to be available:

1. Making existing facilities readily accessible to and usable by disabled persons
2. Job restructuring
3. Part-time or modified work schedules
4. Reassignment to a vacant position
5. Acquisition or modification of equipment or devices
6. Appropriate adjustment or modifications of examinations
7. Training materials or policies
8. Provision of qualified readers or interpreters
9. Other similar accommodations[54]

Employers are expected to provide the accommodations a disabled employee will need to enter or remain in the workforce, unless the employer can show that accommodating the employee results in undue hardship. The law states that the factors to be evaluated in determining undue hardship will be overall size and financial resources of the institution, the number of persons employed at the facility in question, the type of operations conducted at the facility in question, and the impact on operations and expenses.[55] Once again, the EEOC is primarily responsible for enforcing the ADA and ruling on questions of undue hardship and reasonable accommodation. A successful plaintiff under the ADA may obtain an injunction, reinstatement, back pay, compensatory damages, litigation costs, and a reasonable award for attorney fees.[56]

The Supreme Court, in 1999, was asked to decide whether mitigating measures should be considered in determining whether an impairment is "substantially limiting" and therefore protected by the ADA. EEOC guidelines required employers to determine whether an impairment was substantially limiting *without* considering any mitigating measures used. In this Supreme Court decision, twin sisters with 20/200 or worse vision applied for the job of airline pilot. The airline required pilots to have at least 20/100 uncorrected vision. With glasses, the twins' vision was 20/20, and so they sued the airline under the ADA contending that the airline had discriminated against them because the airline's criteria perceived them as disabled. The Court found, however, that an employer does not necessarily violate the ADA by creating physical criteria for a job, as long as the preferred attributes do not rise to the level of substantially limiting impairments.[57] In other words, employers have the right to develop job descriptions that include legitimate physical criteria that relate to job performance. If, for example, the job description for a gym teacher requires that the teacher be able to demonstrate all activities included in the physical education curriculum, a wheelchair-bound applicant for the position would be unlikely to prevail in a claim of disability discrimination.

In a second case, the Court said that mitigating measures should be considered[58] in determining whether an impairment is substantially limiting and therefore protected by the ADA, overturning the EEOC's guidelines on this issue. In this case, UPS fired a mechanic with medically controlled high blood pressure because he could not drive the vehicles he worked on, an essential part of his job description. He sued claiming disability discrimination under the ADA, but the Court found that since his condition was controlled with medication, he was not disabled under the ADA, nor did UPS regard him as disabled. Instead, he was regarded as unqualified because he could not get a Department of Transportation health certification. This case is important in that it emphasizes the need to consider the effect of medications, prostheses, and other mitigating devices in determining whether an employee's condition falls within the purview of the substantially limiting impairments protected by the ADA. Teachers with contact lenses that substantially correct vision impairments and medications that substantially lower high blood pressure are not protected by the ADA. This decision, however, also has implications for the development of job descriptions. While qualifications should not be unnecessarily discriminating, they can and should reflect legitimate employer concerns. Although the twins in this most recent decision may have had 20/20 vision with contacts, an airline has a legitimate concern with the quality of their vision should they lose a contact and a legitimate right to incorporate this concern into the context of the job description and qualifications for the position.

THE AGE DISCRIMINATION IN EMPLOYMENT ACT

The Age Discrimination in Employment Act (ADEA), passed in 1967, prohibits discrimination based on age for employees and job applicants over forty,[59] and it was amended in 1974 to cover state and political subdivisions including school districts. The ADEA prohibits any employment practices that adversely affect the job status of employees over forty[60] and retaliation against employees supporting the age discrimination complaints of others.[61] School districts are most likely to violate the ADEA in the way that they advertise jobs and in their hiring preferences. For example, districts that refuse to hire teachers with more than minimal experience may be guilty of age discrimination since experience equates with age in education.[62] Such policies have a disparate impact on teachers over forty. Age can only be a factor in employment decisions if the employer can show that an older employee cannot perform safely and efficiently. For example, a bus company can have a policy setting thirty-five as the upper age limit for new bus drivers.[63] The ADEA allows the development of age-based retirement, pension, and insurance plans,[64] but no employee can be forced to retire solely on the basis of age, except for policy-level personnel, who may be forced to retire at sixty-five.[65]

Employer liability for age discrimination works in the same way as liability for Title VII discrimination. That is, the employee has the burden of showing that the disputed action was based on age discrimination and that all other reasons given by the employer are lies. However, as with Title VII discrimination, an employer can escape ADEA liability by showing that there were other legitimate reasons for the job action, and it would have been taken even if age had not been a consideration.[66]

Once again, the EEOC is responsible for enforcing the ADEA, investigating complaints, and instituting court actions where appropriate. If the EEOC does not institute court action itself, as with Title VII, it may give the employee a "right to sue" letter, allowing the employee to bring a private civil action. Employees who win their suits may recover twice the amount of any lost wages, in addition to reinstatement or promotion,[67] but they may not recover damages for humiliation or mental suffering.[68] School districts found guilty of age discrimination may also lose their federal funding.[69] Many states have their own versions of the ADEA, but as with earlier civil rights legislation, the ADEA model defines the floor, not the ceiling for protection in these statutes.

It should be noted that recent Supreme Court rulings have cast a shadow on the potential effectiveness of the ADEA as a federal deterrent to age discrimination. In the year 2000, the Supreme Court brought enforcement of the federal version of the ADEA into question. Essentially, in *Kimel v. Florida Bd. of Regents,*[70] the

Court found that Congress exceeded its authority under the Fourteenth Amendment when it included state employees under the coverage of the ADEA. The Court found that the Eleventh Amendment prohibits federal suits against nonconsenting states. This is a legally technical decision that essentially says the Eleventh Amendment of the Constitution does not allow the federal government to pass a federal law allowing a state employee to sue a state agency such as a school without the state's permission. This decision may affect the enforceability of ADEA suits in states that do not have their own versions of age discrimination laws in place. Human resource administrators, in order to be safe, should know their own states' age discrimination laws and avoid basing employment decisions on age unless declining skills, safety, or efficiency are an issue.

THE FAMILY AND MEDICAL LEAVE ACT

In 1993, in an effort to recognize and assist the family as the primary source of care in emergency situations, Congress passed the Family and Medical Leave Act.[71] This law allows all eligible employees up to twelve workweeks per year of unpaid leave to care for a newborn child; to care for, or spend additional time with, an adopted child or foster child; to care for a spouse, child, or parent with a serious health condition; or to recover from a serious health condition.[72]

Eligible employees are those who have worked at least 1,250 hours for the employer during the previous twelve-month period.[73] The regulations for implementing the FMLA define "a serious health condition" as a condition that will require medical attention and that will incapacitate the employee for more than three calendar days; however, serious medical episodes covering briefer time spans, such as asthma or diabetes emergencies are also covered.[74] It should be noted that FMLA leave can be taken all at once, or intermittently, when (1) the employer agrees to part-time use and (2) when it is medically necessary to use such leave due to the employee's serious health condition or the serious health condition of a spouse, child, or parent.[75] If intermittent leave is required for planned treatments or procedures such as chemotherapy, the employee may be transferred to another position in order to mitigate the effect of such intermittent absence.[76]

The basic prescriptions of the FMLA could well be an Excedrin headache for a school district administrator or human resource manager. However, teachers are subject to special continuity rules under the FMLA. These rules state that

1. if a teacher takes FMLA leave five weeks before the end of an academic term and the leave lasts at least three weeks, ending during the last three

weeks of the term, the teacher may be required to continue such leave through the end of the term, in order to avoid disruption of instruction;

2. if FMLA leave, other than for the teacher's own serious illness, begins during the last five weeks of the term, lasts at least two weeks, and ends during the last two weeks of the term, the teacher may also be required to continue such leave through the end of the term, in order to preserve course continuity;

3. if FMLA leave taken by a teacher for reasons other than the teacher's own serious illness begins during the last three weeks of an academic term and will continue for more than five working days, the teacher may be required to continue leave through the end of the academic term.[77]

If, on the other hand, a teacher wishes to take FMLA leave intermittently and that leave will be more than 20 percent of the working days, the teacher may be required to take the leave continuously or to transfer to another position, equivalent in pay and benefits, that will not be as seriously affected by intermittent leave.[78] Under the 20 percent rule, a teacher who requests more than one out of five days of intermittent FMLA leave per week can be transferred to a position in which the teacher's absence will have less impact on the continuity of the instructional program.

The overlap between sick leave, personal leave, and FMLA leave has been a concern for school districts, but the law has provided some guidance. If paid leave following the birth of a child is already provided, that leave must be extended on an unpaid basis up to a total of twelve weeks.[79] In addition, an employee who has accumulated sick leave, personal leave, or vacation leave may be required to use such leave for any or all of the twelve weeks of leave available under the FMLA.[80] Many collectively bargained agreements have adopted versions of these provisions.

Where possible, the law requires an employee to give at least thirty days advance notice before using FMLA leave,[81] in order to minimize program disruption,[82] and a health care provider's note may be required to certify the reason for the leave and its probable duration.[83] The term "health care provider," however, encompasses a wide range of practitioners including dentists, podiatrists, and psychologists.[84] The law's use of loosely defined qualifiers such as "where possible" and "health provider" reflects its overall intent to be user friendly.

FMLA leave differs from other unpaid leave in that it comes with certain protections intended to minimize employee stress in dealing with a family crisis and the demands of work. Employees taking FMLA leave retain their health benefits throughout the leave period,[85] although if the employee fails to return for reasons other than a serious health condition or circumstances beyond the employee's control, the employee may be required to pay the health premiums paid during the leave.[86] More important, employees returning from FMLA leave must be restored to positions previously held or to equivalent positions with the same pay, benefits, and working conditions[87] and with seniority and benefits accrued before the leave intact. Seniority and benefits, however, do not continue to accrue during the leave period.[88]

FMLA complaints are received and investigated by the Secretary of Labor,[89] but covered employees can bring suit against an employer directly[90] in state or federal court within two years of the violation, three if "willfulness" can be shown.[91] Remedies include reinstatement, back pay, or, if there has been no loss of pay, compensation for any expenses incurred as a direct result of providing care, up to a sum equal to twelve weeks' pay with interest, and this amount is then doubled.[92]

Problems arise for school districts that do not clarify when FMLA leave is to begin and end and how it is to dovetail with other existing employee leave. To avoid confusion, human resource administrators should speak with teachers and other school employees before FMLA leave begins and document how and when leave will be allotted before it is taken. A written summary of exactly how leave is allotted and which is paid and which is unpaid can help avoid potential grievances and future litigation. If an employee qualifies for FMLA leave, it is futile to resist the employee's right to use it. Rather, it is important to monitor how and when it will be used.

WORKERS' COMPENSATION

While the Federal Employees' Compensation Act covers federal employees,[93] state workers' compensation statutes administered by the state Bureaus of Workers' Compensation or state Industrial Commissions, in a similar fashion, protect the interests of state employees injured on the job. Specifically, these state laws provide that an employee who sustains an injury in the course of employment and arising out of the injured employee's employment may file a claim for compensation. Injured employees are entitled to receive compensation for loss incurred because of injury, occupational disease, or death and for medical, nurse, hospital services and medicines, and funeral expenses in the case of death.[94]

Workers' compensation laws came into being as an alternative to cumbersome litigation and its inherent effect on business efficiency. Workers' compensation laws make the employer strictly liable to an employee for injuries sustained by the employee that arise out of and in the course of employment, without regard to the negligence of the employer or that of the employee.[95] The employer contributes premiums to a state fund that essentially insures all employees and, in the event of injury, pays them in accordance with a legislated compensation schedule. Awards vary with the gravity and duration of injury. Injured employees covered by Workers' Compensation are assured that they will receive financial support without having to sue the employer. For their part, since workers' compensation is an *exclusive* remedy for on-the-job injuries, employers are assured that they will not have to respond to a suit and submit to the vagaries of courtroom decisions. Initially, Workers' Compensation was introduced as a way of saving both parties time and money in lengthy litigation. Where the Act applies, the employee receives Workers' Compensation, but forfeits the right to sue the employer for higher stakes, unless the employee can show the employer is guilty of "intentional tort." The definition of intentional tort often blurs with mere negligence and so has itself been the focus of much litigation.[96]

One major hurdle human resource administrators face in dealing with workers' compensation claims is that of determining whether a claim has arisen out of, or in the course of, employment. As with any insurance policy, paying every claim without regard for its validity can be a costly proposition resulting in surging premiums as well as large payouts. Not every claim is valid. Consider two teachers attending a district-wide conference. One is injured when the chair she is occupying collapses; the other is struck by a car in the parking lot as he tries to leave the conference, without permission, one hour before it is over. The first question a vigilant administrator must ask is which of the teachers was injured in the course of employment or arising out of employment.

Another major concern for school administrators must be responding promptly to concerns, complaints, and situations that could conceivably rise to the level of "intentional tort." Addressing unsafe conditions, issuing relevant health warnings, and making prompt repairs to building and equipment are just a few of the ways in which district administrators can be sure that they and the district are not guilty of deliberate intentional tort and that workers' compensation works as intended.

UNEMPLOYMENT COMPENSATION

Unemployment compensation provides employees who are laid off *through no fault of their own* a financial subsidy to see them through the period of *involuntary* unemployment. Unemployment Compensation is a function of state law for public school employees, and the specifics of the laws implementing unemployment compensation may vary from state to state. In most states, boards of education can choose one of two methods for financing this legally mandated benefit. The board may either make an annual contribution determined by statutory formula to the state's unemployment compensation fund, or the board may self-insure.[97] In either case, the contribution is equivalent to an insurance premium paid to assure that should employees become unemployed through no fault of their own, they will be financially assisted until they can secure other suitable employment for which they are qualified. Unemployment compensation laws, as workers' compensation laws, protect both teaching and nonteaching employees in public schools.

The proverbial fly in the ointment of administrating unemployment compensation benefits lies in the determination of when an employee is *involuntarily* unemployed. There are some guidelines specific to public school administration. For example, in most states, teachers are not entitled to unemployment compensation for the summer months between the end of one school year and the beginning of the next, if they have a reasonable assurance of reemployment. Teachers who are tenured, that is, who have continuing contracts, cannot file unemployment compensation forms during July and August. On the other hand, if a teacher has been notified that the board does not intend to renew the teacher's contract for the next school year because the board has instituted a reduction in force, that teacher is eligible for unemployment compensation. In the latter example, the teacher is not being fired or released from service for just cause; the teacher is simply being laid off because the district has determined that it must trim its staff and budget. In contrast, teachers who voluntarily resign their positions, or who are fired for documented just cause, are not entitled to unemployment compensation. Unemployment compensation is also not available to striking employees or to teachers who have elected to resign or to go on sabbatical leave.

Teachers who believe they have been wrongfully discharged will sue for reinstatement and to recoup lost unemployment compensation benefits. If their suits succeed, they will be awarded back pay or unemployment compensation, not both. Knowing this, human resource administrators must give clear, documented, and dated notice of the reasons for employee separation from service. Teachers terminated for just cause must be given written termination statements backed by documentation supporting the cause for termination. Likewise, teachers who resign should receive formal restatement letters acknowledging and accepting their voluntary resignations. Teachers who are released as part of a planned reduction in force, should also be informed of their status in a clear and legally timely fashion, and school districts should be prepared to deal with their claims for unemployment compensation.

Unemployment compensation claims can be a drain on a school district's finances. With that in mind, it is essential that human resource managers bring victims of a reduction in force back into the workforce as soon as possible or assist them in getting other suitable employment. In states where teachers do not bargain, school districts may unilaterally determine how they will handle a reduction in force. Where teachers do collectively bargain, the contract will usually provide the protocol for riffing. In most cases, teachers in an affected field without tenure and with the fewest years of experience will be laid off first. Teachers who are riffed, however, retain a hold on jobs in their area of certification that may become available. While the district is under no obligation to recall teachers to exactly the same positions they had before a reduction in force, they are obligated to notify them when any position for which they are qualified becomes available. Tenured teachers who have been riffed are restored to service in their area of certification in the order of seniority they held in the district, and then nontenured teachers are restored in the order of their seniority. Teachers and other school employees who are laid off through no fault of their own may continue to draw unemployment compensation until they have found other suitable employment or refuse a recall offer made by the school district. In the meantime, however, school districts that pay unemployment compensation claims are spending money but receiving no service from the employees they are compensating.

COBRA—THE CONSOLIDATED OMNIBUS BUDGET RECONCILIATION ACT OF 1985

While employees who are laid off from work through no fault of their own are entitled to unemployment compensation, a board of education has neither the obligation nor the authority to continue fringe benefits for a teacher whose contract has been suspended as part of a reduction in force. However, unless an employee has been released for "gross misconduct," the employee is entitled, under COBRA,[98] to continue participation in the district's group health plan for a period up to eighteen months. In addition, the employee's spouse and dependent children are also entitled to continued coverage in such plans for up to thirty-six months, if they would otherwise lose coverage due to the death of the covered employee, divorce or legal separation, or leaving dependency status. This continued coverage must be provided even if the former employee has access to health care through a spouse's employer.[99] The employee, spouse, or child, however, must pay for the premiums for continued coverage, unless the employer has agreed otherwise, and this coverage may be up to 102 percent of the regular group rate.[100] Employers are required to notify departing employees of their rights under

COBRA at the time of separation,[101] and boards that fail to notify departing employees of their rights under COBRA may be liable for ensuing medical costs should the employee or family members fall ill.

THE FOURTEENTH AMENDMENT

The Fourteenth Amendment is a key factor in human resource management. It provides that no person may be deprived of "life, liberty, or property, without due process of law" and that no person may be denied "the equal protection of the laws." In essence, the Fourteenth Amendment is a protective catchall, assuring public school employees that they will be entitled to all the rights and benefits provided by the Constitution and federal laws no matter where they work. It also assures them fair treatment when they are threatened with the loss of life, liberty, or property interests such as jobs, salaries, and benefits of employment. Procedural due process equates with fair treatment and requires

1. a notice of the reason for the adverse action taken;
2. an opportunity to respond to these reasons and charges;
3. the opportunity to confront and cross-examine witnesses;
4. the opportunity to be represented by counsel;
5. the opportunity to appeal an adverse decision.

Tenure

A *property* interest is a legitimate claim of entitlement to continued employment that is created by state law.[102] A teacher's property interest in a particular position comes into being when a teacher is tenured. Nontenured teachers are issued yearly contracts and can be terminated at the end of any school year. Tenured teachers, on the other hand, are said to have continuing contracts and cannot be terminated except for just cause. In order to get tenured status, teachers have to work in a given district for a period of time defined by state teacher tenure laws, to engage in extended academic study beyond the bachelor's level, and to pass the muster of administrative observation and evaluation prescribed by law and/or contract. Ideally, an award of tenure signifies that a school district has put a teacher to the test and found the teacher to be a professional worthy of continued employment. Teachers who are tenured have an expectation of returning to a position in their area of certification year after year.

Liberty Interests

Liberty interests include such fundamental Constitutional rights as freedom of expression and association, but also include a teacher's freedom to take advantage of employment opportunities. Adverse employment decisions should not be based on teachers' exercise of liberty interests. To do so is to deprive teachers of their Constitutional rights. In addition, adverse decisions that damage a teacher's reputation foreclose their employment options, again depriving them of a liberty interest.

The Fourteenth Amendment comes into play when teachers are disciplined, dismissed, or nonrenewed. The Fourteenth Amendment accords employees both *substantive* and *procedural due process*. They are promised equal protection of the Constitution and all federal laws, therefore the school district policy, rule, or regulation giving rise to discipline or dismissal cannot conflict with the rights and privileges accorded the employee by the Constitution and federal law. For example, a teacher cannot be fired for voicing an opinion on a matter of public concern.[103] A school district policy that restricts a teacher's free expression on matters of public concern would deprive the teacher of substantive due process because the policy itself is unconstitutional. On the other hand, if a teacher is given no notice or reason for an adverse employment decision, not permitted to respond to charges, not allowed to confront and cross-examine witnesses, not represented by counsel, and not allowed to appeal an adverse decision, the teacher is being deprived of procedural due process.

It follows that the Fourteenth Amendment affects human resource management in two respects: First, human resource managers must be sure that rules, regulations, and job descriptions that affect employees are not substantively in conflict with Constitutional or federal law. Second, when a district does take an employment action likely to result in an employee's loss of life, liberty, or property interests, the human resource manager must be certain that the employee has been accorded procedural due process. Decisions affecting life, liberty, or property interests must never be made cavalierly.

CONCLUSION

This is by no means an exhaustive list of the federal laws affecting public school employment. The laws discussed have been chosen because they deal with issues that are presently at the forefront of human resource management and will be referred to in subsequent chapters dealing with other aspects of human resource management. As stated earlier, many states have their own legislation mirroring the federal laws discussed. These state laws can give employees more rights than those accorded under federal law, but they cannot give employees fewer rights and protections. That being said, teacher tenure laws are the exclusive province of state law and central to public education human resource management. These laws must be reviewed on a state-by-state basis.

Many of the laws discussed have posting requirements. Posters summarizing the laws are usually available free from the issuing governmental agencies and should be displayed in all relevant workplaces. Employers who do not take steps to notify their employees of rights accorded them under state and federal law may be subject to fines and penalties, as well as civil liability.

A LEGAL PERSPECTIVE

On February 21, 2001, the Supreme Court ruled that state employees in two separate suits could not sue their state employers for damages for violations of the Americans with Disabilities Act.[104] Employees filed lawsuits against agencies of the Alabama state government. In one, a registered nurse sued the University of Alabama Hospital, a state facility, for demoting her when she returned to work after breast cancer treatment. In the other, a security officer sued Alabama's Department of Youth Services for failing to arrange his work conditions to accommodate his chronic asthma and other medical problems.

Alabama responded to both suits by invoking its right to immunity under the Eleventh Amendment, which bars private suits for damages in federal court against states that have not given consent to be sued. The Supreme Court agreed with the state of Alabama, concluding that Congress had exceeded its authority in making states vulnerable to private lawsuits. In speaking for the 5–4 majority, Chief Justice Rehnquist said that it was not enough for Congress to take account of general societal discrimination against people with disabilities. Instead, Congress needed to demonstrate to a high level of proof that the states themselves had been engaged in a "pattern of unconstitutional discrimination." This decision follows a line of cases holding that Congress may not impose obligations on the states that go beyond what the Constitution itself commands. Rehnquist concluded that because the ADA did in fact impose such obligations, it could not be a valid abrogation of states' immunity.

This case, and those that preceded it, will have a telling impact on public education human resource management. States are separately responsible for the creation and maintenance of public education. If they are immune from private suits based on the ADA, the ADEA, and other federally created civil rights statutes, so are public schools, and these federal laws lose the vital element of enforcement needed for successful implementation. This is an evolving area of law, and public school human resource administrators must monitor its subsequent effect on employment practices.

THEORY INTO PRACTICE

Read each of the following fact patterns, and resolve the issues presented in light of the statutes discussed in this chapter.

1. A male teacher in your school complains that other teachers are spreading the rumor that he is gay. As a result of these rumors, his students have made rude comments to him, and several parents have asked him to resign. He says he is the victim of daily abusive comments and behavior by both colleagues and students. As the building administrator, discuss how you will address this problem.
2. Comment on the legality of each of these interview questions:
    a. How old are you?
    b. Do you speak Spanish?
    c. You have an unusual last name. What nationality are you?
3. Teachers in your district do not collectively bargain. A teacher on pregnancy leave is returning to work and has insisted that she be returned to her former position as a kindergarten teacher. The teacher has K–8 certification, and you, the principal, have given her a fifth grade assignment. She objects to this new assignment. Who will win this dispute and why?
4. A teacher in your school has recently told you that he is HIV positive and has asked your help in dealing with the disease. What legal protections, if any, does this teacher have?
5. Is your school district justified in paying the female principal of the elementary school less than the male principals of the middle school and high school? Why or why not?
6. Two candidates were interviewed for an English teaching position. One is a woman with a master's degree and ten years of successful teaching experience. The other is also a woman with a bachelor's degree and no experience. The district would like to save money by hiring the teacher with less experience. What drawbacks are there to this course of action?
7. A teacher in your school recently learned that her child has cancer. She wants to spend as much time as possible with the child during the lengthy period of treatment. What legal recourse does she have in dealing with this difficult situation?

8. A tenured teacher in your school has received unsatisfactory evaluation ratings for two years, despite district efforts to provide support and resources for improvement. The teacher is also a vocal critic of the school's administration. Can this teacher be fired? What law will the teacher be likely to use in a defense?
9. In an effort to save money, a district conducts a reduction in force in the areas of art and music. What benefits, if any, can these teachers retain?
10. You, the principal, ask a teacher to drive a student who has missed the bus home. On the way, the teacher's car is in a serious accident. The child escapes uninjured, but the teacher is paralyzed for life and will no longer be able to work. What recourse does this teacher have?

NOTES

1. 42 U.S.C.S. § 2000e-16 (2002), Pub. L. No. 88-352 (1964).
2. Pub. L. No. 92-261, effective March 24, 1972.
3. 42 U.S.C.S. § 2000e-2 (2002).
4. 42 U.S.C.S. 2000e-2 (2002).
5. 42 U.S.C.S. § 2000e-5(f)(1) (2002).
6. 42 U.S.C.S. § 2000e-5(f) (2002).
7. McDonnell Douglas Corp. v. Green, 411 U.S. 792, 803 (1973).
8. 42 U.S.C.S. § 1981 (2002), Pub. L. No. 102-166 (1991).
9. *See* 42 U.S.C.S. § 1981A (b)(3) (2002).
10. 42 U.S.C.S. § 1981A (b)(3) (2002).
11. 29 U.S.C.S. § 623 (2002).
12. 29 U.S.C.S. § 216(b) (2002), Bishop v. Jelleff Associates, 398 F. Supp. 579 (D.C., Cir., 1974).
13. 42 U.S.C.S. § 2000e-5(g)(1) (2002).
14. 42 U.S.C.S. § 2000e-2(k) (2002).
15. Albemarle Paper Co. v. Moody, 422 U.S. 405 (1975).
16. Texas Dep't of Comty. Affairs v. Burdine, 450 U.S. 248 (1981).
17. St. Mary's Honor Ctr. v. Hicks, 509 U.S. 502 (1993).
18. Price Waterhouse v. Hopkins, 490 U.S. 228 (1989).
19. 42 U.S.C.S. § 2000e-5(g)(2) (2002).
20. *See,* Congressional Record, H.R. 7152, 88th Cong., 77 (1963) and 110 Cong. 2567–2571 (1964).
21. "Labor Law Reports—Employment Practices," with foreword, *Office of Federal Contract Compliance Manual,* 2d ed., Report 86, No. 580, July 3, 1975 (New York, N.Y.: Commerce Clearing House, 1975).
22. Equal Employment Opportunity Commission, *Affirmative Action,* vol. I (Washington, D.C.: Government Printing Office, 1974), 18–64.
23. *United Steelworkers, Etc.,* 443 U.S. 193 (1979).

24. *Wygant,* 476 U.S. at 267 (1986).

25. 20 U.S.C.S. § 1681 to 1688 (2002), Pub. L. No. 95-555 (1978).

26. *See, e.g.,* N. Haven Bd. of Educ. v. Bell, 456 U.S. 512 (1982).

27. 20 U.S.C.S. § 1681(a) (2002).

28. *See, e.g., N. Haven Bd. of Educ.,* 456 U.S. 512.

29. Franklin v. Gwinnett County Pub. Schs., 503 U.S. 60 (1992).

30. Harris v. Forklift Sys., Inc., 510 U.S. 17 (1993).

31. Meritor Sav. Bank, FSB v. Vinson, 477 U.S. 57, 70–71 (1986).

32. *See,* Burlington Indus., Inc. v. Ellerth, 524 U.S. 742 (1998), and Faragher v. City of Boca Raton, 524 U.S. 775 (1998).

33. *Burlington Indus., Inc.,* 524 U.S. 742, 765.

34. *See,* Oncale v. Sundowner Offshore Sers. Inc., 523 U.S. 75 (1998).

35. 42 U.S.C.S. § 2000e-16 (2002), Pub. L. No. 95-555 (1973).

36. *See,* Cleveland Bd. of Educ. v. LaFleur, 414 U.S. 632 (1974).

37. Newport News Shipbuilding and Dry Dock Co. v. EEOC, 462 U.S. 669 (1983).

38. LaFleur, 414 U.S. 632 (1974).

39. 29 U.S.C.S. § 206(d) (2002), Pub. L. No. 88-38 (1963).

40. *See,* Garcia v. San Antonio Metro. Transit Authority, 469 U.S. 528 (1985).

41. Brennan v. Woodbridge Sch. Dist., 8 E.P.D. ¶ 9640 (D. Del. 1974).

42. 29 U.S.C.S. § 216(b) (2002).

43. 29 U.S.C.S. § 701 to 797 (2002), Pub. L. No. 93-112 (1973).

44. Dep't of Health, Education, and Welfare, "Nondiscrimination on the Basis of Handicap," 41 Fed. Reg. 96 (May 17, 1976).

45. 42 U.S.C.S. § 12101 to 12150 (2002), Pub. L. No. 101-336 (1990).

46. 42 U.S.C.S. § 12102(2) (2002).

47. 42 U.S.C.S. § 12208, 12211 (2002).

48. 42 U.S.C.S. § 12111(8) (2002).

49. 42 U.S.C.S. § 12112(a) (2002).

50. 42 U.S.C.S. § 12112(c)(2)(B) (2002).

51. 42 U.S.C.S. § 12112(b)(6)(7) (2002).

52. 42 U.S.C.S. § 12112(c)(3) (2002).

53. 42 U.S.C.S. § 12114(b), (d), 12210(b) (2002).

54. 42 U.S.C.S. § 12111(9) (2002).

55. 42 U.S.C.S. § 12111(10) (2002).

56. 42 U.S.C.S. § 2000e-5(g)(k) (2002).

57. Sutton v. United Air Lines, Inc., 527 U.S. 471 (1999).

58. Murphy v. United Parcel Serv., Inc., 527 U.S. 516 (1999).

59. 29 U.S.C.S. §§ 621 to 634 (2002), Pub. L. No. 90-202 (1967).

60. 29 U.S.C.S. § 623(c) (2002).

61. 29 U.S.C.S. § 623(d) (2002).

62. 29 U.S.C.S. § 623(e) (2002).

63. Hodgson v. Greyhound Lines, Inc., 499 F.2d 859 (7th Cir. 1974), *cert. denied,* 419 U.S. 1122.

64. 29 U.S.C.S. § 623(f)(2)(B) (2002).

65. 29 U.S.C.S. § 631(c) (2002).

66. Miller v. Cigna Corp., 47 F.3d 586 (3d Cir. 1995) (en banc).

67. 29 U.S.C.S. § 216(b) (2002).

68. Rogers v. Exxon Research & Eng'g Co., 550 F.2d (3d Cir. 1977), *cert. denied,* 434 U.S. 1022 (1978).

69. 42 U.S.C.S. §§ 6101 to 6107 (2002), Pub. L. No. 94-135 (1975).

70. *Kimel,* 52 U.S. at 62 (2000).

71. 29 U.S.C.S. § 2601 to 2619 (2002), Pub. L. No. 103-3 (1993).

72. 29 U.S.C.S. § 2612(a) (2002).

73. 29 U.S.C.S. 2611(2) (2002).

74. 29 C.F.R. § 825.114 (2002).

75. 29 U.S.C.S. § 2612(b)(1) (2002).

76. 29 U.S.C.S. § 2612(b)(2) (2002).

77. 29 U.S.C.S. § 2618(c) (2002).

78. 29 U.S.C.S. § 2618(c) (2002).

79. 29 U.S.C.S. § 2612(d)(1) (2002).

80. 29 U.S.C.S. § 2612(d)(2) (2002).

81. 29 U.S.C.S. § 2612(e)(1) (2002).

82. 29 U.S.C.S. § 2612(e)(2)(A) (2002).

83. 29 U.S.C.S. § 2613(a) (2002).

84. 29 U.S.C.S. § 2613(a) (2002).

85. 29 U.S.C.S. § 2614(c) (2002).

86. 29 U.S.C.S. § 2614(c)(2) (2002).

87. 29 U.S.C.S. § 2614(a) (2002).

88. 29 U.S.C.S. § 2614(a) (2002).

89. 29 U.S.C.S. § 2617(b) (2002).

90. 29 U.S.C.S. § 2617(a) (2002).

91. 29 U.S.C.S. § 2617(c) (2002).

92. 29 U.S.C.S. § 2617(a) (2002).

93. 5 U.S.C.S. § 8101 to 8153 (2002), Pub. L. No. 89-554 (1966).

94. *See, e.g.,* OHIO REV. CODE ANN. §§ 4123.01 to .99 (Anderson 2001).

95. J. R. Nolan and M. J. Connolly, *Black's Law Dictionary*, 5th ed. (St. Paul, Minn.: West Publishing, 1979), 1439.

96. *See, e.g.,* Fyffe v. Jeno's Inc., 570 N.E.2d 1108 (1991) and the cases cited therein.

97. *See, e.g.,* OHIO REV. CODE ANN. §§ 4141.242, 4141.25 (Anderson 2001).

98. 42 U.S.C.S. § 300bb-1 to -8 (2002), Pub. L. No. 99-272 (1986).

99. Geissal v. Moore Med. Corp., 118 S. Ct. 1869 (1998).

100. 42 U.S.C.S. § 300bb-2 (2002).

101. 42 U.S.C.S. § 300bb-6 (2002).

102. Bd. of Regents of State Colls. v. Roth, 408 U.S. 564 (1972).

103. *See, e.g.,* Pickering v. Bd. of Educ., 391 U.S. 563 (1968).

104. Bd. of Trustees of the Univ. of Alabama v. Garrett, 121 S. Ct. 955 (2001).

Chapter Six

Planning and Recruitment

An essential part of human resource administration is the ability to project personnel needs. The number of administrators, teachers, and support staff needed to implement an educational program will be influenced by legislation, contract, district goals and profiles, and the status of personnel already employed. Each of these factors becomes a parameter of effective planning and will be discussed in this chapter.

LEGISLATED PARAMETERS FOR PERSONNEL PLANNING

Individual states, as noted earlier, are vested with the ultimate control of public education. State legislatures have the fundamental power to select the public school curriculum, and their decisions in matters of curriculum are final. State legislatures may, however, delegate this authority to school district boards of education. Such delegation gives the local school board the right to prescribe the district's courses of study. Nevertheless, states usually legislate a basic curriculum, requiring school boards to include certain designated subjects in the programs they provide. Figure 6.1 lists some of the common curricular requirements prescribed by state law.

Some state laws dealing with public school curricula also impose a broad general requirement that every course of study be infused with the principles of democracy and ethical behavior and require that boards of education adopt policies reminding teachers they hire of their duty to instill ethical principles and democratic ideals. Many state laws also address the way subjects will be taught, prescribing student performance objectives in subject areas and grade levels, administering proficiency tests to monitor achievement in given subject areas, and requiring districts to offer appropriate intervention services for students who have difficulty in performing satisfactorily. Ultimately, state laws can fully

Subject	Content
Language Arts	Reading Writing Spelling Literature
Mathematics	Computation Estimation Problem Solving
Social Studies	U.S. History Government World History Geography
Science	Earth Science Biology Chemistry Physics
Health	Nutrition Sex Education Safety/First Aid Drug Abuse
Fine Arts	Art Music
Physical Education	Hand/Eye Coordination Sports Appreciation Lifetime Fitness

Figure 6.1   Common Curricular Requirements Prescribed by State Law

control what is taught and how it is taught and, in so doing, have a direct effect on a school district's staffing. For example, when states mandate all-day kindergarten programs, limit the number of special education students in a class, or mandate remediation for students in poorly performing schools, they are requiring school districts to hire teachers trained to meet these state mandates in the numbers required to bring state objectives to fruition.

Under the watchful eyes of state governments, public school curricula have exploded in recent years as states have attempted to address social as well as educational needs in the classroom. Courses of study now include first aid, community service, and values clarification courses in addition to reading, writing, and arithmetic, and school districts are required to develop programs and hire teachers to address these new state concerns. With this in mind, human resource administrators, be they principals, personnel directors, or assistant superintendents, must be alert to legislatively mandated programs and make them part of the district's personnel planning process.

CONTRACT PARAMETERS FOR PERSONNEL PLANNING

Even in school districts that do not collectively bargain, safety, health, and educational standards set by state law will limit the size of classes and the number of teacher assignments in a given school day. In school districts that do collectively bargain, negotiated contracts can have a direct impact on these same concerns. Contracts frequently set limits on the class size, the number of instructional assignments teachers can receive, and the way in which substitute coverage will be provided. These factors, as well as sick leave, pregnancy leave, and personal leave provisions in state laws and district contracts, have a direct effect on school staffing needs and personnel planning.

In human resource planning the devil is in the details and numbers. For example, the length of school day and year and the actual length of class periods will play a role in determining the final staffing cost of an educational program because length of day, year, and class periods determine the structure of a district's program and the number of teachers needed to implement an educational program in which contact hours are often prescribed by state law. Similarly, contracts will inevitably touch on staffing issues with clauses that address hours and terms and conditions of employment. Figure 6.2 explores some typical contract clauses and their potential effect on staffing and human resource management.

Staffing is the largest expenditure in the school budget. Thus, human resource managers must pay attention to every aspect of program planning that may in any way affect staffing and increase the costs of the educational program. Collectively bargained contracts exist to protect the interests of teachers and staff. In so doing, they cannot help but have a direct impact on personnel planning. There are no freebies in collective bargaining. Rights won by unions in bargaining not only place constraints on personnel planning, but they inevitably come with a price tag. Therefore, human resource managers must cost out the price of concessions proposed in bargaining.

DISTRICT PROFILES AND GOALS

A district's goals are its long-range expectations for the students it serves. Not all districts have the same long-range expectations for their children; therefore, a vital part of successful human resource management is to discover and accept the goals of a given community. The assumption that all parents want all stu-

Contract Clause	Potential Effect
Number of different teacher assignments, i.e., preparations within areas of certification	Will force district to hire more teachers to cover different assignments within an area of certification.
Start and end of school day	Will determine number of classes that can be offered and must be covered.
Class size	Will determine staffing needs in case of overloads.
Length and number of planning periods for classroom teachers	Will create need for teachers to cover classes during planning release time.
Duty-free lunch period for classroom teachers	Will create need for student supervision.
Sick leave, personal leave, parenting leave	Will create need for temporary and long-term substitute coverage.

Figure 6.2   Contract Clauses That May Affect Human Resource Management

dents to go to college may not always be true. In comfortable blue collar and farming communities, the school boards representing these communities may value strong vocational programs more than advanced placement offerings. In contrast, urban districts struggling to provide the basics may feel their tax dollars are better spent on remedial programs that will fill basic gaps in student learning. Successful human resource management must be responsive to differing district expectations.

This does not mean that educational leaders should not try to inspire all communities to grow and aspire to new levels of achievement for their children. It does mean, however, that part of the planning function should be the development of a community profile, which includes community input on what matters in public education. School district surveys and community studies can go a long way toward informing administrative practice. In the end, school budgets and programs developed without community input and support are doomed to defeat. Figure 6.3 lists some of the factors to be evaluated in developing a community profile and an educational program that reflects community needs and concerns.

School district goals and objectives are not the only way in which communities affect human resource planning. The economic rise and decline of communities will have an even more direct impact on the number of teachers and support staff needed to deliver an education program. When major businesses and industries leave a community, enrollment and tax base both inevitably decline, and when they come into a community, they can cause unanticipated district overcrowding and cost increases, which hopefully are offset by a growing tax

- District Description: Urban, Suburban, Rural
- Population Size
- Major Businesses
- Major Industries
- Types of Housing
- Average Cost of Housing
- Size of Average Family
- Average Income
- Number of School-Aged Children
- Highest Level of Parental Education
- Percent of Graduates Attending Colleges
- Percent of Graduates Employed
- Number of Single-Parent Homes
- Number of Families without Children
- Number of Senior Citizens
- Major Recent Economic Changes

Figure 6.3   A Community Profile: Factors to Consider

base. Therefore, school districts must assess present and potential community growth as a pivotal part of their own personnel planning function.

Enrollment studies over five-year periods can be useful in assessing trends that can inform planning. For example, enrollment at a particular level of the school program often correlates with housing and income trends. Burgeoning elementary programs are often indicative of an influx of young married couples with relatively low incomes. In contrast, burgeoning high school programs are frequently found in communities with relatively more expensive housing and families with parents in their forties. Enrollment studies should be a corollary to the community profile discussed earlier, and together they will provide a basis for a district's staffing plan. The gathering of data is a significant part of human resource planning. In this day of tight budgets and the demand for increased accountability, school district administrators will be asked to validate need before spending money. State mandates, contractual restrictions, community growth and need profiles, and enrollment studies support requests for increased spending.

PERSONNEL STATUS

Another integral part of planning for staffing involves assessing the status of those already employed in a district. Inventory cards, completed at hiring, should be annually updated to reflect an employee's current status and future plans. Figure 6.4 summarizes some of the basic information that can be part of an employee inventory. Figure 6.5, the reverse side of this inventory card,

Personnel Information	Changes
Name: _____	_____
Address:_____	_____
Home Phone: _____	_____
Position: _____	_____
Degrees: _____	_____
Years in District: _____	_____
Certification: _____	_____
Prior Positions in District: _____	_____
Tenure Status: _____	_____
RIF Status [If Applicable]: _____	_____

Figure 6.4   Personnel Inventory Form

Please Indicate Your Plans for the Upcoming School Year

I will return to my current assignment.	☐ yes	☐ no
I will return to a new assignment.	☐ yes	☐ no
I am requesting a voluntary transfer.	☐ yes	☐ no
[Indicate school and position below.]		
I am requesting leave.	☐ yes	☐ no
[Indicate type and period of time below.]	☐ yes	☐ no
I am requesting retirement information.	☐ yes	☐ no

Other Pertinent Information and Requests:

Signature: _____   Date: _____

Figure 6.5   Employee Intent Form

gathers information regarding employment plans for the upcoming school year. This annual review of present and future status is central to district planning.

Projected use of sick leave, pregnancy leave, and retirement will all affect staffing. Good personnel planning projects needs created by these options. Personnel administration is always a complex puzzle with many pieces. Law, contract, district input, and current personnel status are all pieces of that puzzle that must be addressed in projecting staffing for a sound educational program.

THE JOB DESCRIPTION

Once personnel needs have been assessed, the next step in the process of recruitment is the development of job descriptions. Job descriptions are official and legally binding statements describing a position's qualifications and responsibilities. Job descriptions require the employing district to clarify its expectations, and they require the applicant to attest to qualifications and abilities that address those stated expectations. Job descriptions should never be taken lightly. They become legally binding documents for both the employer and the employee that can be called on as evidence of a contract breach on either side.

In 1996, the National School Boards Association suggested a process for preparing job descriptions that entailed the following steps:

1. Superintendent recommendation of all positions to be covered by written job descriptions
2. Board approval of a job description development program
3. Coordination of responsibility for implementation
4. Development of job descriptions
5. Coordinator review of draft descriptions
6. Editing of job descriptions for style, format, and content
7. Supervisor and jobholder review for currency and accuracy
8. Superintendent approval of job descriptions
9. Preparation of job description manual
10. Submission to the board for approval[1]

Job descriptions should include school mission statements and objectives, qualifications, responsibilities, outcomes, and evaluation criteria. Supervisors and employees currently assigned to the same or similar posts best develop these aspects of the job description. Figure 6.6 is a Position Inventory Form to be completed by the employee currently holding the position, the position supervisor, or the proposed supervisor, if the position is new.

Position Title	_____
Requirements at Hiring:	_____
	_____
	_____
Present Responsibilities:	_____
	_____
	_____
Recommended Changes in Job Description, i.e., Requirements and Responsibilities	_____
	_____
	_____
Years of Service:	_____
Years of Supervision:	_____
Signature: _____	Date: _____

Figure 6.6   A Position Inventory Form

Preparation of viable job descriptions is no easy task. Job descriptions that are legally defensible require an analysis of the following job features:

1. What are the responsibilities of the position?
2. Why are these responsibilities significant to the position?
3. How should performance of these responsibilities be evaluated?
4. What skills are needed for this position?
5. What educational background is required for this position?
6. What job-specific training and experience are required for this position?
7. How does this job relate to the work of others?
8. What physical demands will be placed on the successful applicant?
9. What environmental conditions will affect performance?
10. How will performance be evaluated?

The job description becomes the basis for both selection and evaluation. It is the employee's official notice of pre-employment and post-employment requirements.

Figure 6.7 illustrates a job description for an elementary teacher, and figure 6.8 is a job description/job advertisement for an elementary principal.

As discussed in chapter five, Title VII's basic purpose is to ensure equality of employment opportunities by eliminating employment practices and policies that discriminate on the basis of race, religion, gender, and national origin. The Act also prohibits employment practices that, while not overtly discriminatory, may have a disparate impact on members on one of the protected classes.[2] This kind of discrimination can sometimes be found in job descriptions that include physical or performance demands that tend to preclude members of protected classes from applying. Disparate impact claims are usually based on statistics showing that, despite the intent of the employer, members of a protected class were the victims of discrimination as the result of the employer's business practices. Employers are allowed to maintain otherwise discriminatory employment practices only if they can show that such practices and policies are job-related and consistent with business necessity and that there is no alternative employment practice available that would be equally effective and have a less discriminatory impact.[3] Employees win disparate impact cases by showing that the employer refused to adopt other equally effective practices that would not have a discriminatory effect or that the employer's policy was not job-related or a business necessity.

The Americans with Disabilities Act, the Age Discrimination in Employment Act, and the Pregnancy Act, discussed in chapter five, similarly protect the disabled, those over forty, and pregnant women from employment decisions that may have a disparate impact on their employment opportunities. That is why job descriptions and the job advertisements they give rise to must be carefully reviewed for discriminatory qualification and responsibility statements. Rarely in public education does race, creed, gender, national origin, age, or pregnancy give rise to the level of a *bona fide occupational qualification* (BFOQ). While religiously affiliated private schools may consider applicants' creeds in making hiring decisions, public schools cannot follow suit. In addition, rarely can jobs be found in public education that could not be done by both genders and older employees. A BFOQ is not established by stereotyped assumptions as to what jobs women can or cannot do.[4] Although the temptation might exist for school administrators to avoid hiring teachers over forty, teachers who are disabled, and teachers who are pregnant, they are not at liberty to do so, and job descriptions and advertisements cannot contain qualifications that are veiled excuses for discriminatory preferences.

Stated qualifications and responsibilities must be related to the job. For example, it is legitimate to require a special education teacher in a self-contained program for severely disabled students to be able to lift two hundred pounds or

ELEMENTARY TEACHER

Qualifications:
- A Bachelor's Degree in Elementary Education
- An Elementary, K–8, Teaching Certificate
- Teaching Experience in an Elementary School

Reports to and
Is Evaluated by: The School's Principal or Assistant Principal

Job Goals: To provide structured learning experiences for students in grades one through eight that reflect the state and district curriculum

Specific Duties:
- Initial student assessment at the beginning of the school year

- Development of appropriate instructional and behavioral objectives for each student assigned

- Development of weekly lesson plans incorporating the state and district curriculum, and addressing all levels of Bloom's Taxonomy

- Regular evaluation of student progress in attaining stated objectives

- Effective and regular communication with parents, including at least two formal meetings a year

- Active participation in the development of appropriate individual education plans for special education students

- Effective collaboration with the school's teachers and administrators

- Ongoing participation in professional growth activities

- Service on at least one school committee

- Compliance with all provisions of board policy and contract

Figure 6.7   Elementary Teacher Job Description

ELEMENTARY PRINCIPAL

Position Available:	August 1, 2002
Compensation:	• 213 workdays
	• $61,896 starting base pay; actual pay dependent on training and experience
	• Excellent benefits, plus 4 weeks vacation
	• Two-year contract
Responsibilities:	• Principal of Kennedy Intermediate School
	• Major Responsibilities: instructional leadership and general school administration
Qualifications:	• State Certification for Elementary Principal or equivalent certification
	• Excellent teaching experience K–8
	• Strong instructional leadership skills
	• Strong interpersonal skills
	• Strong organizational skills
	• Understanding of contemporary elementary education skills/training to work with students, staff, and parents
	• Fiscal management skills
	• Administrative experience preferred

Figure 6.8   Elementary Principal Job Description/Job Advertisement

more if the teacher will be expected to help students move from desk to wheel-chair. This qualification may eliminate teachers who are themselves disabled from the applicant pool, however, the qualification in this instance is indeed a business necessity, a BFOQ. On the other hand, that same qualification for an English teacher is unlikely to pass legal muster, since there are other ways of providing for the needs of the occasional special education student likely to attend English class and need to be lifted. Options exist that would eliminate the disparate impact this qualification might have on disabled applicants for the position of English teacher; for example, the student's special education teacher or an aide could be made available during the class. While the requirement may be reasonable for a swimming instructor to be sighted for safety reasons, a sight requirement appears less reasonable when hiring a history teacher.

In the past, the courts have allowed a school district to consider gender in hiring a guidance counselor because the school argued that it had a compelling need for at least one counselor of each gender in order to assure that students of both genders would have the opportunity to discuss personal matters with a guidance counselor.[5] However, such gender-preferenced qualifications are the exception, not the rule. In this day and age of gender equity, trying to justify gender-specific jobs in public schools is very difficult. In the final analysis, the job description should merely state all degrees, certifications, skills, and training needed for a given position, and position responsibilities and objectives, and the position should be filled by whichever applicant best fits the published job description.

As noted, an important part of every job description should be a delineation of specific responsibilities. Before applying, applicants should understand what they will be held responsible for and who will be responsible for evaluating their performance in a given position. An organizational chart can be helpful in giving applicants a sense of the organizational pecking order, and a road map for organizational etiquette. Figure 6.9 is an example of a typical organizational chart, illustrating a district's responsibility and reporting structure. In this particular organizational chart, principals and assistant principals are primarily responsible for supervising teachers.

Finally, job descriptions should discuss the type of contract being offered. Is the contract limited or continuing? If limited, for what specific period of time will the applicant be employed? Are there any provisos to the contract being offered, that is, state certification, proof of good health or drug-free status? As explained earlier, school districts can require a medical exam *after* a contract has been offered, if all employees are subject to the same requirement. Likewise, it goes without saying that school districts can only put certified teachers into classrooms. While teachers' unions have thus far successfully resisted drug testing for teachers, most school districts do require drug testing at the time of hiring for all other school employees. Job descriptions may also premise hiring on the completion of successful background checks.

Salaries will usually be linked to job descriptions and qualifications. Positions requiring more rigorous qualifications and more extensive experience usually come with greater degrees of responsibility and, therefore, merit higher pay. In public schools, salary scales correlate monetary compensation for teachers with education and experience. This is particularly true in districts that collectively bargain. Even in districts that do not bargain, salary scales are helpful in allowing the district to acknowledge an employee's value by higher placement at time of hiring and in giving the new employee a view of potential increases, assuming satisfactory performance.[6] Salary, however, should never be an afterthought. The basis for

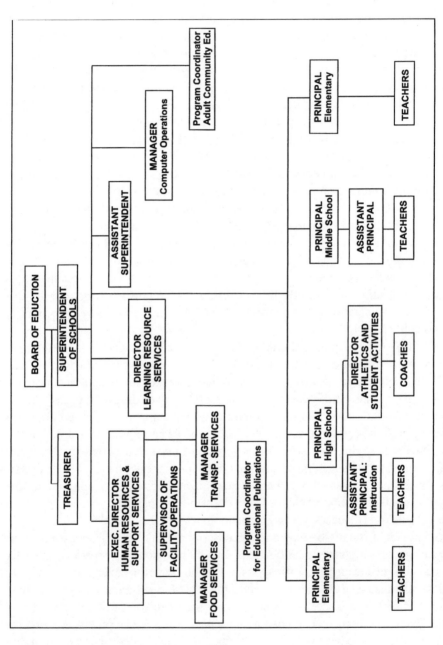

Figure 6.9 Organization Chart by Position

salary should be clearly justified by the job description and the applicant's qualifications in response to the job description. Salary placement that cannot be justified may be viewed as discriminatory under Title VII or the Equal Pay Act.

ADVERTISING THE JOB

The same laws that legislate against discriminatory concerns in the development of the job description apply to the development of the job advertisement. School districts must be mindful of advertisements that may have a disparate impact on applicants in protected categories. The Equal Employment Opportunity Commission (EEOC) has provided an administrative rule of thumb for determining when an employment practice may be considered to have a disproportionate impact on a protected group.[7] An employment practice is deemed to have a disproportionate adverse impact whenever the rate of selection for any protected group is less than 80 percent of the rate for the group having the highest selection rate.

Figures 6.10 and 6.11 give examples of job advertisements for the position of principal at the elementary level and at the junior–senior high school level. As one can see, the primary difference between job advertisements and job descriptions is their brevity. Job advertisements are concise, eye-catching inducements to application. Job descriptions are detailed explications of the district's expectations enclosed with applications sent to prospective applicants. Both should be developed with a conscious attempt to avoid disparate impact.

In districts with a history of discriminatory hiring, an affirmative action plan may require that districts advertise in minority newspapers and use minority placement centers in order to actively pursue compliance with EEOC guidelines. Human resource managers should monitor the steps they take to ensure equal employment opportunities for protected categories. One way to do this is to ask applicants, on the district's application form, how they heard about the position. Their responses can guide the choice of future publications and channels for advertising district positions.

THE APPLICATION PROCESS

Most school districts have formal applications for positions within the district. These applications ask for personal data, educational preparation, certification, work experience, and references. Some applications, however, seek information that may be perceived as discriminatory and therefore illegal. Figure 6.12 lists the type of information that is lawful to request and the type of information that is unlawful to request.

ELEMENTARY PRINCIPAL K–5

Middlebury Community School
Middlebury, Iowa

"Four-star" school district seeks visionary, child-centered leader with background in elementary teaching and administration. (Preferred but not required)

Required application materials include:
- Letter of interest
- Resume
- University credentials, including transcripts
- Middlebury Community School application
- Administrative license

The Middlebury Community School Corporation offers a competitive salary and fringe benefit package. Applications will be accepted until March 23, 2002. Send materials to:

Figure 6.10   Sample Job Advertisement—Elementary Principal

Jr.–Sr. PRINCIPAL

Walden, Massachusetts

Seeking a dynamic principal for 400-student Jr.–Sr. High. Must possess strong leadership and interpersonal skills and a demonstrated commitment to academic excellence. Candidate will be skilled in program and curriculum development, supervision and evaluation, scheduling, and change theory. Start July 1, 2002. Application—March 23, 2002. Send a complete application package: letter of application, resume, transcripts, certification, and three current letters of recommendation to:

Figure 6.11   Sample Job Advertisement—Jr.–Sr. High Principal

Here is a series of questions that the New York State Division of Human Rights has compiled as being lawful and unlawful pre-employment inquiries. As New York appears to be stricter than most states and the federal government, by following these recommendations, lawyers suggest that a company may be less likely to find itself in difficulty with the authorities because of pre-employment inquiries.

Subject	Lawful	Unlawful
Race or Color		Complexion or color of skin. Coloring.
Religion or Creed		Inquiry into applicant's religious denomination, religious affiliations, church, parish, pastor, or religious holidays observed. Applicant may not be told, "This is a (Catholic, Protestant, or Jewish) organization."
National Origin		Inquiry into applicant's lineage, ancestry, national origin, descent, parentage, or nationality. Nationality of applicant's parents or spouse. What is your mother tongue?
Sex		Inquiry as to sex. Do you wish to be addressed as Mr.? Mrs.? Miss? or Ms.?
Marital Status		Are you married? Are you single? Divorced? Separated? Name or other information about spouse Where does your spouse work? What are the ages of your children, if any?
Birth Control		Inquiry as to capacity to reproduce, advocacy of any form of birth control or family planning.
Age	Are you between 18 and 70 years of age? If not, state your age.	How old are you? What is your date birth?

Figure 6.12a   Legal and Illegal Pre-employment Questions

Disability	Do you have any impairment, physical, mental, or medical, that would interfere with your ability to perform the job for which you have applied? If there are any positions or types of positions for which you should not be considered, or job duties you cannot perform because of physical, mental, or medical disability, please describe.	Do you have a disability? Have you ever been treated for any of the following diseases . . . ?
Arrest Record	Have you ever been convicted of a crime? (Give details.)	Have you ever been arrested?
Name	Have you ever worked for this company under a different name? Is any additional information relative to change of name, use of an assumed name, or nickname necessary to enable a check on your work record? If so, explain.	Original name of an applicant whose name has been changed by court order or otherwise. Maiden name of a married woman. If you have ever worked under another name, state name and dates.
Address or Duration of Residence	Applicant's place of residence. How long a resident of this state or city?	
Birthplace		Birthplace of applicant. Birthplace of applicant's parents, spouse, or other close relatives.
Birth Date		Requirement that applicant submit birth certificate, naturalization, or baptismal record. Requirement that applicant produce proof of age in the form of a birth certificate or baptismal record.
Photograph		Requirement or option that applicant affix a photograph to employment form at any time before hiring.
Citizenship	Are you a citizen of the United States? If not a citizen of the United States, do you intend to become	Of what country are you a citizen? Whether an applicant is naturalized or a native-born citizen; the date

Figure 6.12b   Legal and Illegal Pre-employment Questions

	a citizen of the United States? If you are not a United States citizen, have you the legal right to remain permanently in the United States? Do you intend to remain permanently in the United States?

Requirement that applicant state whether he or she has ever been interned or arrested as an enemy alien. | when the applicant acquired citizenship.

Requirement that applicant produce naturalization papers or first papers.

Whether applicant's spouse or parents are naturalized or native-born citizens of the United States; the date when such spouse or parents acquired citizenship. |
| Language | Inquiry into languages applicant speaks and writes fluently. | What is your native language?

Inquiry into how applicant acquired ability to read, write, or speak a foreign language. |
Education	Inquiry into applicant's academic, vocational, or professional education and the public and private schools attended.	
Experience	Inquiry into work experience.	
Relatives	Name of applicant's relatives, other than a spouse, already employed by this company.	Names, addresses, ages, number, or other information concerning applicant's spouse, children, or other relatives not employed by the company.
Notice in Case of Emergency	Name and address of person to be notified in case of accident or emergency.	
Military Experience	Inquiry into applicant's military experience in the Armed Forces of the United States or in a State Militia.

Inquiry into applicant's service in a particular branch of the United States Army, Navy, etc. | Inquiry into applicant's general military experience. |
| Organizations | Inquiry into applicant's membership in organizations that the applicant considers relevant to his or her ability to perform the job. | List all clubs, societies, and lodges to which you belong. |

Figure 6.12c   Legal and Illegal Pre-employment Questions

A rule of thumb in constructing a district's job application is that no questions irrelevant to the position should ever be asked. Nine times out of ten, irrelevant questions can have discriminatory implications. For example, while one's marital status is irrelevant to one's ability to do the job, once asked, the question does give rise to the perception of potential gender discrimination.

District Forms

Figure 6.13 is an example of a legally defensible school district employment application.

Although the application form itself is a central part of recruitment, as figure 6.13 indicates, the application process should include all the following elements:

1. a completed and signed district application form;
2. an applicant resume;
3. a copy of a valid teaching certificate;
4. an official copy of all undergraduate and graduate transcripts;
5. a copy of the National Teacher Examination scores.

The advertised deadline should be strictly adhered to as the closing date for receiving this information. Consistency is central to good human resource management. To make exceptions is to once again invite the perception of discriminatory behavior, and, in the final analysis, applicants who cannot comply with advertised dates for submitting materials are unlikely to be the best candidates for employment.

School districts frequently include an Affirmative Action Compliance Form with the application materials they send. Figure 6.14 is an example of this form. Although it is worthwhile for districts to monitor the success of their affirmative action efforts, sending this form with the district's application is not a good idea in that applicants who return the form with their applications walk away with the perception that they were asked, albeit on a separate form, to racially and ethnically identify themselves. Districts would be better served by providing applicants with a separate envelope or addressed postcard for submitting this information alone.

The Resume

Applicants often wonder why it is necessary to submit both an application and a resume when applying for a job, since they both include much of the same information. However, from a human resource manager's perspective, the application standardizes the information a district will need in making its decision. On the other hand, the resume and application can serve as a check on each other. While the information in both should be identical, it sometimes is not.

APPLICATION FOR SCHOOL EMPLOYMENT

TEACHER / ADMINISTRATOR / SUBSTITUTE TEACHER / TUTOR
SUPPLEMENTAL DUTY / COMMUNITY EDUCATION INSTRUCTOR

THE CANDIDATE MUST FORWARD TO THE DIVISION OF HUMAN RESOURCES A
RESUME, COMPLETE TRANSCRIPTS OF COLLEGE CREDITS, COLLEGE PLACEMENT
OFFICE FILE (THREE CURRENT REFERENCES IF NOT IN ONE'S PLACEMENT OFFICE
FILE), NTE SCORES (IF REQUIRED AT THE TIME OF INITIAL STATE CERTIFICATION),
AND EVIDENCE OF CERTIFICATION OR ELIGIBILITY FOR CERTIFICATION FOR THE
POSITION SOUGHT.

(TYPE OR PRINT)

I. PERSONAL INFORMATION   DATE _____
                                    SOCIAL SECURITY NUMBER _____
   NAME _____
              LAST   FIRST   MIDDLE
   ADDRESS (CURRENT) _____
                        NUMBER & STREET   CITY

   _____
        STATE   ZIP   AREA CODE   PHONE NUMBER
   ADDRESS (PERMANENT) _____
                        NUMBER & STREET   CITY

   _____
        STATE   ZIP   AREA CODE   PHONE NUMBER
   I WISH TO BE CONSIDERED FOR:
      REGULAR TEACHER _____ SUBSTITUTE TEACHER _____ TUTOR _____
      ADMINISTRATOR _____ SUPPLEMENTAL DUTY _____
      COMMUNITY EDUCATION INSTRUCTOR (certificated position) _____

II. EMPLOYMENT INFORMATION
    A. PRESENT POSITION _____
    B. POSITION FOR WHICH YOU ARE APPLYING:
       1st Choice _____
                        GRADE OR LEVEL   SUBJECT
       2nd Choice _____
                        GRADE OR LEVEL   SUBJECT
    C. WHEN WOULD YOU BE AVAILABLE FOR THIS POSITION? _____
    D. CERTIFICATE(S) HELD:

AREA OF CERTIFICATION	STATE	CERT. #	TYPE	ENDORSEMENT(S) (if any)	EXPIRATION DATE

    E. LIST ANY ACTIVITIES OR CLUBS YOU WOULD BE WILLING TO ADVISE OR COACH:
       _____

Figure 6.13a   Application for School Employment

III. EDUCATION (PLEASE LIST MOST RECENT EDUCATION FIRST)

SCHOOL AND LOCATION	DEGREE	MAJOR	GPA

IV. SUBSTITUTE TEACHING (IF YOU CHECKED SUBSTITUTE ON PAGE 1, FILL OUT BELOW)
DAYS AVAILABLE: _____

GRADE LEVEL(S) OR SUBJECT(S) PREFERRED: _____

V. REFERENCES (INCLUDE PRINCIPALS, SUPERINTENDENTS, OR OTHERS FOR WHOM YOU HAVE WORKED RECENTLY)

NAME	ADDRESS, CITY, STATE, ZIP, PHONE #	REFERRAL PERSON'S POSITION

VI. HAVE YOU EVER BEEN OFFERED OR WORKED UNDER A CONTINUING CONTRACT?   YES _____ NO _____

VII. TEACHING AND OTHER WORK EXPERIENCE, INCLUDE MILITARY (LIST MOST RECENT EXPERIENCE FIRST)

FROM: MO. YR.	TO: MO. YR.	NO. MONTHS	TITLE OF POSITION	SALARY–FINAL

NAME OF EMPLOYER	DUTIES
ADDRESS PHONE #	
NAME OF SUPERVISOR	REASON FOR LEAVING

FROM: MO. YR.	TO: MO. YR.	NO. MONTHS	TITLE OF POSITION	SALARY–FINAL

NAME OF EMPLOYER	DUTIES
ADDRESS PHONE #	
NAME OF SUPERVISOR	REASON FOR LEAVING

Figure 6.13b   Application for School Employment

VIII. OTHER CONSIDERATIONS

HAVE YOU EVER WORKED FOR OR APPLIED FOR A POSITION WITH THIS DISTRICT BEFORE?

YES _____ NO _____

DATE APPLIED _____ DATES WORKED _____

IF SO, UNDER WHAT NAME? _____

ARE YOU AUTHORIZED TO BE EMPLOYED IN THE UNITED STATES?

YES _____ NO _____

HAVE YOU EVER BEEN CONVICTED OF ANY FELONY OR ANY MISDEMEANOR OTHER THAN A TRAFFIC VIOLATION WHICH HAS NOT BEEN EXPUNGED?

YES _____ NO _____ IF YES, PLEASE EXPLAIN.

HAVE YOU EVER BEEN DISMISSED FROM OR REFUSED RE-EMPLOYMENT IN AN ADMINISTRATIVE OR TEACHING POSITION? YES _____ NO _____

IX. IN YOUR OWN HANDWRITING, WRITE A BRIEF STATEMENT BELOW INDICATING THE REASONS WHY YOU WANT TO TEACH IN THIS DISTRICT'S SCHOOLS.

I certify that all statements I have made in this application are true, complete, and correct to the best of my knowledge and that I am aware that any false statements, misrepresentations, or omissions of the facts will be sufficient cause for dismissal.

I understand that the Board of Education may want to verify the statements I have made in this application. I hereby give my permission for the Board of Education, either at this time or any time during my employment, to request and review any of my educational records, employment records from previous employers, court records, and police records from any local, state, or federal agency keeping such records. I also authorize the Board of Education to obtain oral and written recommendations from the persons listed on this application, from all previous employers, and from persons listed as personal references. I fully release the Board of Education and all previous employers and persons contacted for references from any and all claims that might arise from the exchange of information regarding prior job performance and/or qualifications for employment. I understand that any employment continuation will be dependent on the results of the fingerprinting check through the Bureau of Criminal Identification and Investigation and successful completion of a drug/alcohol screen.

_____   _____
              Date   Signature of Applicant

PLEASE RETURN THIS APPLICATION TO:

Division of Human Resources
NAME & ADDRESS OF SCHOOL DISTRICT

"AN EQUAL OPPORTUNITY EMPLOYER"

THIS SCHOOL DISTRICT DOES NOT DISCRIMINATE ON THE BASIS OF SEX, RACE, COLOR, RELIGION, AGE, DISABILITY, OR NATIONAL ORIGIN IN THE EDUCATIONAL PROGRAMS THAT IT OPERATES AND THE REQUIREMENTS OF TITLE IX OF THE EDUCATIONAL AMENDMENTS OF 1972, TITLE VII OF THE 1964 CIVIL RIGHTS ACT, AND SECTION 504 OF THE REHABILITATION ACT OF 1973. NOT TO SO DISCRIMINATE EXTENDS TO EMPLOYMENT IN SUCH EDUCATIONAL PROGRAMS. THE OFFICE OF THE ASSISTANT SUPERINTENDENT HAS BEEN ASSIGNED THE RESPONSIBILITY FOR COORDINATING EFFORTS TO COMPLY WITH THESE ACTS.

Figure 6.13c   Application for School Employment

Racial/Ethnic Data

The following information is asked in order to monitor our Affirmative Action Program and to ensure equal employment opportunity. Institutions receiving federal funds are required to collect and maintain data on the race, sex, and ethnic identity of all applicants for employment.

Date: _____ (month) _____ (day) _____ (year)
Position applying for: _____
Sex:_____ Male _____ Female   U.S. Citizen: _____ Yes _____ No
Birth date: _____ (month) _____ (day) _____ (year)

_____ White   (should include persons having origins in any of the original
                           peoples of Europe, North Africa, the Middle East, or the
                           Indian subcontinent)
_____ Black   (should include persons having origins in any of the black
                           racial groups of Africa)
_____ Hispanic   (should include persons of Mexican, Puerto Rican, Cuban,
                           Central or South American, or other Spanish culture or
                           origin, regardless of race)
_____ Asian   (should include persons having origins of any of the oriental
                           peoples of the Far East, Southeast Asia, or the Pacific
                           Islands; this includes China, Japan, Korea, the Philippine
                           Islands, and Samoa)
_____ Native American   (should include persons having origins in any of the original
                           peoples of North America)

NOTE: The above information will not be used in evaluating your application and will be
       kept separately only in our Affirmative Action file. You are not required to
       complete this form, though your cooperation would be greatly appreciated.

Figure 6.14   Affirmative Action Compliance Form

Finally, a resume provides insight into what the applicant perceives to be important, as well as the applicant's personal penchant for organization and presentation. The resume gives the district a sense of the applicant's style.

Transcripts

Official transcripts are an essential part of the application process. They are an official record of the applicant's academic performance and an indicator of persistence and dedication to a task. As such, transcripts must play a central role in the selection process. Hence, school administrators find difficulty in defending employment decisions regarding the hiring of teachers that do not give deference to academic success. While it may be argued that teachers who have known failure themselves are better teachers for that experience, hiring applicants with poor academic track records is risky and flies in the face of common sense and effective human resource management.

Certificates

States control the process of teacher certification. Usually, certification or licensing requires the completion of a college degree that includes a stated number of credits or courses in education, including applicable field experiences, and proof of good character. Some states also require prospective teachers to pass the National Teachers Examination. Figure 6.15 compares the statutory requirements for certification in California and Pennsylvania.

Most states presently require some form of standardized test for entry into teacher education programs, program completion, initial certification, and/or certification renewal.[8] The Supreme Court has upheld use of the National Teachers Examination, although the test has been shown to have a disparate impact on minority applicants for teaching certificates.[9] Essentially, the test has been found to be a fair method for assessing needed skills, and the concept of disparate impact cannot abrogate the need to have the very best teachers in the nation's classrooms.

The Supreme Court has also allowed school districts to require prospective teachers to sign oaths, narrowly limited to affirming support for the government and a pledge not to act forcibly to overthrow the government.[10] However, while pledges requiring faithful performance of duties and support for the federal and state Constitutions have been upheld,[11] oaths requiring applicants to swear they are not members of subversive organizations have not been allowed,[12] because in the latter case, constitutionally protected freedom of association is proscribed.

Citizenship can also be a requirement for teacher certification. The Supreme Court upheld a New York law denying certification to teachers who were eligible for certification, but refused to apply for naturalization.[13] The Court held that teaching is an integral governmental function, so bound up with the operation of the state as a governmental entity as to permit the exclusion from those functions of all persons who have not become part of the process of self-government.[14] Essentially, the Court found that the state's interest in furthering its educational goals justified its mandate for teacher citizenship.

In states that have established certification subject areas, a teacher must possess a valid certificate to teach a specific subject.[15] However, some states allow persons who have not followed the traditional path to licensure to teach, for limited time periods, in public schools.[16] Such temporary licensure may require only that the individual have either a bachelor's degree or higher degree in the subject to be taught or that the individual have significant experience relating to that subject.[17] In the face of looming teacher shortages, such emergency certification will probably become more popular. That being said, school districts not employing certified teachers risk loss of financial accreditation and fiscal support.[18] They also open themselves up to lawsuits in courses

| California | CAL. EDUC. CODE ANN. § 44225 |

The commission shall do all of the following:

(a) Establish professional standards, assessments, and examinations for entry and advancement in the education profession. While the Legislature recognizes that the commission will exercise its prerogative to determine those requirements, it is the intent of the Legislature that standards, assessments, and examinations be developed and implemented for the following:

(1) The preliminary teaching credential, to be granted upon possession of a baccalaureate degree from a regionally accredited institution in a subject other than professional education, completion of an accredited program of professional preparation, and either successful passage of an examination or assessment that has been adopted or approved by the commission in the subject or subjects appropriate to the grade level to be taught, to include college-level reading, writing, and mathematics skills, or completion of an accredited program of subject matter preparation and successful passage of the basic skills proficiency test as provided for in Article 4 (commencing with Section 44250). The commission shall uniformly consider the results of the basic skills proficiency test in conjunction with other pertinent information about the qualifications of each candidate for a preliminary credential, and may award the credential on the basis of the overall performance of a candidate as measured by several criteria of professional competence, provided that each candidate meets minimum standards set by the commission on each criterion. Upon application by a regionally accredited institution of higher education, the commission may categorically grant credit to course work completed in an accredited program of professional preparation, as specified by this paragraph, by undergraduates of that institution, where the commission finds there are adequate assurances of the quality of necessary undergraduate instruction in the liberal arts and in the subject area or areas to be taught.

(2) The professional teaching credential, to be granted upon successful passage of a state examination or assessment in the subject or subjects appropriate to the grade level to be taught, to include college-level basic reading, writing, and mathematics skills, and completion of a period of beginning-teacher support that includes assessments of ability to teach subject matter to pupils, ability to work well with pupils, classroom management, and instructional skills. A candidate who successfully passes the examination or assessment pursuant to paragraph (1) shall be deemed to have passed the state examination or assessment in the subject or subjects to be taught pursuant to this paragraph.

| Pennsylvania | PA. STAT. ANN. tit. 24 § 1225 |

The Department of Public Instruction shall have the power, and its duty shall be—

(a) To provide for and to regulate the certificates and the registration of persons qualified to teach in such schools;

(b) To certify as qualified to practice the art of teaching in such schools any applicant eighteen (18) years of age, of good moral character, not addicted to the use of intoxicating liquor or narcotic drugs, and who has graduated from a college, university, or institution of learning approved as herein provided, and who has completed such professional preparation for teaching as may be prescribed by the State Board of Education, and to register such person upon such proof as the State Board of Education may require that such applicant possess such qualifications.

Figure 6.15 Statutory Requirements for Teacher Certification: California and Pennsylvania

such as chemistry, industrial arts, and physical education, where students may be injured as the result of improper instruction.

Teaching certificates have been found by the courts to be licenses, subject to state renewal requirements.[19] Teachers who do not renew their teaching licenses prior to expiration can be fired,[20] and should not be hired. Thus, application review must take notice of the expiration dates on teaching and administrative certificates. States also have the authority to revoke teacher licenses for a variety of other reasons, including immorality, incompetency, breach of contract, and neglect of duty. No single definitive list of reasons for revocation exists, but license revocation can be based on a teacher's behavior both inside and outside of the classroom. For example, the courts have upheld a state's decision to revoke the license of a teacher who appeared on television in disguise to discuss nonconventional sexual behavior as a member of a "swingers club."[21]

In summary, proof of teacher licensure is an important part of the application process. Possession of a license indicates that the applicant has complied with at least the state's minimum certification standards and is prepared to teach. Nevertheless, local school boards are not precluded from setting their own higher standards in their job descriptions, as long as those standards are applied in a uniform and nondiscriminatory fashion.[22] Licensing is a beginning, not an end in assuring that educators are prepared.

A LEGAL PERSPECTIVE

Recruitment is a process wrought with legal land mines. Law and contract define the way school districts must proceed at every step. Personnel need projections, job descriptions, job advertisements, and the application process itself must all be developed in the context of law and contract if they are to be effective and withstand the tests of time and litigation.

THEORY INTO PRACTICE

1. Develop a profile for your school district and a statement of its perceived goals.
2. Analyze the staff at your school with respect to race, gender, and age. Should your district have an affirmative action plan in light of your analysis?
3. Evaluate your district's organizational chart. Does the chart truly represent the way the district functions?

4. Compare the job descriptions for teachers and administrators in your district with respect to stated qualifications and responsibilities.
5. Review advertisements for teaching and administrative positions. Do any, either directly or indirectly, contain age or gender preferences?
6. How do school districts that do not collectively bargain determine teachers' salaries?
7. Review your district's application form. Does it contain any illegal or inappropriate requests for information?
8. Complete your district's application form, and compare the information you have provided with that appearing in your current resume.
9. What are your state's requirements for teacher licensing and for license renewal?
10. What grounds does your state use for revoking a teacher's license?

NOTES

1. National School Boards Association, *The School Personnel Management System* (Arlington, Va.: National School Boards Association, 1996), 157.

2. 42 U.S.C.S. § 2000e-2(k) (2002).

3. 42 U.S.C.S. § 2000e-2(k) (2002).

4. EEOC Sex Discrimination Guidelines, 29 C.F.R. § 1604.02(a)(1)(ii).

5. Stone v. Belgrade Sch. Dist. No. 44, 703 P.2d 136 (Mont. 1985).

6. C. Knutson, "Development of a Master Salary Schedule," in *Wage and Salary Administration: A Handbook for School Business Officials*, ed. C. W. Foster (Chicago, Ill.: Research Corporation of the Association of School Business Officials, 1969), 15.

7. Uniform Guidelines on Employee Selection Procedure, Section 4(d), codified at 29 C.F.R. § 1607.

8. M. McCarthy, "Teacher-Testing Programs," in *Educational Reform Movement of the 1980's,* ed. J. Murphy (Berkeley, Calif.: McCutchan Publishing, 1990), 189–214.

9. Nat'l Educ. Ass'n v. South Carolina, 434 U.S. 1026 (1978).

10. Cole v. Richardson, 405 U.S. 676 (1972).

11. Ohlson v. Phillips, 397 U.S. 317 (1970).

12. Keyishian v. Bd. of Regents of the Univ. of the State of New York, 385 U.S. 589 (1967).

13. Ambach v. Norwick, 441 U.S. 68 (1979).

14. *Ambach,* 441 U.S. 68, 73–74.

15. Tate v. Livingston Parish Sch. Bd., 444 So. 2d 219 (La. Ct. App. 1983), *writ denied,* 446 So. 2d 314 (La. 1984).

16. *See, e.g.,* OHIO REV. CODE ANN. § 3319.301 (Anderson 2001).

17. *See, e.g.,* OHIO REV. CODE ANN. § 3319.301(A) (Anderson 2001).

18. Wagenblast v. Crook County Sch. Dist., 707 P.2d 69 (Or. Ct. App. 1985).

19. Fields v. Hallsville Indep. Sch. Dist., 906 F.2d 1017 (5th Cir. 1990), *cert. denied,* 498 U.S. 1026 (1990).

20. Frey v. Adams County Sch. Dist. No. 14, 771 P.2d 27 (Colo. Ct. App. 1989), *aff'd,* 804 P.2d 851 (Colo. 1991).

21. Pettit v. State Bd. of Educ., 513 P.2d 889 (Cal. 1973).

22. Dennery v. Bd. of Educ. of Passaic County Reg'l High Sch. Dist., 622 A.2d 858 (N.J. 1993).

Chapter Seven

Review, Interview, and Selection

Successful recruitment will usually attract a significant number of potential candidates for a position. Applications, transcripts, proof of certification, and resumes will begin arriving, and the process of filing and reviewing the paperwork each applicant submits begins. Review, interview, and selection are stages of a process, and figure 7.1 is a schematic description of the steps in that process.

THE PAPER SCREENING

The first step in the review process is the paper screening. Even before seeing an applicant, the paperwork submitted will give the reviewer a distinct impression of who the applicant is. Getting all requested information in to the district on time is the first hurdle a serious applicant must jump. In order to keep the process on schedule, human resource administrators must set deadlines for submission, and, in order to avoid the perception of discriminatory treatment, human resource administrators must remain faithful to those deadlines. Bending the rules regarding what is to be submitted and when is a surefire way to get in trouble. Ultimately, the question becomes where to draw the line in making allowances for time and content, and that question will inevitably be followed by more questions from applicants who perceive themselves to be hurt by allowances made or not made. The only certain way to avoid the curse of concessions is simply not to make them. Position advertisements with posted deadlines, and job descriptions with stated qualifications must be honored in all parts at every step of the process. Applications that are incomplete or not on time should be eliminated from consideration.

Application screening should correlate with the job qualifications appearing on the job description. Applicants who do not have the qualifications listed should be removed from consideration. For example, if the job description required a candidate to have a master's degree and at least five years of experience, a candidate with a bachelor's degree and one year of experience should be screened out

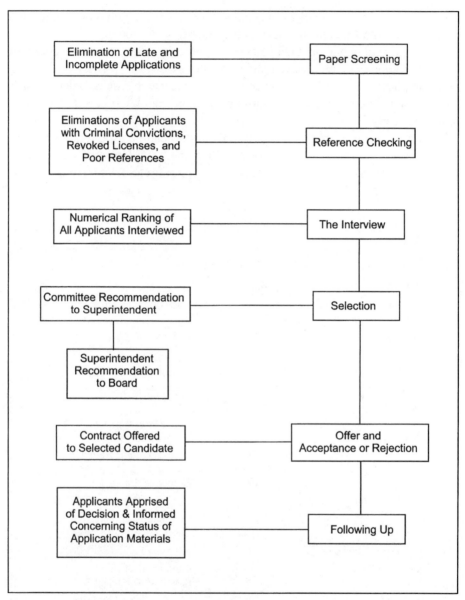

Figure 7.1 Review, Interview, and Selection: The Process of Hiring

at this stage. While at first glance this may seem a bit hard-nosed, consider the consequences of the alternative, that is, hiring an applicant with neither the advertised degree nor experience. Rejected, qualified applicants can be expected to question such a decision, and in looking for reasons, they will review their own legal options for challenging a decision perceived as blatantly unfair. There are no secrets in human resource management. It is a business built on formality, and every form reviewed in the application process becomes a public record, accessible to the general public, including rejected applicants. The fairness and equity of the selection process are always open to public review. The privacy of the individual applicants is not really an issue because their names can be deleted. Their qualifications in comparison with those of the applicant hired become the focus of an equity review.

Figure 7.2 is an example of a simple form that can be used to keep the selection process on track. This form monitors the completion of other forms used in the selection process and requires a signature and date to ensure procedural accountability.

Activity	Completed	Documentation
POSITION: _____		
DATE: _____ REASONS FOR VACANCY: _____		
Review and Approve Job Announcement	☐	Copy of Job Description
Post Position	☐	Posting
	☐	Mailing List
Receive Inquiries	☐	List of Applications Sent
Check on Advertising Effectiveness	☐	Applicant Response Form
Receive and Review Applications	☐	Application Screening Form
Paper Screening for Interview	☐	Paper Screening Results
	☐	Numerical Evaluation
Reference Check	☐	Telephone Reference Check Form
	☐	Criminal Background Check Report
Candidate Interview	☐	Interview Ranking List
Identification of Finalists	☐	Candidate Ranking List Based on Numerical Ratings
Board of Education Decision	☐	Board Meeting Minutes
Reviewed by: _____		
Date: _____		

Figure 7.2   Selection File Checklist

Qualifications must always be evaluated with reference to the posted job description. Figure 7.3 is a form that can be used to correlate posted job qualifications with submitted material. In this example, the form lists the qualifications posted for a school guidance counselor.

Once candidates who are qualified for the advertised position are identified, the next step in the process of review is to rate and rank the applicants based on their submitted paperwork. Each applicant comes with a unique paper background highlighting experiences and achievements. Some candidates will be stronger than others in areas important to the position. Figure 7.4 is an example of a form that can be used in rating the credentials of a candidate for an administrative position. This form in essence develops a numerical profile of areas of strength and weakness in the applicant's credentials.

Numerical ratings are used to bring objectivity to this part of the process, but there is optional space for briefly commenting on the reasons for below average or superior ratings. Ideally, those who will be interviewing the successful candidates should individually complete this numerical review. Individual ratings at this stage of the selection process avoid the pitfalls of what those who study organizational behavior call *groupthink*. Groupthink is a collective pattern of defensive avoidance that leads to a deterioration

---

Candidate: _____

For Administrative Position: _____

Job Qualifications (From Posting)		Qualifications Met	
1.	Master's degree in guidance and counseling	☐ yes	☐ no
2.	State certification	☐ yes	☐ no
3.	Three (3) years successful experience in a public school	☐ yes	☐ no
4.	Experience in conducting small group specialized counseling	☐ yes	☐ no
5.	Experience in the development of individual education plans for special education students	☐ yes	☐ no

All Qualifications Met: ☐ yes ☐ no

Screened by: _____

Date: _____

Figure 7.3   Application Screening: Job Description versus Applicant Qualifications

Candidate: _____

Position: _____

		0	1	2	3	4	5	6	7
		Below Average		Average		Above Average			Superior

										Information Missing	Comments
A.	Experience Related to:										
	Administration	1	2	3	4	5	6	7		I.M.	
	Supervision	1	2	3	4	5	6	7		I.M.	
	Curriculum Development	1	2	3	4	5	6	7		I.M.	
	Staff Selection	1	2	3	4	5	6	7		I.M.	
	Urban Education	1	2	3	4	5	6	7		I.M.	
	Suburban Education	1	2	3	4	5	6	7		I.M.	
	Teaching	1	2	3	4	5	6	7		I.M.	
	Areas Taught	1	2	3	4	5	6	7		I.M.	
	Levels Taught	1	2	3	4	5	6	7		I.M.	
	Related Noneducational Experience	1	2	3	4	5	6	7		I.M.	
B.	Academic Preparations:										
	Degrees Earned	1	2	3	4	5	6	7		I.M.	
	Academic Grades	1	2	3	4	5	6	7		I.M.	
	Fields of Study	1	2	3	4	5	6	7		I.M.	
	Honors	1	2	3	4	5	6	7		I.M.	
	Special Training	1	2	3	4	5	6	7		I.M.	
C.	Experience Related Directly to This Position:	1	2	3	4	5	6	7		I.M.	

Figure 7.4   Rating Credentials to Identify the Best-Qualified Administrative Candidates for Interviewing

of mental efficiency, reality testing, and moral judgment.[1] Groupthink occurs when decision-making groups are cohesive, insulated from outside criticism, and subject to strong directive leadership by one or more group members. Vocal members with strong opinions essentially silence less vocal members of the group by creating an illusion of group unanimity. Individual members of the group assume that everyone else agrees and that the silence of others implies consent and agreement with whatever opinions are on the table and with whatever decisions are made. Group members invent justifications for whatever actions they take and dismiss rival or critical opinions.[2] In the end, the need to belong overrides the need to be true to one's own beliefs. Decisions made in an environment that fosters groupthink are more likely to be poor because *the group* is keeping individuals from evaluating and sincerely choosing among alternatives.[3] Groupthink uses the desire for social acceptance to stifle the criticism and dissent central to finding the best solution to a problem. In human resource management, groupthink can also set the stage for stereotyping and for the discussion of factors prohibited by law. In contrast, individual review and rating of applicant credentials will allow a fairer, more objective, numerical ranking of the candidates.

REFERENCE CHECKING

One of the most important tasks in the review process is reference checking. One need only look at the stories of child abuse by school personnel that appear almost daily in the news to appreciate the significance of checking the background of every person one hires to work in a school. The completed application serves as a starting point for reference checking; for asking applicants to name former employers, places, and periods of employment; and to provide addresses and phone numbers. Gaps in an applicant's employment history should send up a red flag. Although many women take leave for child rearing, one cannot assume that this accounts for gaps in the employment history. It is important that applicants under serious consideration be asked, before selection for interviewing, what they were doing during unaccounted for periods of time and, where possible, verify their explanation.

Several questions should appear on every application in order to help with the background check and to deal with the prospect of deception. Every candidate should be asked whether they have been *convicted* of a crime. There is a difference between being *arrested* and being *convicted*. A person can be arrested and, through the judicial process, be found innocent of the charge filed. However, a person who has been *convicted* of a crime has been found guilty as charged in a court of law. While it would be unfair to remove an applicant who had been arrested from consideration, convicted felons should have no place in a public school's job pool. Also important is to use the term *crime*, as opposed to *felony*, in posing this question, because many felony charges, especially sex offenses, are reduced to misdemeanors as part of plea bargaining agreements. Questions that are too technical can allow an applicant to evade the truth.

Another important question that should appear on the application is why the applicant left each of the positions listed in the work history. The applicant's reasons for leaving can then be compared with the responses former employers give to this same question during telephone reference checks. The application should also contain a signed release giving the school district permission to take the steps it deems necessary in completing a thorough background check. Some experts have gone even further, recommending that school districts add liability waivers to employment applications. By signing the application, applicants waive their rights to find out what references say about them, as well as their right to hold references, including former employers, law enforcement agencies, federal records, and child and protective service agencies, legally responsible for comments.[4] Finally, every application should include a statement notifying the candidate that lies on the application, if discovered after hiring, will be ground for dismissal. Figure 7.5 gives examples of how these points are handled on a typical application.

Qualified Privilege

Human resource managers are often called on to both give and receive references for job applicants, and this is probably one of the areas of greatest concern for managers who fear the potential repercussions of total honesty. However, such fears have no foundation. The law of defamation recognizes a *qualified privilege* to tell the whole truth in situations such as these. A qualified privilege exists whenever a statement is made in good faith, without actual malice, on a subject in which the speaker has a valid interest or duty, to a person having a corresponding interest or duty.[5] There is no reason why school districts should not be totally honest with one another. Statements made in the context of employer–employee relationships, particularly references, fall under the protective umbrella of qualified privilege if they are made in good faith, without actual malice, on a subject in which the speaker has a valid interest or duty, to a person having a corresponding interest or duty. Courts have freely granted qualified privilege protection to communications between school officials,[6] and some states have laws specifically protecting an employer's right to give references.[7] Such laws provide that no employer shall be liable in damages to any employee for information disclosed to a prospective employer concerning job performance unless the employee can show that the employer knew that the information was false, intended to mislead the prospective employer, was acting with discriminatory intent, or was otherwise acting maliciously and in bad faith.[8] As of August 1997 twenty-six states had adopted laws aimed at protecting public employers from defamation suits in cases where they provided good-faith responses to requests for information about employees.[9] Ethically

My witnessed/notarized signature on the (school district) application for employment authorizes school district personnel and security/police departments to conduct a complete background investigation and authorizes release of all information in connection with my application for employment. This investigation may include such information as criminal or civil arrests and convictions, driving records, previous educational or training institutions, previous employers, personal and developed references, professional references, and other appropriate or available sources. I waive my right of access to any of the information and, without limitation, hereby release the school district and the reference source from whom the information was received, from any liability in connection with its release or official use. This release includes all the sources mentioned above as well as the following specific examples: local police/sheriff and other state or federal law enforcement agency; information from any local, state, or federal record, or central record exchange of data or data on any and all criminal arrests or convictions; and any information from any other state department of social services or child protection services unit, and any other locality to which they may refer for information regarding any findings or investigations involving me, relating to child abuse, neglect, or domestic violence.

I hereby certify that all entries and statements are true, correct, and complete on this application and are subject to verification and relied on in considering my application. I also understand that any omissions, false answers, or statements made by me on this application, or any supplement to it, regardless of time of discovery, may be sufficient grounds for failure to employ me or for my discharge should I become employed by the school district.

_____

Date   Signature of applicant

Witness: _____

Date   Signature   Print Name

(NOTARY if applicable)

Note: School officials should review individual state laws with their attorneys before adopting this or any similar waiver.

I understand that the Board of Education may want to verify the statements I have made in this application. I hereby give my permission for the Board of Education, either at this time or any time during my employment, to request and review any of my educational records, employment records from previous employers, court records, and police records from any local, state, or federal agency keeping such records. I also authorize the Board of Education to obtain oral and written recommendations from the persons listed on this application, from all previous employers and from persons listed as personal references. I fully release the Board of Education and all previous employers and persons contacted for references from any and all claims that might arise from the exchange of information regarding prior job performance and/or qualifications for employment. I understand that any employment continuation will be dependent on the results of the fingerprinting check through the Bureau of Criminal Identification and Investigation and successful completion of a drug/alcohol screen.

_____ _____

Date   Signature of Applicant

Figure 7.5 Applications and Background Checks [Waiver and Statement Acknowledging Truth of Statements]

and legally, if one is in a position to know the quality of a prospective employee's performance, one has a protected duty to share that information when asked by a potential employer with a corresponding duty to inquire, and questions answered in good faith and without malice are not libelous or slanderous. Truth is its own defense to a charge of libel or slander.

Nevertheless, in spite of public policy, laws and court decisions upholding the right of school officials to freely share employment information, many districts have adopted a practice euphemistically referred to as *passing the trash,* under which they either ignore the truth or refuse to comment at all to questions about an applicant's past performance or reason for leaving the district. Since the 1980s, school district attorneys, concerned with the threat of litigation, have advised school districts to adopt policies of limited or no disclosure about past employees.[10] A recent nationwide study, however, shows that only a single case exists in which a teacher had successfully sued an administrator for defamation based on information provided to a prospective employer.[11] On the other hand, the courts are beginning to punish administrators who engage in passing the trash. For example, the California Supreme Court ruled that a student molested by a middle school vice principal could go forward with her suit against the administrators in three other districts who had written glowing recommendations for him without mentioning that he had been investigated for alleged improprieties with students in their districts and had been forced to leave at least two of the three earlier districts.[12]

Negligent Hiring

Negligent hiring is the other side of this troublesome coin. When school districts simply do not bother checking the backgrounds of prospective employees and asking for references, they can and should also be held liable for the tortuous acts of those unchecked employees. All employers have a duty to protect foreseeable victims from harm by those they hire, and for school districts this duty is particularly weighty considering the age and vulnerability of their charges. To establish a cause of action for negligent hiring, a plaintiff must show that the employer knew, or in the exercise of ordinary care should have known, that an employee was unfit or dangerous at the time of the employee's hiring and that the employee was the proximate cause of the plaintiff's injuries.[13]

In pursuit of school safety, many states now require fingerprinting and criminal background checks for all applicants for school positions. There are also agencies in place to assist with background checks. The Teacher Identification Clearinghouse, maintained by the National Association of State Directors of Teacher Education and Certification (NASDTEC), provides a nationwide database of teachers whose certifications have been denied, revoked, or suspended over the past ten years. States, not individual districts, join the clearinghouse, which distributes a monthly update of the names, known aliases, birth dates, and Social Security numbers of all persons whose certification was withheld by member states, and as of July 1990, forty-two states had signed clearinghouse agreements.[14] For districts who are not members of the clearinghouse, *The Guide to Background Investigations* outlines procedures for obtaining criminal, court, workers' compensation, education, and driving records, and gives each state's policies regarding access to this information.[15]

Telephone reference checks are the local district's required effort to check the validity of information the applicant has provided. Figure 7.6 is an example of

---

POSITION: _____

CANDIDATE: _____

Address: _____

Phone: _____

Candidate's Certification Status: _____

Reference Contacted: _____

Position: _____

Period during which reference knew candidate: _____

Capacity in which reference knew candidate: _____

Public Relations Skills:

a. with Staff...............................	Poor	Fair	Good	Excellent
b. with Unions.............................	Poor	Fair	Good	Excellent
c. with Community Groups.....................	Poor	Fair	Good	Excellent
d. with Minorities...........................	Poor	Fair	Good	Excellent
e. with Supervisors	Poor	Fair	Good	Excellent
f. with Board of Education	Poor	Fair	Good	Excellent

Professional Stamina:

a. Ability to react under pressure	Poor	Fair	Good	Excellent
Examples:				
b. Ability to respond intelligently under pressure...........................	Poor	Fair	Good	Excellent
Examples:				
c. Ability to cope under situations of extended pressure	Poor	Fair	Good	Excellent
Examples:				

Professional Character:

a. Initiative	Poor	Fair	Good	Excellent
b. Ability to make decisions	Poor	Fair	Good	Excellent
c. Ability to be part of a team	Poor	Fair	Good	Excellent
d. Loyalty.................................	Poor	Fair	Good	Excellent
e. Judgment..............................	Poor	Fair	Good	Excellent

Greatest Asset: _____

Most Significant Handicap: _____

Other Comments: _____

INTERVIEWER:

DATE:

TIME:

Figure 7.6   Telephone Reference Check

a form that can be used to standardize the gathering of information during a telephone reference check.

In the interest of equity, it is important that such standardization be established. References, their relationship to the applicant, and the period of contact should be identified, and the same questions regarding performance should be asked of each person interviewed. All reference information, including criminal background checks and telephone reference checks become part of applicant files for later review by the interviewing committee.

THE INTERVIEW

The opportunity to meet face-to-face with applicants is a vital part of the hiring. However, interviewing, like hiring, is a part of a process not a single event. That process includes five steps:

1. Selecting the Interview Committee
2. Training the Interview Committee
3. Developing the Interview Questions
4. Conducting the Interview and Numerically Rating Applicants
5. Numerical Tallying and Selection

Selecting the Interview Committee

Deciding who is on an interview committee is the important first step in the process. Ideally, committee members should be stakeholders in the outcome of the interview, that is, they should have an interest in the newly hired employee's success. Principals, teachers, board members, parents, and students all qualify as stakeholders and legitimate members of committees that interview prospective administrators and teachers. Human resource managers putting together interview teams, however, must take care in choosing members who will review candidates with an open mind. Every effort should be made to select interviewers who are not bigots and whose participation will be respectful and circumspect.

Training the Interview Committee

Interviewers who are not aware of the legalities surrounding the interview process are likely to lead the school district down a path of unnecessary litigation. Therefore, it is important to provide preliminary training for the interview committee that will help them understand how various state and federal laws will affect pre-employment questioning.

Figure 7.7 summarizes the discriminatory status of some often asked questions and can help committee members avoid asking for information that is not legally justified. Every question asked during an interview must be job-related. Questions that are not job-related will, nine times out of ten, lend themselves to the applicant's perception of discrimination.

The following lists provide questions that can or should not be asked on employment application forms and in pre-employment interviews or other pre-employment inquiries. Some of the questions listed as potentially discriminatory may be asked legally if they relate to bona fide occupational requirements of a particular job or if there are affirmative action considerations.

SUBJECT	JOB-RELATED, NONDISCRIMINATORY QUESTIONS	NOT JOB-RELATED, POTENTIALLY DISCRIMINATORY QUESTIONS
Name	Applicant's full name. Have you worked for this business or organization under a different name?	Applicant's maiden name
	Is any additional information relative to a different name necessary to check on your work record? If yes, explain.	Original name of applicant whose name has been changed by court order or otherwise
Address/ Residence	What is your mailing address?	Where did you live previously?
	How long a resident of this state or city? (for tax purpose)	
Sex, Marital Status, Family	Statement of district policy regarding work assignment of employees who are related	Questions that indicate applicant's sex, marital status, and number and/or ages of children or dependents; provisions for child care, questions regarding pregnancy, childbearing, or birth control
	Name and address of parent or guardian if applicant is a minor	Name or address of relative, spouse, or children of applicant
		With whom do you live?
Race, Color	None	Questions regarding applicant's complexion, color of skin, eyes, hair, etc.

Figure 7.7a Avoiding Discriminatory Pre-employment Inquiries

Age	Statement that hiring is subject to verification that applicant meets legal age requirements	Age
		Birth date
	If hired, can you show proof of age?	Questions that tend to identify applicant over age 40
National Origin	Languages applicant reads, speaks or writes	Questions of nationality, lineage, ancestry, national origin, descent, or parentage of applicant, applicant's parents, or spouse
		How applicant acquired the ability to read, write, or speak a foreign language
Birthplace, Citizenship	Can you, after employment, submit verification of your legal right to work in the United States?	Requirements that applicant produce naturalization papers or alien card prior to employment
	Statement that proof of legal right to work in the United States may be required after employment	Birthplace or citizenship of applicant, applicant's parents, spouse, or other relatives
Physical Condition, Handicap	Do you have any physical condition or handicap that may limit your ability to perform the job applied for? If yes, what can be done to accommodate the limitation?	Questions regarding receipt of Workers' Compensation
		Do you have any physical disabilities or handicaps?
Physical Description, Photograph	Statement that photograph may be required after employment	Questions as to applicant's height and weight
		Request applicant, at his or her option, to submit a photograph
Religion	Statement of regular day, hours, or shifts to be worked	Questions regarding applicant's religion
Arrest, Criminal Record	Statement that, if recommended for employment, applicant would be required to give permission for a criminal records check	Have you ever been arrested?

Figure 7.7b   Avoiding Discriminatory Pre-employment Inquiries

Dependents		Do you have any children?
		How old are your children?
		Do you have any dependents?
		What child care arrangements have you made?
Driver's License	May be asked about only if driving is necessary for the job	Do you have a valid driver's license?
Education	Inquiry into academic, vocational, or professional education of the applicant and the schools attended	
Emergency Notification	Name and address of person to be notified in case of accident or emergency	Name and address of nearest relative to be notified in case of emergency
Experience	Inquiries into work experience	
Health/ Pregnancy (Post-offer/ Pre-employment Only	Do you have any impairments, physical, mental, or medical, that would interfere with your ability to do the job for which you have applied? Are there any positions for which you should not be considered or job duties you cannot perform because of a physical or mental handicap? Inquiries into contagious or communicable diseases that may endanger others	Are you pregnant? Are you using any contraceptives? Are you planning to have a family? Requirements that women be given a pelvic examination Do you have a disability or handicap?
Height or Weight		Any inquiries regarding applicant's height or weight. Post-offer/pre-employment physical examinations are optional
Relatives	Names of applicant's relatives already employed by the school system	Requirement to furnish address of any relative

Figure 7.7c   Avoiding Discriminatory Pre-employment Inquiries

Special Skills	Inquiries into special skills such as typing, foreign languages, writing, operating computers, etc.	
Organizations	Inquiry into membership in professional organizations or hobby groups relevant to the job	Inquiry into membership in specific organizations the name or character of which reveal personal information that could be used to discriminate against the applicant

Figure 7.7d   Avoiding Discriminatory Pre-employment Inquiries

Some other do's and don'ts that should be shared with the interview committee include:

1. making the candidate comfortable so that the committee can get a true picture of attitudes and motivation;
2. letting the candidate do most of the talking;
3. phrasing questions in such a way that they do not suggest an answer;
4. avoiding questions that can be answered with simply a "yes" or "no";
5. monitoring one's own nonverbal communication;
6. avoiding arguments or the appearance of cross-examining the applicant;
7. pausing between questions and applicant answers as a way of encouraging the candidate to continue and reveal information that might have been withheld.

Developing the Interview Questions

The interview committee develops the questions they will ask in advance. Once again, in the interest of fairness and equity, each candidate should be asked the same questions, preferably in the same sequence, and by the same committee members. Standardizing the interview process is an important part of avoiding discriminatory behavior. Add-on questions or extraneous comments by individual interviewers should be avoided.

Interview questions can be structured or unstructured and should address major areas of concern related to the job. In interviewing prospective teachers, these areas may include questions about teaching methodology, curriculum, student discipline, communications with parents, and familiarity with technology, as well as the applicant's attitudes regarding multiculturalism, professional growth, and accountability. Figure 7.8 provides a list of questions in each of these categories that can be adapted for use in interviewing prospective teachers. Figure 7.9 provides a similar list of questions in areas related to the hiring of an administrator. In addition, candidates can be asked to prepare unstructured responses to situational problems posed by the interview committee. Applicants for the position of principal, for example, can be asked to review the videotape of a lesson being taught and to prepare a written critique of the teacher's performance with suggestions for improvement.

Conducting the Interview and Numerically Rating the Applicants

At the end of each interview, committee members will be asked to use the information they have gleaned from the interview to numerically rate the candidates. Figure 7.10 gives an example of an interview evaluation form for a teaching position, and figure 7.11 adapts this form for evaluating a prospective administrator. As noted earlier, these evaluations are best done without

---

JOB PERFORMANCE

1. How do you plan a lesson?
2. How would you pretest students?
3. How would you incorporate Bloom's Taxonomy into your lesson plan?
4. How would you evaluate student learning?
5. How do you perceive the role of the classroom teacher?

MULTICULTURAL/DIVERSITY SENSITIVITY

1. How would you promote tolerance of diversity?
2. Give examples of ways you would foster an appreciation for multiculturalism.

EXCEPTIONAL EDUCATION NEEDS

1. What role should regular classroom teachers play in the instruction of students with special needs?
2. How will you address the needs of children with physical and emotional concerns?
3. What strategies would you use to ensure classroom unity?
4. What strategies will you use to ensure minority student achievement?
5. Do you believe all children can achieve, and what evidence supports your opinion?

TECHNOLOGY

1. How should technology interface with education?
2. How will you use technology to enhance your own teaching?

PROFESSIONAL GROWTH AND DEVELOPMENT

1. Where do you see yourself five years hence?
2. What immediate professional growth plans do you have?
3. What are your interests outside of the classroom?

BELIEFS

1. What is effective teaching?
2. How should teachers be evaluated?
3. What can you personally do to make education more effective?

Figure 7.8   Interview Questions for Prospective Teachers

JOB PERFORMANCE
1. How would you deal with a staff member who is either continuously late to work or excessively absent?
2. Please outline the process for evaluating teachers that you believe to be most effective.
3. Identify the essential elements of a plan for improvement for a teacher whose performance is not satisfactory.
4. A teacher who has been employed by the district for many years is not performing satisfactorily. How would you proceed?
5. A popular teacher is doing an outstanding job. How would you approach the required evaluation of this employee?
6. Describe reliable indicators of an effective classroom.
7. What have you done to assist a teacher in improving his/her areas of weakness and supporting his/her strengths and growth?

MULTICULTURAL/DIVERSITY
1. How would you effectively promote or facilitate development of a multicultural environment?
2. Cite specific examples where you have initiated programs and opportunities to meet the diversified needs of students.
3. How have/will you promote multicultural awareness and appreciation for diversity?
4. What are your visions on multicultural education?
5. What strategies have you used to bring about unity and to increase inclusiveness in ethnically and economically diverse student populations?
6. What strategies have you utilized to increase student achievement of minority students where that has been a concern?

EXCEPTIONAL EDUCATION NEEDS
1. What do you see as regular education's role in special education?
2. What are your experiences and beliefs about fulfilling the needs of special education students?
3. What are your experiences and beliefs about fulfilling the needs of students at risk?
4. Describe your experiences in developing school programs for students with special needs.

LEADERSHIP QUALITIES
1. Why would you like to be a (principal)?
2. What qualities do you consider essential for an effective (principal)?
3. Share the details of the implementation process by which you introduced an innovative practice in your current building/district.
4. What is your vision for this building/district in the next decade?
5. Describe how you prepare for and spend a typical workday.
6. What leadership attributes do you believe to be your strengths? Cite examples in which you demonstrated these qualities.
7. What are some beliefs and practices related to education administration that you absolutely will not compromise? Cite examples where you held to these beliefs/practices in the face of adversity.
8. How do you initiate/facilitate change? Cite an example.
9. Highlight the basic elements of delegation and share an example of how you typically delegate responsibilities.

Figure 7.9a   Interview Questions for Prospective Administrators

10. How do you get staff members excited about new ideas/change?
11. How do you motivate staff members?
12. What are the most important functions of an administrator in this position?
13. What are appropriate organizational/community activities for an administrator in this position?
14. If you were observed in your normal workday, what would be seen that would help others to understand your leadership style?
15. What is your vision for your school/position? What special talents do you bring to facilitate this vision?
16. How have you provided educational leadership for classroom teachers?

STUDENT DISCIPLINE
1. What role should a principal take in student discipline?
2. When is it appropriate for the principal to intervene in a student disciplinary concern?
3. Describe the process or system you believe to be most effective in addressing student discipline?
4. What techniques for managing children's behavior have you used?

RELATIONSHIPS/COMMUNICATION
1. What type of relationship would you establish with the employees you supervise?
2. How have/would you encourage the involvement of parents and community members in the educational process?
3. How have/would you promote articulation and cooperation between departments?
4. What are the elements of effective communication?
5. What type of relationship would you like to have with students and staff? How would you develop these relationships?
6. How can cooperation and camaraderie be maintained in spite of competition for limited resources?
7. Please share a time in which you worked with parents and the community in some kind of school–community partnership. What did you do?
8. Just as the student population has become more diverse, so has the parent population. How have/would you make parents feel more a part of their child's education and increase their level of comfort in a school setting?
9. What role have you taken as an educator and a leader in interacting with the community?
10. Describe a situation in your current position in which you had to deal with a volatile or sensitive encounter concerning a student, staff member, or parent. How was this situation resolved?

TECHNOLOGY
1. How have/would you utilize technology to be more effective as an administrator?
2. What new technology and applications do you foresee for the future of education?
3. How does technology interfere with education at this level?

PROFESSIONAL GROWTH AND DEVELOPMENT
1. How have/would you ensure an effective staff development program for your staff members?
2. What professional development activities have you pursued in the past year? How have you found them to be beneficial?
3. What are your main goals and aspirations for your professional career?

Figure 7.9b   Interview Questions for Prospective Administrators

4. How do you determine your effectiveness as an administrator?
5. How do you balance the demands and stress of educational administration with other demands and needs in your life?
6. What are your interests outside of educational administration?
7. What is it about being an administrator that brings you the greatest satisfaction?

PROBLEM SOLVING/DECISION MAKING
1. Share your beliefs/experiences with site-based decision making.
2. What areas lend themselves best to site-based decisions, and what areas should not be open to a site-based decision-making process?
3. Which administrative duties do you find to be the most enjoyable? Which do you find to be the least enjoyable?
4. What has been your greatest professional challenge? How did you address the challenge?
5. How do you determine when to have a staff meeting and the meeting's agenda?
6. You have just received a grievance from the union for a new practice you have implemented. What would you do?
7. A teacher has come to you with a request that you believe has merit but is not permitted by the Master Contract. What would you do?
8. How would staff members describe your decision-making style? Describe one instance in which a difficult decision had to be made and how you reached the decision.
9. How would you resolve a situation in which a staff member, student, and parent are in serious disagreement?
10. How do you handle conflict between staff members?
11. What are the most critical problems facing education today? What steps would you like to see initiated to address these problems?
12. How would you proceed with developing your annual budget?
13. Give an example of how you have dealt with a staff member who was resistant to change when change was necessary.
14. A student is referred to you because he/she has been missing school with increasing frequency. How would you work toward reducing the student's absenteeism?

STAFF SELECTION
1. What qualities and characteristics do you look for in prospective employees?
2. What process do you find effective in selecting new staff members?

CURRICULUM AND INSTRUCTION
1. How do/can you determine if students are receiving the learning experiences they need?
2. How have you supported teachers in developing an innovative practice, learning model, or curriculum development?
3. We have more and more children who present academic and behavioral challenges, yet do not meet the criteria for special education services. What strategies would you suggest to teachers as they attempt to meet the diversified needs of these children?
4. How have you supported diverse learning styles and teaching styles?

Figure 7.9c   Interview Questions for Prospective Administrators

CANDIDATE: _____

POSITION: _____

	0	1	2	3	4	5	6	7
	Below Average		Average		Above Average			Superior

A. Instructional Skills: Not Applicable   Comments

Demonstrated Lesson
Planning Ability   1 2 3 4 5 6 7   N.A.

Demonstrated Knowledge
of Subject   1 2 3 4 5 6 7   N.A.

Demonstrated Ability to
Select Appropriate
Leaning Activities   1 2 3 4 5 6 7   N.A.

Demonstrated Ability to
Individualize Instruction   1 2 3 4 5 6 7   N.A.

Demonstrated Ability to
Incorporate All Levels of
Bloom's Taxonomy   1 2 3 4 5 6 7   N.A.

B. Communication Skills:

Demonstrated Ability to
Communicate Well
During the Interview   1 2 3 4 5 6 7   N.A.

Demonstrated Examples of
Successful Communications
with Various Segments of
the Educational
Community (Parents,
Teachers, Students,
Administrators)   1 2 3 4 5 6 7   N.A.

Publications   1 2 3 4 5 6 7   N.A.

C. Professional Skills:

Demonstrated Creativity   1 2 3 4 5 6 7   N.A.

Demonstrated Initiative   1 2 3 4 5 6 7   N.A.

Demonstrated Follow-
Through   1 2 3 4 5 6 7   N.A.

Demonstrated Familiarity
with Professional Trends   1 2 3 4 5 6 7   N.A.

Demonstrated Experience
Related to Posted Position   1 2 3 4 5 6 7   N.A.

Demonstrated Ability to
Cope with Pressure   1 2 3 4 5 6 7   N.A.

Figure 7.10   Interview Evaluation Form for Teaching Candidates

CANDIDATE: _____

POSITION: _____

	0	1	2	3	4	5	6	7	
	Below Average		Average		Above Average			Superior	

A. Administrative Skills:									Not Applicable	Comments
Demonstrated Planning Ability	1	2	3	4	5	6	7	N.A.	
Demonstrated Organzation Ability	1	2	3	4	5	6	7	N.A.	
Demonstrated Ability to Select and Train Staff	1	2	3	4	5	6	7	N.A.	
Demonstrated Ability to Educate Staff	1	2	3	4	5	6	7	N.A.	
Demonstrated Staff Support Programs	1	2	3	4	5	6	7	N.A.	

B. Communication Skills:									
Demonstrated Ability to Communicate Well During the Interview	1	2	3	4	5	6	7	N.A.
Demonstrated Examples of Successful Communications with Various Segments of the Educational Community (Parents, Teachers, Students, School Boards, & Other Professionals))	1	2	3	4	5	6	7	N.A.
Publications	1	2	3	4	5	6	7	N.A.

C. Professional Skills:									
Demonstrated Creativity	1	2	3	4	5	6	7	N.A.
Demonstrated Initiative	1	2	3	4	5	6	7	N.A.
Demonstrated Follow-Through	1	2	3	4	5	6	7	N.A.
Demonstrated Familiarity with Professional Trends	1	2	3	4	5	6	7	N.A.
Demonstrated Experience Related to Posted Position	1	2	3	4	5	6	7	N.A.
Demonstrated Ability to Cope with Pressure	1	2	3	4	5	6	7	N.A.

Figure 7.11   Interview Evaluation Form for Administrative Candidates

group discussion that may pollute the process and introduce discriminatory perceptions and comments.

A recent trend has some school districts employing outside agencies to interview prospective applicants. For example, the Gallup Organization offers school districts their *Teacher Perceiver* interview program. The *Teacher Perceiver Interview* is an individually administered interview composed of sixty open-ended questions designed to permit individual self-expression with regard to different job-related issues and to predict job-related behaviors of individuals through a study of twelve themes that the Gallup Organization considers central to predicting successful teaching.[16] The *Teacher Perceiver* analyzes applicant-free responses and listens for cues correlating with the twelve identified themes Gallup has identified as predictive of success in the classroom.

SELECTION

Final selection of the successful candidate for any position in a public school should rest on the objective, personal, and numerical rankings assigned each candidate by the members of the interviewing committee. Selection based on any other criteria is open to criticism in that it ignores concerns for fairness, equity, and independent input in the selection process. Politics, bigotry, and groupthink decisions should have no place in the selection process. If they do, they set the stage for ethical and legal challenges. School districts are small communities in which the vagaries of process easily become the object of gossip and public concern. Human resource managers owe it to the school district they represent and to themselves to conduct the business of recruitment, interview, and selection in a way that is above reproach.

Offer and Acceptance

Every valid contract requires offer and acceptance. Contracts also require consideration for services rendered. In public education, successful candidates should be offered contracts clearly specifying job expectations and clarifying the salary and benefits to be received. However, there is a legal protocol in education that prescribes official hiring.

Board Approval

Once the interview committee has rendered its collective opinion, a recommendation can be made to the superintendent, and with the approval of the superintendent, it can be conveyed to the board of education. The authority to select and appoint teachers is vested solely in the board of education,[17] and the board carries the ultimate responsibility in all matters relating to the employment and reemployment of teachers.[18] This power may not be delegated to the superintendent of schools or to any other person.[19] Superintendents can recommend, but they cannot insist. Thus, all school district appointments are subject to approval by the board of education.

Neither administrators nor interviewers can officially hire the successful applicant, no matter how impressed they may be. All offers of employment must be premised on approval by the board of education. This important qualification can cause problems if not fully understood by the applicant. Thus, to create a presumption of hiring before the board has officially acted is legally precarious for interviewers or administrators.

Once the board has approved a candidate's appointment, an official contract can be offered and a request for timely acceptance should be relayed to the successful candidate. Successful candidates need to fully understand the terms and conditions of the contract being offered, including placement on the pay scale, entitlements under the contract, and position responsibilities. The law requires offer and consideration premised on informed agreement to perform as required by contract.

Following Up

Once the successful candidate has officially accepted the position offered, it behooves human resource administrators to notify unsuccessful candidates of the board's decision and to let them know the status of their files and applications. Human resource management that is sensitive and considerate can also, in the long run, be economical and timesaving. The files of finalists, those interviewed but not chosen, should not be discarded. It is wise to keep these files arranged according to their final numerical ranking for at least one year, should something go awry or additional needs arise. These finalists are the best viable options in the event the chosen candidate refuses the position offered, performs poorly, or other emergency openings evolve. With this in mind, figure 7.12 is offered as a sample communication informing unsuccessful candidates of the board's appointment, while keeping the prospect of future employment an option.

A LEGAL PERSPECTIVE

While the process of review, interview, and selection might seem to some to be overly cumbersome, it is designed to ensure equity for all candidates and, done

Dear (Applicant),

The Board of Education has decided to offer (Name of Successful Applicant) a contract for the position of (Principal, Teacher, etc.). This letter is sent to thank you for your interest in this position and to inform you that your application and materials will remain on file with our Human Resource Director for one year.

Should a position for which you are qualified become available, we will contact you.

Sincerely,

Figure 7.12   Notifying Unsuccessful Candidates

properly, to ensure the selection of the best candidate for the position. Shortcuts are not economically or legally sound. Inevitably, they lend themselves to the perception of discrimination, corruption, nepotism, or inconsistency. Therefore, it is important to establish standardized procedures and forms to monitor the process and mitigate discriminatory behavior. A record of objective recruitment, evaluation, and selection is the best defense to charges of discrimination, corruption, nepotism, or inconsistency.

THEORY INTO PRACTICE

1. Describe the process your school district uses in hiring teachers and administrators.
2. Who is in charge of supervising this process, and how is this person selected?
3. What criteria are used to select applicants for interviewing?
4. Describe the reference-checking process currently used in your school district.
5. Interview those persons who give references in your district, and discuss any district policy regarding the information that can be released to inquiring employers.
6. How are interviews conducted in your district?
7. Review and evaluate any forms your district may use during the review, interview, and selection processes.
8. How does your district notify unsuccessful candidates of hiring decisions?
9. What happens to the applicant files of unsuccessful candidates in your district?
10. Has your district encountered any problems during the course of interview and selection?

NOTES

1. I. Janis, "Groupthink," *Psychology Today* 5, no. 6 (1971): 43–46, 74–76.

2. I. Janis, *Groupthink,* rev. and enl ed. of *Victims of Groupthink* (Boston, Mass.: Houghton Mifflin, 1982).

3. N. Maier and J. Thurber, "Innovative Problem-Solving by Outsiders: A Study of Individuals and Groups," *Personal Psychology* 22, no. 3 (1969): 237–249.

4. "Liability Waiver Can Improve Reference Checks," *Inside School Safety* 2, no.1 (Frederick, Md.: Aspen Publishers, 1997) (quoting J. Barry Hylton, a school security consultant).

5. Hahn v. Kotten, 331 N.E.2d 713 (1975). This case provides a good discussion of the concept of qualified privilege.

6. Ranous v. Hughes, 141 N.W.2d 251 (Wis. 1966); McAulay v. Maloff, 369 N.Y.S.2d 946 (N.Y. Civ. Ct. 1975); Creps v. Waltz, 450 N.E.2d 716 (1982).

7. *See, e.g.,* OHIO REV. CODE ANN. § 4113.71(B) (Anderson 2001).

8. OHIO REV. CODE ANN. § 4113.71(B) (Anderson 2001).

9. C. Hendrie, "'Passing the Trash' by School Districts Frees Sexual Predators to Hunt Again," *Education Week* 18, no. 5 (1998): 3. Editorial Projects in Education, 1998, citing a study done by Fredric J. Hartmeister, assistant professor of education at Texas Tech University in Lubbock, Texas.

10. Hendrie, "'Passing the Trash,'" 3–4.

11. Hendrie, "'Passing the Trash,'" 3–4, citing the research of F. J. Hartmeister, assistant professor of education at Texas Tech University in Lubbock, Texas.

12. Randi W., a minor, v. Muroc Joint Unified Sch. Dist., 929 P.2d 582 (1997).

13. Malorney v. B & L Motor Freight, Inc., 496 N.E.2d 1086 (1986).

14. A. Baas, "Background Checks on School Personnel," *ERIC Digest,* ser. EA 55 (1990) (ERIC Clearinghouse on Educational Management, Eugene, Oregon, 1990.)

15. R. Long, *The Guide to Background Investigations* (Tulsa, Okla.: National Employment Screening Services, 1989) (Address: 8801 S. Yale, Tulsa, OK 74137-3575).

16. The Gallup Organization, *Teacher Perceiver: Overview, Background, and Research* (Lincoln, Nebr.: The Gallup Organization, 1997), 1.

17. *See, e.g.,* OHIO REV. CODE ANN. § 3319.07 (Anderson 2001).

18. Justus v. Brown, 325 N.E.2d 884 (1975).

19. State *ex rel.* Werden v. Williams, 29 Ohio St. 161 (1876).

Chapter Eight

Welcoming New Employees

INDUCTION

New teachers, as all new employees are required to make physical, social, and emotional adjustments to any new position, and they must become familiar with the community, the school, the curriculum, and a whole new set of colleagues and potential friends. Few periods compare in impact and importance with the first year of teaching.[1] This first year is often a year of trial and tribulation as new teachers and teachers new to a particular building must virtually sink or swim. Teaching is one of the few professions in which beginners are expected to fulfill the same responsibilities as veterans.[2]

Unlike other professions, education expects novices to be self-sufficient and successful from the start and provides little or no assistance or time to adapt.

No allowances are made for the many challenges new teachers face. Teaching is more difficult today because of the increasing numbers of at-risk children in public schools, a more extensive and varied curriculum that is prescribed by state and local authorities, and the introduction of new technology.[3] As a result of these obstacles to success, research has found that

1. Almost 15 percent of new teachers leave after the first year
2. Between 40 and 50 percent leave teaching after fewer than seven years
3. As a group, the most academically talented teachers are the least likely to stay in the profession
4. Younger teachers, when compared with more experienced teachers, report more emotional exhaustion and a greater degree of depression[4]

As much as 40 percent of all voluntary resignations occur within the first year of employment in any organization, representing a costly recruiting expense for school districts.[5] In view of these costs and the feedback researchers are getting from new teachers, it is easy to see why induction programs are important. Induction programs help new employees make a comfortable transition into their new assignments by acquainting them with school and community, introducing them to colleagues, providing them with necessary information, and giving them the material and resource support they will need to succeed. The National Association of Secondary School Principals actually considers induction a continuation of teacher education with a significant amount of learning taking place during the process.[6] In many respects, induction is an extension of student teaching for novice teachers.

Objectives

Induction is not an event. Induction is a process that translates system philosophy into cultural reality by describing and interpreting roles, relationships, and behaviors necessary for individual, unit, and organizational effectiveness.[7] The stated objectives of any induction program should be

1. to improve teacher effectiveness;
2. to encourage teacher retention by giving support and assistance;
3. to promote the professional and personal well-being of new teachers;
4. to communicate district and school culture;
5. to satisfy state mandates.[8]

With these objectives in mind, the induction process should have many different components.

What to Include

The initial stage of induction occurs before school begins. Most districts plan a meeting or series of meetings during which they disperse information in a marathon fashion that often challenges the physical, mental, and emotional stamina of even the most dedicated novice. This is not to say that there is no need for such orientation programs. However, they should be planned and structured to ensure that their purpose is not lost in a program that simply overwhelms participants. Educational administrators are always in search of the silver bullet, the single event that will do everything for everyone, but educational problems are rarely resolved by a single meeting, no matter how long or presumably informative. Remember, induction is not an event, it is a process.

There is so much information that new teachers need to know. Community induction, alone, should include information about geography, economics, housing, area churches, educational resources, medical resources, recreational facilities, child care, restaurants, and shopping malls. Then there are all the bits and pieces of administrative information that teachers need to know in order to do the job. Figure 8.1 offers a list, in no way meant to be definitive, of some of the basic information and materials essential to effective induction.

In addition to these necessities, an effective induction program will also provide some *comfort essentials*, welcoming gifts, or tokens, from the school district and the community. Effective schools enlist the community in the service of education as providers of education resources through businesses, museums, and other settings.[9] Some districts provide welcome gift baskets with coupons and samples from local stores, businesses, and industries. Gift certificates to local office supply stores are particularly helpful to new teachers. One district provides a copy of Harry Wong's book, *The First Days of School*,[10] and a symbolic umbrella to every new teacher. These small tokens of appreciation and welcome help to personalize and humanize the process. More ambitious induction programs provide more formidable tokens of appreciation. For example, in many urban areas, teachers can now get deep discounts on federally

Teacher Assignment

Negotiated Agreement

Teacher Handbook

Student Handbook

Curriculum

Text Books/Teacher Guides

Keys

School District Calendar

Personnel Directory with Names, Positions, and Phone Numbers

Map of School/District

Teaching Materials [chalk, pens, pencils, paper]

Catalog of Available Audiovisual Equipment

Samples of Administrative Forms:

>   [Discipline Referral, Work Orders, Observation/Evaluation, Leave Requests, Hall Passes, Attendance Reports, Report Cards, Special Education Referrals, Mid-Quarter Progress Reports.]

Figure 8.1   Induction Information

owned houses through the *Teacher Next Door* program.[11] Helping teachers find affordable housing to buy or rent has become an important incentive in addressing the growing problem of teacher shortages and retention. In big ways and small, every gesture will have an impact on that vital first meeting that often makes or breaks the professional relationship.

Initial Orientation

First impressions are always important and very hard to overcome. Therefore considerable thought should be given to the structure of those first meetings for new employees and employees new to the district. Figure 8.2 outlines a three-day program designed to introduce new employees to the school district, the community, the assigned school, and classroom.

Often districts compress the orientation process into one- or two-day programs that rarely give new employees time to breathe let alone assimilate information and adapt to their new roles and communities. Programs that are too rushed and overwhelming with information become part of the very problem induction hopes to resolve. Such programs produce confusion and frustration, as well as a first impression of district insensitivity that may last for a very long time.

As the schedule in figure 8.2 suggests, each day of orientation should include some opportunity for informal human contact and physical activity. All educators know that prolonged lecturing is an ineffective approach to teaching because students tend to tune out after the first forty-five minutes of even the best talk. Nevertheless, there are school district administrators who think nothing of subjecting new employees to one or two days of four-hour lectures relieved only by thirty-minute lunch breaks and five-minute trips to the restroom.

In this same vein of concern for human endurance, something should be said about the location of orientation programs. Again, first impressions are difficult to overcome. Herding new employees into a cold or overheated auditorium or cafeteria in which nothing seems to work the way it was intended is hardly the best start to a working relationship. Presenting administrators and program coordinators will come and go as they complete their piece of the program, but the newly employed captive audience will be forced to endure several hours in the chosen environment—hard chairs, poor lighting, and all. If orientation programs are to be effective, participants must be comfortable. Heating, lighting, audiovisual preparedness, organized distributions, and food are an essential part of the orientation planning process. Ample supplies of hot coffee and tea, or cold soda and donuts, can go a long way in making a difficult situation tolerable, and hourly ten-minute breaks set the stage for needed socialization. In short, sensitivity to comfort plays a key role in effective induction.

	Introduction to Community & District	Introduction to School & Colleagues	Introduction to Classroom & Curriculum

AM	Superintendent: Welcome
	
	Human Resource Director:
	Personnel Information
	  Contract
	  Benefits
	  Employee Handbook
	  Forms and Procedures
	
	Bus Tour of City
		Principal: Welcome
		
		Assistant Principal:
		Building Information
		  Student Handbook
		  Teacher Directory
		  Keys
		  Forms & Procedures
		
		Staff Members:
		Introduction to Mentors
		
		Student Government:
		Tour of Building
			Meeting with Department and Mentor
			
			Preparation of Classroom
			
			Provision of Materials/Texts
			
			Development of Lesson Plans

	Lunch with Board of Education Members	Lunch with Parent Teachers Association	Lunch with Mentor and Colleagues

PM	Director of Curriculum:
	Presentation of District Objectives
	
	Director of Special Education:
	Overview of Special Education
	
	Presentation of Welcoming Gift Baskets
		Staff:
		Resource Presentations
		  School Nurse
		  School Psychologist
		  School Counselors
		  Media Specialist
		  Subject Area Specialists
		  Special Education Coordinator
			Lesson Plan Review with Mentor
			
			Distribution of Class Lists
			
			Meetings with School Nurse, Special Education Director, and Counselor Regarding Students with Special Needs

Figure 8.2   An Orientation Program Plan

Ongoing Induction

One does not become a satisfied contributing member of any organization in the span of one, two, or three days. Induction is a process, and orientation is simply one step in that process. Questions, concerns, and problems will inevitably arise in the course of ongoing employment, and so ongoing induction activities should be planned to help neophytes over the hurdles of being the new kids on the block. Figure 8.3 is an example of a plan of monthly meetings addressing some of the issues most likely to arise in that critical first year of teacher employment.

September	→ → → →	Classroom Control Referrals Techniques Problems
October	→ → → →	Parent Conferencing Examples Problems
November	→ → → →	Lesson Planning Suggestions Problems
December	→ → → →	Teacher Evaluation Procedures Problems
January	→ → → →	Grading Tests Other Ways to Evaluate Problems
February	→ → → →	State and District Testing Examples How to Prepare Students
March	→ → → →	Professional Development Opportunities Expectations
April	→ → → →	Dealing with Failing Students Parent Notification Resources Suggestions
May	→ → → →	Ending the School Year Activities Expectations Problems
June	→ → → →	Final Responsibilities

Figure 8.3   An Ongoing Induction Plan

Day-to-day induction will also occur if teachers have the time and place to meet, talk, and exchange information in an informal setting. Teachers' lounges that are clean, comfortable, and convenient can provide that kind of setting for important ongoing socialization and induction. Community newspapers, professional journals, newsletters, computers with Internet connections, and up-to-date bulletin boards posting professional notices and opportunities should be placed in teachers' lounges to create an environment in which social and professional interests can both be nurtured.

A media facility and program that supports professional development is yet another tool in continuing induction. There should be a section of every school library dedicated to educational professional development, an area housing the latest books, journals, audiotapes, and videos addressing educational research and practice, and this section's supervision should be part of the media specialist's job description to let teachers know what is available and to respond to their suggestions for adding to the collection. Teachers themselves can organize a school research and development committee responsible for previewing and reviewing research and practice publications on a regular basis and then sharing content and opinions with colleagues in a newsletter dedicated to research and review. This kind of program creates the expectation of continuing professional awareness that should be an integral part of every effective school's culture.

Little things mean a lot in the course of ongoing induction. For example, an up-to-date teacher/school employee directory with photos and basic facts about each staff member's subject area, years in the system, and outside interests can help new staff get to know their colleagues, and school newsletters announcing births, engagements, weddings, and retirements will continue this process of socialization. A social committee, assigned the task of acknowledging milestones in the lives of staff with token gifts and get-togethers is a keystone in creating a culture of sustained camaraderie.

Assigned service on standing school committees is yet another way in which new teachers can get to know their colleagues and their schools. Be it a textbook committee, a social committee, or simply a school improvement committee, membership spurs communication and understanding. Isolation is probably the greatest threat to new teacher retention. Novices who feel they have no one to talk to, no one to ask for help, and no role to play in the life of the school are more likely to leave the school and profession within that first year.

In the spirit of eliminating first-year isolation, two final suggestions are offered for ongoing induction. The first is relatively simple and entails only brief, but daily, personal contact by principals with every teacher in a given school. Time spent need not be lengthy, and conversation need not be weighty, but every principal should touch base with every teacher every day. A walk through the halls, a visit to the cafeteria, and a stop in the teachers' lounge are all ongoing opportunities for administrators to continue the process of induction. Nothing brings home a sense of belonging more than name and face recognition. Principals must always have their thumbs on the pulses of their schools, and what better way to do this than by paying daily attention to its vital signs, its teachers.

The second, and final, suggestion is for ongoing professional induction centers to have a program encouraging new teachers to log, that is, write about, pivotal events in that first year of service and their reaction to those events. Successful professional induction creates reflective practitioners.[12] Every teacher, but particularly those new to the profession and the school, should be encouraged to examine what they do and the environment in which they are asked to work, that is, to become reflective practitioners. Portfolio development can be one avenue in this quest for professional reflection. A portfolio plan for new teachers might include logged entries addressing the following areas:

1. A record of critical incidents and teacher responses to those incidents
2. A list of perceived personal and professional achievements in the first year of performance
3. A list of emerging concerns arising out of the teacher's first year of performance
4. The teacher's objectives for addressing those concerns in the near future
5. A plan for evaluating objective attainment

MENTORING

While each of the programs discussed helps continue the process of induction outside of the classroom, there is a definite need for induction programs to provide help to new teachers inside of the classroom. More often than not, new teachers get the worst assignments and the heaviest teaching loads.[13] Under the guise of paying one's dues or indoctrination, teachers with the least experience are given students most in need of teachers with experience. Students who create problems that may be beyond the ability of new teachers should be assigned to more experienced teachers, and new teachers, as part of their induction, should get specific instruction about the special characteristics of the community, neighborhood, and students they serve.[14] When that is politically or logistically impossible, mentoring may be the only way to salvage a bad situation.

Done well, mentoring programs improve teaching, raise teachers' self-confidence, and increase teacher retention.[15] Several studies show mentoring helps beginning professionals acquire increased teaching competence.[16] Questions of who should mentor, what training they should have, and how a mentoring program should be implemented are central to providing effective mentoring for new teachers.

Selection

Not every experienced teacher should be a mentor. The most important qualities for effective mentors are good communication skills, outstanding classroom skills, the respect of their peers and the desire to participate in a mentoring program.[17] Research indicates mentors succeed when they are older than the teachers they work with, are of the same gender, and teach in the same discipline.[18] In light of these findings, a mentor program should begin by inviting voluntary participation by experienced teachers who are ready, willing, and able to help their new colleagues.

Successful mentoring programs are never haphazard affairs. Primarily, prospective mentors must be screened with respect to their own classroom performance. Teachers who have their own problems in or out of the classroom will be unlikely to offer the kinds of advice and support new teachers need. However, mentor teachers must be more than simply teachers without any visible or recorded problems of their own. Teachers selected to mentor must have evaluations reflecting outstanding, not merely adequate, classroom skills. Mentors are the kinds of teachers other teachers in the building look up to and admire, professionals who effectively communicate with both students and staff.

Human resource managers who want to implement mentoring programs must review, interview, and select mentors with as much care as they would teachers.

Training and Implementation

It should not be assumed that teachers selected as mentors would automatically know how to mentor. Mentor training must always reflect the needs of new teachers. New teachers have been found to need help in handling discipline, classroom management, lesson planning, understanding written and unwritten school rules, developing social skills, and developing techniques for handling parent conferences.[19] In response to instructional concerns, mentor training should include instruction in the techniques of lesson planning, clinical supervision, application of Bloom's Taxonomy, data gathering, lesson analysis, conferencing, and cognitive coaching. Successful mentors help new teachers to plan meaningful lessons with stimulating learning activities. They help new teachers to learn to analyze what they do and to question the decisions they make in developing and implementing a lesson. Mentors gather data to objectively show teachers the consequences of the pedagogical choices they have made, and they help them to use this information in creating learning experiences that are more effective. Finally, experienced teachers, even the good ones, are not necessarily good mentors until they have learned to communicate. Successful mentoring requires the ability to know why some methods work and others do not, to share this understanding, and to help new teachers acquire their own ability to discern what is effective and what is not.

The Pathwise Program

Ohio's new *Teacher Education and Licensure Standards* include "the Entry Year (EY) Program" that mandates mentoring to foster professional growth.[20] In this program mentors offer the support needed to help new teachers meet "real world," full-time classroom and building challenges. New teachers in the EY program are mentored for one academic year in methods that strengthen particular areas of teaching practice including four domains:

1. Organizing content knowledge for student learning
2. Creating an environment for student learning
3. Teaching for student learning
4. Teacher Professionalism[21]

Mentor teachers receive training in how to support and guide beginning teachers through the use of a system known as *Pathwise*, developed by the Educational Testing Service as a framework for mentor teacher feedback. Mentors receive regional support and networking activities through one of Ohio's regional professional development centers. They work continuously with entry year teachers to enhance their professional growth and understanding of the planning, preparation, and presentation of various learning activities, and the variety of ways to assess such activities.[22] School districts using Pathwise mentoring are encouraged to incorporate a teacher's service as a mentor into the mentor teacher's own individual professional development plan as an activity that counts toward state licensure renewal.[23]

Although the classroom must always be the focus of any good mentoring program, good mentoring must go beyond the classroom door as well. Mentors also serve a political and social function. They provide political information and advice, publicize their protégés' accomplishments, protect their protégés, and counsel them regarding career moves.[24] Under the best of circumstances, the mentor is a combination of caring friend and critic.

Obstacles to successful mentoring include lack of time to meet and observe, personality conflicts, lack of administrative support, unclear roles or lack of training for the role of mentor, and mismatches in assignment or philosophy of teaching.[25] What should be immediately obvious is that each of these obstacles can be administratively controlled.

Time is the proverbial red herring proffered to defeat every new effort to improve the quality of public education. But time can be provided if administrators are willing to be a bit creative. If every building administrator agreed to personally relieve a mentor teacher for one teaching period a day, the job of mentoring could easily be done, and as an added benefit, the administrator would have a more realistic comprehension of the demands of classroom teaching. Even in buildings in which administrators feel they themselves cannot provide such needed relief, a substitute teacher can and should be provided. In the end, the cost of dedicated substitute coverage will be far less than the combined costs of further recruitment, parental dissatisfaction, and possible dismissal litigation.

Personality conflicts are another condition of success easily controlled by an alert human resource manager. Just as there is an art to successful teaching, so there is an art to successful human resource management. Successful human resource managers avoid or resolve personality conflicts by actively getting to know the people they put together. New teachers and mentors should never be randomly thrown together. Thus, a human resource professional familiar with both parties should match them. Age, gender, experience, assignments, and teaching philosophies must all be given due consideration in making mentoring assignments. Every job has its specialized new demands. Educators who gave up the classroom for central office or building administration must realize that the burden of correcting papers and assigning grades was replaced by an equally demanding chore, that of anticipating employee need and response in a variety of situations. Human resource managers make equally weighty choices based on demographic and experiential data every time they assign a mentor to a new teacher.

Another essential part of successful mentoring is clear role definition. Mentors exist to assist, not to assess. At no time are they part of the evaluation process. Evaluation is a legally prescribed activity that is the province of licensed administrators, not teachers. In districts with negotiated agreements, mentors, who are classroom teachers, cannot also be official evaluators and remain part of the bargaining unit. Thus, it becomes incumbent on administrators who want to develop mentoring programs to clearly define the job as assistive rather than assessive, collegial rather than administrative. In districts that negotiate, mentor job descriptions will likely be a subject of collective bargaining.

Finally, ongoing administrative support is necessary for successful mentoring. Mentoring has great potential as a palliative to the woes of first year teaching. However, mentoring cannot succeed if it is not taken seriously from the start and accorded administrative notice and respect. Mentoring is not a fad or passing educational fancy. Mentoring is a proven technique for helping new and inexperienced teachers become part of the profession that should work in any school that takes the time and makes the effort to do it right. Time, effort, and acknowledgment are the proof of administrative support.

Evaluation and Planning

The effectiveness of every educational program must be evaluated, and mentoring programs are not the exception. At the end of that critical first year, new teachers should be given the opportunity to comment on the mentoring experience, and their comments should be the basis for program adjustments. New teachers who have been mentored can provide firsthand feedback on the effectiveness of the program. Figure 8.4 is an example of a survey that can be used to assess the effectiveness of the mentoring program at the end of the first year.

INDUCTION FOR CLASSIFIED STAFF

Classified staff include any of the myriad nonteaching, unlicensed employees who provide the support services needed to effectively run a public school.

Please respond to the following questions anonymously.

1. How often did you meet with your mentor?

2. In which of the following areas did your mentor provide assistance?

    ☐ Lesson Planning   ☐ Parent Conferencing
    ☐ Lesson Analysis   ☐ Understanding the Rules
    ☐ Data Collection   ☐ Developing Social Skills
    ☐ Use of A-V Equipment   ☐ Special Education
    ☐ Use of the Media Center   ☐ Individualization of Instruction
    ☐ Record Keeping   ☐ Discipline
    ☐ Classroom Management

3. Please note other areas in which you feel your mentor helped you.

4. Were there areas in which your mentor did not help you? Explain.

5. How would you change the mentoring program to make it more effective?

Figure 8.4   A Survey for Evaluating the Effectiveness of Mentoring

They include the school secretaries, custodians, bus drivers, cafeteria workers, and clerks. Classified employees are grouped by job description and sometimes by bargaining unit. They, like teachers, come and go in the course of a school year and should also have access to formal induction programs. Job expectations and roles change for classified employees just as they do for teachers,[26] and induction programs can be used to clarify situational expectations. Just as for new teachers, orientation programs should induct new classified employees into the social and performance-related aspects of the job.[27]

Objectives

The objectives for classified staff induction programs must be tailored to the specific roles and responsibilities of each group. The workplace rules and responsibilities of secretaries will be distinctly different from those of custodians and teaching aides. Figure 8.5 provides sample induction agendas for several classified positions.

INDUCTING ADMINISTRATORS

They say it is lonely at the top, and many new administrators have come to know the truth of that cliché. While administrative positions are usually filled from the teaching ranks, there is a wide gulf between the demands of the two kinds of positions. Time management, informed decision making, and public relations replace concerns for lesson planning and instructional execution when teachers become administrators. Unfortunately, few school districts have internships for prospective administrators equivalent to student teaching for prospective teachers. The logistics and demands of classroom teaching make it difficult for up-and-coming administrators to take any significant amount of time from their present teaching assignments for immersion in administrative training. As a result, becoming a new administrator is a lot like diving naked into a pool of ice cold water and praying desperately on the way down that you will be able to catch your breath and remember how to swim.

There are, however, a few life jackets than can help cushion the plunge. To begin with, administrative job descriptions should clearly list responsibilities, and organizational charts, discussed earlier, should help new administrators identify their role within the administrative structure. Just as teachers receive keys, curricula, contracts, and handbooks as part of their induction, so, too, should new administrators receive the documents and materials they will need to understand the school's work rules and performance expectations. Figure 8.6 summarizes some key items every new administrator should receive.

FOR TEACHER AIDES	FOR CUSTODIAL STAFF	FOR CLERICAL STAFF
1. Discussion of Job Descriptions	1. Discussion of Job Descriptions	1. Discussion of Job Descriptions
2. Role in Classroom	2. Introduction of Custodial Staff	2. Introduction of Office Manager and Personnel
3. Confidentiality Issues	3. Work Order Processing	3. Discussion of Office Etiquette
4. Reporting Absences/Contract Review	4. Workplace Safety	4. Introduction to Files and Formats
5. Professional Growth Opportunities	5. Building and Safety Codes	5. Demonstration of How to Use Equipment
6. Protocol for Evaluating Performance	6. Emergency Response	6. Protocol for Evaluating Performance
7. Safety in the Classroom	7. Requesting Supplies	7. Professional Growth Opportunities
8. Classroom Management Issues	8. Professional Growth Opportunities	8. Confidentiality Issues
9. Discipline	9. Performance Evaluation	9. Reporting Absences/Contract Review
10. Emergency Response	10. Reporting Absences/Contract Review	10. Emergency Response

Figure. 8.5   Sample Agendas for the Induction of Classified Employees

Job Description	District Calendar
Teacher and Support Personnel Negotiated Agreements	Secretary
Teacher and Support Personnel Job Descriptions	List of Specific Areas of Responsibility
Organizational Chart	Opportunities for Professional Growth
Teacher Handbook	Emergency Response Guide
Student Handbook	Personal Log Book
Employee Directory Correlating Names and Positions	Building Map
Set of Keys or a Master Key to Building Rooms	Appointment Calendar

Figure 8.6   Induction Materials Every New Administrator Should Receive

Objectives

The objectives for administrative induction focus on giving the new administrator a view of the *big* picture. The program should prepare administrators to become macro, as opposed to, micromanagers, informed and capable problem solvers. Effective administrative induction will do five things:

1. Introduce the new administrator to the culture of the district and the school
2. Define the role of the administrator in that culture
3. Introduce and explain administrative procedures and protocols
4. Highlight available resources
5. Give the new administrator a framework for addressing and resolving day-to-day problems

In the final analysis, the job of every public school administrator consists of developing appropriate, legal, and effective solutions to a host of problems as yet unidentified. Administrator induction gives the administrator a toolbox and instructions for doing that.

Procedures

One other way for a new administrator to learn about a school's culture and procedures is by conducting a series of scheduled interviews with key figures in the school organization including department heads, curriculum specialists, the secretarial staff, the custodial staff, the counseling staff, the school psychologist and nurse, and the school or district's bookkeeper.[28] Questions about each person's role within the organization and their perception of that role's effectiveness in light of ongoing challenges will prepare the new administrator to better understand and deal with problems that might arise. Interviewing gives new administrators the opportunity to develop important working relationships while at the same time gaining insights and information that only face-to-face questioning can provide.

Beginning administrators can also be helped by detailed work plans that include projected dates for completion of various assignments.[29] These plans can be developed with the help of assigned supervisors or administrative mentors familiar with the demands of the job. Figure 8.7 is an abbreviated example of one such work plan.

Since administrative positions are usually filled from the teaching ranks, aspiring administrators rarely have the opportunity to immerse themselves in an internship comparable to student teaching prior to actual appointment. Thus, mentoring becomes an important option for addressing any gaps in field experience. An effective mentoring program for new administrators provides

Tasks	*Steps and Contracts*	*Completion Dates*
Teacher Observations	Meet Department Chairs [Plan process]	September 15
	Review Forms and Procedures	September 30
	Develop Priority Visits	September 30
	Observe	December 15
Teacher Evaluations	Complete Observations	December 15
	Meet with Department Chairs	
	[Gather input and data]	January 5
	Review Law and Contract	January 10
	Prepare Forms	January 15
	Schedule Evaluation Meetings	January 20
	Finalize Reports	Before meetings
	Give Teachers Copies	February 15
Supervise Attendance Reporting	Meet with Attendance Clerk	September 10
	Prepare Memo on Reporting	September 12
	Distribute Memo Outlining Process to Teachers . . .	September 13
	Arrange for Collection of Daily Attendance	
	Reports	Ongoing
	Monitor Process	Daily
	Arrange to Distribute Final Report	Ongoing
	Evaluate Process	Ongoing

Figure 8.7   Administrative Work Plan

1. ongoing differentiated assistance tailored to the novice's specific assignment;
2. ongoing general assistance in acquiring knowledge of the district curriculum, responsibilities for implementing that curriculum, and the instructional resources available for such implementation;
3. ongoing differentiated and general assistance with difficult management tasks;
4. ongoing orientation to staff, policies, procedures, and routines.[30]

As with teacher mentors, administrator mentors should be successful, licensed, and experienced administrators who are respected by teachers and administrative colleagues. Administrators who have acted as mentors report that they too were rewarded for their efforts. In their roles as mentors, they were exposed to ideas new administrators brought from other school districts, they learned about research, they felt the satisfaction of once again being teachers, and they enjoyed an affirmation of their own professional competence.[31]

OVERALL EVALUATION, PLANNING, AND MAINTENANCE

Induction programs, as all school programs, should be evaluated annually. As noted earlier, probably the most effective way to do this is to either survey or interview groups of employees regarding the effectiveness of their respective induction experiences. This feedback should then become part of the planning for subsequent induction programs for each group. Involving new employees who have participated in recent induction programs directly in the planning and implementation of subsequent programs is also wise. They will have the best perspective on which parts of past programs were best and least effective.

In keeping with the theme that induction is a process, not an event, a word should be said about how to extend the benefits of formal induction to teachers and support personnel who may be hired *after* the school year has begun. Schools have a duty to provide some form of orientation for these new employees. Left without guidance, they will surely flounder, if not fail entirely. Therefore, the following suggestions are offered for *late induction* activities:

1. If possible, videotape any presentations and keep a file of these presentations in the media center so that employees hired at any time during the school year will have access to the information they provide.
2. Prepare extra packets of materials distributed during induction, and keep these ready for later distribution.

3. Prepare a list of teachers who will be ready, willing, and able to help late entries adjust to their new schools.
4. Formally introduce and welcome employees hired after the school year has begun.
5. Make supervisors responsible for meeting with late hires at least weekly for the first two months of service to assist them in adjusting to the demands of their new jobs.

A LEGAL PERSPECTIVE

Induction has many facets and addresses the needs of many different groups of school employees. All induction programs, however, seek to inform. New employees who understand the school's mission and their place in that mission will be more comfortable in their roles, and they will be more likely to succeed. Nevertheless, the benefits of effective induction programs go far beyond the sense of initial well-being they may generate. Induction programs are the district's forum for giving new employees official notice of rules, regulations, procedures, and expectations tied to their respective new positions. New employees who participate in well-planned induction programs can never say they did not know or were not told what was expected of them. The official notice new employees receive during induction becomes the legal foundation for holding them accountable for their performance.

THEORY INTO PRACTICE

1. Describe your own school's induction program for new teachers.
2. Describe induction programs your school may offer other groups of new employees.
3. What materials do teachers receive as part of their induction program?
4. Interview a new teacher concerning the effectiveness of your school's induction activities.
5. Interview a teacher who was hired after the school year began concerning the efforts your district makes for inducting new employees who were not part of the official induction program.
6. Does your school have a mentoring program for new teachers? Why or why not?
7. Describe your district's induction program for new administrators.
8. What suggestions can you make for improving your district's induction program for new teachers?

9. Think back to your own first year of teaching. What were the most troubling problems you faced?
10. How could the challenges you faced in problem 9 have been addressed?

NOTES

1. M. J. Johnston and K. Ryan, "Research on the Beginning Teacher: Implications for Teacher Education," in *The Education of Teachers: A Look Ahead,* ed. K. R. Howey and W. E. Gardner (New York, N.Y.: Longman, 1983), 136–162.

2. J. Reinhartz, ed., *Teacher Induction* (Washington, D.C.: NEA, 1989)

3. G. Mager, "The Place of Induction in Becoming a Teacher," in *Teacher Induction and Mentoring: School-Based Collaborative Programs,* ed. G. DeBolt (Albany, N.Y.: State University of New York Press, 1992), 3–33.

4. S. Tonnsen and S. Patterson, "Fighting First Year Jitters," *Executive Educator* 14, no. 1 (1992): 29–30.

5. D. Harvey and R. B. Bowin, *Human Resource Management: An Experimental Approach* (Upper Saddle River, N.J.: Prentice Hall, 1996).

6. D. W. Hunt, "Guidelines for Principals," in *Project on the Induction of Beginning Teachers* (Arlington, Va.: National Association of Secondary School Principals, 1969), 3–8.

7. M. Albert and M. Silverman, "Making Management Philosophy a Cultural Reality, Part II: Design Human Resource Programs Accordingly," *Personnel* 61, no. 2 (1984): 28–35.

8. S. Hirsch, "New Teacher Induction: An Interview with Leslie Huling-Austin," *Journal of Staff Development* 11 (1990): 2–4.

9. B. Joyce, et al., *The Structure of School Improvement* (New York, N.Y.: Longman, 1983), 113.

10. H. Wong and R. T. Wong, *The First Days of School* (Sunnyvale, Calif.: Harry K. Wong Publications, 1991).

11. M. Galley, "For Sale: Affordable Housing for Teachers," *Education Week* XX, no. 25 (March 7, 2001): 1.

12. D. A. Schon, *Educating the Reflective Practitioner* (San Francisco, Calif.: Jossey-Bass, 1987).

13. L. Huling-Austin, et al., *Assisting the Beginning Teacher* (Reston, Va.: Association of Teacher Educators, 1989).

14. J. Conant, "The Education of America's Teachers," in *Guidelines for Principals: Project on Induction of Beginning Teachers,* ed. D. W. Hunt (Arlington, Va.: National Association of Secondary School Principals, 1969), 3.

15. D. Ladestro, "Learning from the Experienced," *Teacher Magazine* 3, no. 2 (October 1991): 20–21.

16. W. A. Gray and M. M. Gray, "Synthesis of Research on Mentoring Beginning Teachers," *Educational Leadership* 43 (November 1985): 37–43.

17. H. E. Loucks, "Teacher Induction: A Success Story," *Principal* 73, no. 1 (September 1993): 27–29.

18. C. Galvey-Hjornevik, "Mentoring among Teachers: A Review of the Literature," *Journal of Teacher Education* 37 (1986): 6–11.

19. T. Brzoska, *Mentor Teacher Handbook* (Vancouver, Wash.: Evergreen School District, 1987), 288.

20. Ohio Department of Education, Division of Professional Development & Licensure, *Ohio's Entry Year Program for Teachers: Toward the Implementation of Performance-Based Licensure* (May 1999): 2.

21. *Ohio's Entry Year Program for Teachers,* 3.

22. *Ohio's Entry Year Program for Teachers,* 3.

23. *Ohio's Entry Year Program for Teachers,* 3.

24. E. M. Anderson and A. L. Shannon, "Toward a Conceptualization of Mentoring," *Journal of Teacher Education* 39 (1988): 38–42.

25. T. Ganser, "How Mentors Describe and Categorize Their Ideas about Mentor Roles, Benefits of Mentoring and Obstacles to Mentoring" (paper presented at the annual meeting of the Association of Teacher Educators, Los Angeles, Calif., 1993) (ERIC Document Reproduction Service, no. ED 354237).

26. K. M. Andreson and D. Durant, "Classified Staff Developers Unite!" *Journal of Staff Development* 18, no. 1 (1997): 18–21.

27. T. Bolton, *Human Resources Management* (Cambridge, Mass.: Blackwell, 1997).

28. B. Jentz, *Entry: The Hiring, Start-Up, and Supervision of Administrators* (New York, N.Y.: McGraw-Hill, 1982).

29. Jentz, *Entry: The Hiring, Start-Up, and Supervision of Administrators.*

30. W. R. Drury, "Entry-Year Administrator Induction: A State and Local School District Model," *Spectrum: Journal of School Research and Information* 6, no. 1 (Winter 1988): 8.

31. M. A. Playko and J. C. Daresh, "Mentoring Programs for Aspiring Administrators: An Analysis of Benefits to Mentors," *Spectrum: Journal of School Research and Information* 11, no. 3 (Summer 1993): 14–15.

Chapter Nine

Supervision and Evaluation

REMEDIATION

Two of the major functions of human resource management are supervision and evaluation, and it is important from the outset to recognize that they are not the same. Evaluations are summative comments and opinions of a teacher's performance at the end of a given period of time, while supervision is a formative sharing of information and insights intended to improve teacher performance during that given period of time. Supervision is a process. Evaluation is an event. Law, contract, or district policy can mandate both, but supervision mandated by law is referred to as remediation.

Just as teachers should test what they have taught, so evaluators should appraise teacher performance based on the job description and evaluation instrument the district has developed for a given position, and supervisors should use job descriptions and completed evaluations to structure remediation efforts. Job descriptions and evaluation forms tell teachers what district expectations are. Therefore, supervision and remediation should be guided by the evaluation instrument and procedures. Areas in which a teacher's performance is rated unsatisfactory on an evaluation are areas that should be the focus of supervision and remediation.

Providing remediation is no longer a matter of choice in many states. The courts in the 1990s have interpreted tenure statutes passed in the late 1970s as requiring proof of remediation in nonrenewal and dismissal proceedings.[1] Many states go so far as to give specific plans for remediation, and school districts that ignore state requirements have their efforts to discipline or dismiss teachers reversed in the courts.[2] State laws that include remediation sometimes require specific numbers of observations, as well as a definite period of time for improvement.[3] For example, California requires forty-five days for remediation, while Arizona and New Jersey mandate ninety days.[4] On the other hand, West Virginia merely requires an improvement period for behavior that is correctable, and Minnesota simply requires remedial time.[5]

Regardless of time allocations or the specific numbers of observations and conferences a state law may mandate, the process of remediation follows a formal observation visit and usually includes three basic steps:

1. The teacher must receive formal notice of the supervisor's concerns.
2. The teacher must be given time (as prescribed by law and/or contract) to improve.
3. The teacher must be given help to improve.

Remediation is supervision for needed improvement, an action plan and resources for resolving recognized problems. Remediation begins with administrative observation, and subsequent steps are based on what is learned from data gathered during that observation. Also important to note is that remediation can address problems observed outside of the classroom as well as those observed in the classroom.

Behavior That Is Remediable

Objectionable or unsatisfactory practices that can be eliminated or improved are considered remediable. Not every objectionable or unsatisfactory employee practice is remediable, particularly when the employee is a teacher. Classroom teachers are held to high standards by law and society. Some kinds of objectionable behavior exist that may destroy a teacher's ability to function in the classroom. Sexual impropriety, criminal acts, and unethical conduct are seldom remediable, while incompetence usually is remediable.[6] Even tenured teachers can be fired for engaging in irremediable behavior, but districts have a legal obligation to assist teachers whose behavior is remediable.

To determine whether objectionable teacher behavior is remediable or irremediable, three questions should be asked:

1. Were students, faculty, or schools damaged by the teacher's behavior?
2. If there was damage as the result of the teacher's conduct, could that damage have been avoided or mitigated, and had the teacher been warned?[7]
3. Can the effects of the teacher's conduct be corrected?[8]

There are some objectionable teacher behaviors, which may be peripheral to classroom performance, but will nevertheless render the teacher ineffective in the classroom. Eight factors are used to determine if a teacher's classroom effectiveness is impaired:

1. age/maturity of students;
2. likelihood that a teacher's conduct will adversely affect students or teachers;

3. degree of anticipated adversity;
4. proximity or remoteness in time of conduct;
5. extenuating or aggravating circumstances surrounding conduct;
6. likelihood that conduct may be repeated;
7. motives underlying conduct;
8. whether conduct will have a chilling effect on the rights of teachers.[9]

Poor lesson planning and lesson execution are examples of teacher behaviors that are remediable. With proper warnings, instruction, modeling, and time, most teachers can learn to plan and execute effective lessons. Poor teacher attendance and record keeping are also remediable problems, although note that such behaviors occurring repeatedly over time, even after a teacher has been warned, can come to be considered irremediable. When warnings and administrative assistance are ignored, even behavior initially deemed remediable, will be considered irremediable.

Behavior That Is Not Remediable

Irremediable behaviors are those that do damage students, faculty, and schools or that make it impossible for the offending teacher to be effective. The effects of irremediable behavior cannot be corrected. Offensive sexual behavior is usually irremediable in light of student immaturity, the damage and public outrage engendered, and the likelihood that such behavior would recur, and so the courts have held that sexual misconduct is a condition that cannot be remedied.[10] However, other examples of irremediable behavior may be less obvious. For example, state codes have allowed teachers to be dismissed for incompetence, neglect of duty, insubordination, and other just causes, in addition to a host of varied crimes and misdemeanors.

Insubordination is the refusal to obey an order that a superior is entitled to give and have obeyed, that is, a willful or intentional disregard of the lawful and reasonable instructions of an employer.[11] Neglect of duty, on the other hand, is the failure to do what one is required to do by law or contract.[12] In a case combining these irremediable elements, an auto mechanics teacher, tenured and with twenty years of experience, lost his job for refusing to report to a school district's new shop facility because he thought that the new facility was unsafe and not secure enough to protect his tools and equipment.[13] The teacher had initially agreed to the transfer and later attended a conference where his concerns were heard, although found to be without merit. Despite this history, he failed to report to the new facility for work, leaving the students with a substitute teacher or no teacher at all, and was ultimately fired. The court sustained the school district's decision to fire the teacher for insubordination and neglect of duty, as described by the facts of the case. Teachers who ignore warnings and refuse to follow instructions, thereby placing students at risk, are acting in an irremediable fashion.

Teachers convicted of crimes are also usually deemed to have engaged in irremediable behavior, although the types of crimes may differ significantly. Most administrators would feel fully justified in firing teachers involved with drug use, and the courts have indeed held that teachers who break federal drug laws are no longer qualified to be teachers.[14] This reasoning can be applied to other criminal activity as well, and state laws dealing with teacher termination identify other felonies and misdemeanors meriting teacher dismissal or revocation of license. However, teachers can also be fired for irremediable behavior falling under the elusive heading of "other due and sufficient cause," or "good cause." Good cause includes any ground put forward by the district in good faith and that is not arbitrary, irrational, unreasonable, or irrelevant to the district's task of building and maintaining an efficient school system.[15] Such behavior must necessarily have undermined the teacher's capacity to work effectively with fellow staff members, set an extremely poor example for students and staff, and reflected personal values inconsistent with continued employment as a teacher.[16] These types of irremediable behaviors are matters of personal ethics and common sense, rarely lending themselves to advance administrative warning. For example, a track coach who advised a student to take diet pills to improve her performance was found to be properly terminated for just cause.[17]

In some states "immoral behavior" is considered just cause for termination. Although immorality currently is a concept often difficult to define, one court provided some guidance, holding that immorality is conduct that is hostile to the welfare of the school community.[18] While criminal behavior, whether job-related or not, can always be considered immoral, immoral behavior may not always be criminal. Thus, a high school wrestling coach who involved students in a false weigh-in prior to a wrestling meet was found to be properly dismissed for immorality.[19] In another example, the termination of a teacher was upheld when evidence showed she had improperly disclosed information on a standardized achievement test to her students.[20]

Tenure, Discipline, and Dismissal

Evaluation and supervision directly affect tenure decisions. Teachers are eligible for two kinds of contracts: limited and continuing. Teachers with limited contracts are hired on an annual basis, have no property right to continued employment when the school year is over, and are said to be nontenured. Teachers with limited contracts can have their contracts nonrenewed at the end of any school year. Nontenured teachers who are notified that their contracts will not be renewed may be entitled to evaluation reports, a statement of the reason for nonrenewal, and a hearing, if state law allows, but the board of education is not required to justify or prove its reasons for nonrenewal.[21] This very limited protection, provided by some states, was created in response to teachers' unions' demands for fair dismissal procedures for nontenured teachers. In contrast, tenured teachers have continuing contracts, the expectation of reemployment from one year to the next, and a constitutional right to due process of law before their employment may be terminated. Tenured teachers can only be terminated for just cause, as delineated by state law and proven by a board of education.

Teachers attain tenure based on the status of their licenses, the quality of their teaching, and their years of successful service in a given district. Teachers eligible for tenure are expected to hold professional licenses that indicate they have a master's degree or that they have completed a designated number of hours of graduate work. Tenure status is awarded by individual school districts, not the state, and teacher tenure laws also usually require that eligible teachers work in the awarding district a specific number of years. Last, most state tenure laws prescribe a process including evaluation, and sometimes remediation, before tenure is awarded or denied. When tenure is denied, records of evaluation and remediation will come into question as school districts attempt to prove compliance with the states' teacher tenure laws. Lawsuits arising from tenure decisions rarely question the judgment of school officials in choosing to award or deny tenure. Such decisions are discretionary and a management right, as discussed in an earlier chapter. However, lawsuits arising from tenure decisions are lost based on the failure of school officials to follow the procedures prescribed by state tenure laws, a ministerial function, not left to official discretion. Thus, human resource administrators should be familiar with a state's legislated requirements regarding the number of observations and evaluations, the length of official observations, the responsibility to remediate, and the time to remediate.

Teachers who have tenure should continue to be evaluated as part of quality management and professional growth. However, negotiated agreements or board of education policy will usually control the evaluation of teachers on continuing contract. Evaluation can be considered a term or condition of employment, and therefore a bargainable issue in states that allow teachers to collectively bargain. In states where teachers do not collectively bargain, evaluation procedures will remain management's prerogative. That being said, it must be remembered that tenured teachers have a property right to their jobs and a constitutional right to due process of law before they lose those jobs. Procedural due process requires that a teacher threatened with dismissal be accorded:

1. notice of the reason for their dismissal,
2. an opportunity to confront and cross-examine witnesses and accusers,

3. an opportunity to be represented by counsel,
4. the right to a hearing,
5, the right to appeal a negative decision.

Moreover, specific statutory grounds for dismissal must be actually proven by a board of education before a tenured teacher's contract can be terminated.

Tenured teachers enjoy the same contractual and legal protections when faced with the threat of disciplinary action falling short of actual dismissal. Recorded reprimands and suspensions, with or without pay, can also trigger the due process requirement. Similarly, nontenured teachers threatened with termination *before* their yearly contracts have expired have a right to procedural due process, because such dismissal, without just cause, would be a breach of contract.

THE SUPERVISION PROCESS

The preceding discussion is meant to drive home the legal importance of regular supervision and evaluation in making human resource management decisions. However, regular supervision and evaluation are also professionally and personally important and directly related to the effectiveness of instruction. Teachers who are not supervised feel isolated and undervalued.[22] Good supervision and regular evaluation inform instructional practice, and the characteristics of the information needed by teachers from evaluation sources, including the quality of suggestions and the persuasiveness of the evaluator's rationale for improvement, will determine the value of the evaluation for teachers.[23] Thus, it is important to train supervisors and evaluators to observe, collect, and analyze data, conference, write reports, set goals, and remediate teachers as needed,[24] in short, to make their feedback informative and persuasive, as opposed to an empty exercise in pedantic pedagogy.

Observation

Observations are firsthand visits to classrooms or firsthand impressions of performance outside of the classroom during identified periods of time. Classroom observations entail spending the requisite period of time needed to view the presentation, implementation, and assessment of an identified instructional objective. The law or contract may define the length of such an "official" observation. Official observations provide a basis for judgments rendered in later evaluations. With this in mind, an observation can only be considered in evaluating the teacher's performance if the authorized observer spent the prescribed length of time in the classroom. Out-of-classroom observations also play a part in a teacher's evaluation and include records of conferences and memos addressing teacher performance in areas unrelated to instruction—areas such as teacher attendance, collegiality, cooperation, and appearance. Observations, both in and out of the classroom, if they are to provide valid feedback for supervision, should be data-driven, and this documentation must be shared with the teacher when it is gathered. Teachers need to be made aware of concerns when they arise, not at the point of evaluation, if they are to benefit from remediation.

Data Collection

Classroom observers can collect data in a variety of ways. Acheson and Gall have provided an extensive set of approaches for objective data collection,[25] and the videotape *Another Set of Eyes* can be used to train observers in these techniques.[26] Figure 9.1 summarizes several methods and identifies the kind of concern each method of data collection might address.

Method	Procedure	Sample of Problem Addressed
Verbatim Scripting Taping	Record all or most of what a teacher says.	To draw attention to misinformation.
Selective Verbatim	Record questions or responses.	To analyze cognitive levels of instruction.
Verbal Flow	Use seating chart to show exchange between teacher and students.	Some students ignored. Gender or racial bias.
At Task Analysis	Use seating chart to monitor individual student engagement in learning in timed segments.	Draws teacher attention to periods of distraction for individual students.
Classroom Movement	Monitor teacher and/or student movement in classes such as labs, P.E., art, and shops.	Monitors teacher contact and student engagement in the assignment.
Interaction Analysis	Analyze verbal interactions [what is said] between teachers and students.	Draws teacher attention to excessive lecturing and failure to encourage student participation.
Anecdotal Description	Describe all aspects of the class, in short, objective phrases or sentences, creating an anecdotal summary for analysis.	Draws teacher attention to any factor that may be affecting or impeding learning [announcements, lighting, lack of preparedness].

Figure 9.1 Methods for Collecting Classroom Data

Supervisors can develop their own methods for data collection, by simply identifying their concerns, and then asking themselves how they can show the teacher what they have seen and heard that is the basis for these concerns.

Typically school districts use two types of forms for teacher appraisal: the observation form, used to record classroom visits and to comment on data gathered during those visits, and the evaluation form, used to assess a teacher's overall performance during a defined period of time. Figure 9.2 is an example of an observation form, and figure 9.3 is an example of a district evaluation form.

Employee _____   Observer _____

Grade/Subject _____   Observation Date _____

Appraisal Scale:

  S = Satisfactory [Sufficient to meet the requirement—does not mean perfect or excellent
        performance and may be accompanied by a suggestion for improvement.]
  N.O. = Not Observed
  U = Unsatisfactory [Rating must be supported by documentation.]

Starting Time _____   Ending Time _____

I.   INSTRUCTIONAL PROCEDURES
     ____ Evidence of planning
     ____ Organization of instructional procedures
     ____ Provides for differences in capacities of pupils
     ____ Use of resourceful techniques
     ____ Use of appropriate procedures to evaluate student learning
     ____ Skill in presentation
     ____ Student participation
     ____ Knowledge of subject matter

II. MANAGEMENT SKILLS
     ____ Organization of materials and supplies
     ____ Follows building and Board procedures that relate to classroom functions
     ____ Maintains student discipline
     ____ Organization of classroom

III. PUPIL–EMPLOYEE RELATIONSHIP
     ____ Helps child to develop and maintain good self-concept
     ____ Establishes good rapport

Observer Comments:

Employee Comments:

    _____   _____
        Observer's Signature   Employee's Signature

    Conference Date _____

The signature of the employee does not indicate approval of the ratings or comments but rather that he/she received a copy of this form. If the employee wishes to file a written response, the employee may do so.

Figure 9.2   A Classroom Observation Form

Employee _____   Evaluator _____

Grade/Subject _____

Evaluation Scale

S = Satisfactory [Sufficient to meet the requirement—does not mean perfect or excellent performance and may be accompanied by a suggestion for improvement.]

N.O. = Not Observed

U = Unsatisfactory [Ratings should be based on prior observations and documentation.]

I.   INSTRUCTIONAL PROCEDURES
____ Evidence of planning
____ Organization of instructional procedures
____ Provides for differences in capacities of pupils
____ Use of resourceful techniques
____ Use of appropriate procedures to evaluate student learning
____ Skill in presentation
____ Student participation
____ Knowledge of subject matter

II. MANAGEMENT SKILLS
____ Organization of materials and supplies
____ Renders prompt and accurate reports
____ Follows building and Board procedures
____ Maintains student discipline
____ Organization of classroom

III. PUPIL–EMPLOYEE RELATIONSHIPS
____ Helps child to develop and maintain good self-concept
____ Establishes good rapport
____ Counsels students

IV. PARENT–EMPLOYEE RELATIONSHIP
____ Encourages communication
____ Communicates in a professional manner

V.   STAFF–EMPLOYEE RELATIONSHIP
____ Works in a positive manner with school personnel (Human Relations)
____ Maintains communication

VI. PERSONAL CHARACTERISTICS
____ Reliable
____ Adaptable
____ Appropriate appearance

VII. PROFESSIONAL IMPROVEMENT

Figure 9.3a   A Teacher Evaluation Form

This category is not to be rated but may be commented on when appropriate (professional meetings, workshops, programs, etc.)

Administrator Comments:

Employee Comments:

_____   _____
Observer's Signature   Employee's Signature

Date _____   Date _____

The signature of the employee does not indicate approval of the ratings or comments but rather that he/she received a copy of this form. If the employee wishes to file a written response, the employee may do so.

Figure 9.3b   A Teacher Evaluation Form

Note that the classroom observation and the final evaluation are interrelated documents. Neither stands alone in the appraisal process. Observations documenting problems with classroom performance should not be followed by glowing evaluations making no mention of how, or if, the problems observed were ever resolved. Nor should problem-free observations be followed by negative evaluations. Problems cited for the first time on end-of-year evaluations are lawsuits in the making. How can a teacher be held accountable or disciplined for behavior that was never brought to the teacher's attention? Teachers faced with such evaluations will rightly claim that they were given neither notice of the evaluator's concerns nor time to improve. Evaluations must refer back to formal observations with data collection and analysis documenting the basis for praise or criticism.

As the example in figure 9.3 indicates, evaluation forms often appraise performance beyond the classroom as well, and these comments and ratings on performance peripheral to teaching should also be based on recorded data. For example, if tardiness to class has been a problem, the supervisor should note the times and dates when the teacher was observed arriving late and refer to memos and conferences held to bring the problem to the teacher's attention. If there are no recorded times and dates or memos and conference records, an unsatisfactory rating given at the time of evaluation can and should be challenged. Teacher behavior meriting an unsatisfactory rating on an evaluation should have merited a warning when first observed. Evaluations and observations are interrelated official records of a teacher's performance in and out of the classroom, and notice is the first step in procedural due process.

Data Analysis

Before perception can become reality, there must be data and data analysis confirming perception. An observer can feel that a teacher is not really engaging the students in the learning process, but to convince the teacher that feeling is fact, the observer must show the teacher what the students were actually doing during the class period. The method of data collection known as *At Task Behavior* is one way to provide such feedback. Figure 9.4 is an example of *At Task* data collected and analyzed in preparation for a conference with a classroom teacher.

Data collection and analysis, in order to be effective and legally defensible, must be objective, specific, and numerical. Observers should avoid using words such as *many, some, a few,* and *a lot* to describe what they saw and to analyze

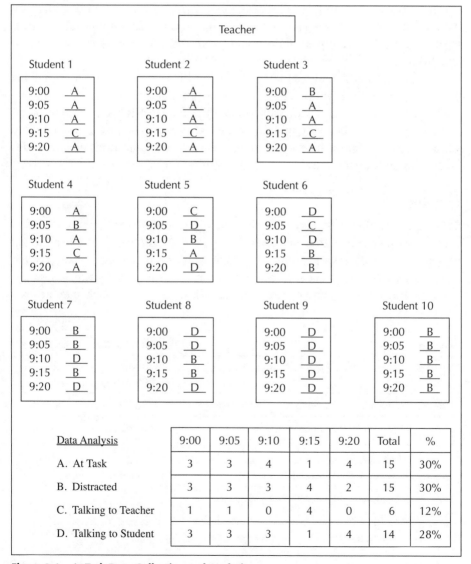

Figure 9.4 At Task Data Collection and Analysis

the data collected. Instead, as shown in figure 9.4, actual numbers and percentages of students engaged, distracted, or misbehaving during each part of the class should be calculated to clearly show the teacher that a problem exists and to give the teacher a method for determining why. Is the seating arrangement contributing to the problem? What was happening in class during the period of greatest distraction?

There are many ways to collect valuable data that will inform instruction, but in each instance the observer should strive for objectivity and specificity. If, for example, the level of teacher questioning is a concern, *selective verbatim* data collection can record teacher questions, and the questions can then be analyzed with respect to the level of Bloom's Taxonomy they reflect. Figure 9.5 is an example of data collected and analyzed for the level of questioning.

Data gathered and analyzed in this way can then be the basis for comments made on official observation and evaluation forms. More important, data gathered and analyzed in this way can become the focus of the supervision or remediation process. For example, a teacher whose questioning never gets beyond the level of application can be helped to structure questions and activities incorporating higher cognitive levels of learning for all lessons.

Conferencing

Supervision conferences may take place before an observation, but postconferences must take place after an observation. Preconferences can be used to set the stage for the observation, outlining the lesson's objective, the makeup of the class, and the lesson's place in the curriculum sequence. Many times, preconferences are, in fact, mandated by contract. In districts in which they are not

Questions	*Level of Bloom's Taxonomy*
What do we call mathematical expressions such as $X + 5 = 8$?	Knowledge
When we solve a linear equation, what do we want to find?	Comprehension
How do we solve this linear equation?	Application
How would you solve $5X = 125$?	Analysis
Describe how you would solve $5X + 5 = 120$?	Synthesis
How would you determine if the value you found for X is correct?	Evaluation

Figure 9.5   A Data-Based Analysis of a Teacher's Level of Questioning

mandated by contract or policy, however, their value has sometimes been questioned in that they can reduce the observation to a show-and-tell event that will be of little actual value to the teacher or the observer. There is something to be said for spontaneous supervision and the unannounced classroom observation. Postconferences, on the other hand, are an essential part of effective supervision and remediation, whether prescribed by contract or not. The postconference provides an opportunity to present data analysis and to work with the teacher to develop ways of eliminating identified problems. The postconference is the heart of remediation.

There is an art to effective postconferencing. In order to make the most of this opportunity to assist teachers, the following steps should be an integral part of postconferencing:

1. Teachers should receive the data collected and the observer's analysis of that data before the postconference. It is difficult to understand and respond intelligently to information one sees for the first time in a supervisory conference.
2. Observers should prepare questions that will help the teacher recognize and address identified concerns. Postconferencing is an excellent opportunity for cognitive coaching, with the emphasis on questioning instead of telling. Cognitive coaches do not give answers, but rather act as catalysts to reflective self-analysis.[27]
3. Observers must schedule adequate, uninterrupted time to conduct the postconference. For supervision to be effective, it must be taken seriously and accorded the respect it pedagogically and legally deserves.

FORMAL SUPERVISION MODELS

There are many different approaches to supervising educational personnel.[28] However, some methods have found formal acceptance in law and contract, while others play a more dubious role in formal supervision, that is, supervision activities that will become part of a teacher's employment record. Models differ with respect to their focus and their procedures, and figure 9.6 compares the focus of the four most frequently used approaches for formal educational supervision.

The Trait Model

The Trait Model for supervising teachers is based on the assumption that teachers and supervisors can agree on the characteristics of exemplary teacher performance in and out of the classroom. Adjectives, phrases, or short sentences are used to describe desired qualities and performance, and are accompanied by a rating scale

Model	Focus	Problem Example
Trait	Teacher Traits	Teacher Dress Issue
Process	Structure of Lesson	Poor Lesson Plan
Instructional Objective	Student Learning	Poor Student Work
Teacher Performance Objective	Teacher Performance Out of Classroom	Teacher Tardiness

Figure 9.6   Models Used to Formally Supervise Teachers

for noting the degree to which the desired quality appears. Under the best of circumstances, as in figure 9.7, the sought-after traits are defined, as is the rating system the district is using, and the supervisor is asked to comment on the reason for a given rating.

While the evaluation of teachers remains a management right, in districts that collectively bargain, evaluation forms and procedures can become negotiable terms and conditions of employment. A commercial model of this kind of supervision is *Praxis III*, a trait rubric developed by the Educational Testing Service for supervising entry year teachers.[29] Praxis assessors are trained to use the rubric and to make professionally defensible judgments regarding the classroom performance of beginning teachers, a process that districts using any trait model should emulate.

The Trait Model can be an effective evaluation instrument and guide for supervision if traits and rating systems are clearly defined and supervisors are trained to use the instrument. This training must include ways to collect data to support ratings and thus make them less subjective and open to legal challenge. In addition, teachers should have an opportunity to become familiar with the instrument, its purpose, and procedures. Traits that are not clearly defined and ratings that are not backed by data make districts legally vulnerable.

The Process Model

Some evaluation plans are based on the premise that if a teacher plans and presents a lesson well, learning will take place. In this approach to evaluating and supervising performance, the focus is on the process of teaching and the steps in that process. Hunter identified six steps in the teaching process that can be used to evaluate teacher planning and execution.[30] Figure 9.8 shows how these steps can be used to analyze the effectiveness of the teaching process.

Steps that are missing or poorly executed will inform supervision. However, the judgments made using this model, to be effective, must also be backed by specific data indicating the presence or absence of each step, and therein lies the problem. Short of making a verbatim script, audiotape, or videotape of the lesson, it will be

Evaluation of _____ Job Title _____

School/Location _____ Classification _____

Evaluator _____ Job Title _____

Criteria to Be Used by Evaluators

1. The evaluator must base the evaluation of the job areas as they relate to work assignments. Judgment of one work area must not influence judgment of others.

2. The evaluation must be based on the employee's characteristic performance over the prescribed evaluation period and not on any single or isolated incident.

3. Evaluations must be based on personal observation and not on hearsay information.

4. The statement following each indicated job area that most closely describes the employee's performance must be checked.

5. Explanations or other comments should be noted in the space provided below each of the individually listed job areas.

6. The evaluator must indicate an overall judgment of the employee's job performance in the area labeled "Summary" on this form.

Definition of Evaluation Terms

1. "Exceptional" is defined as performing well above the level required by the employee's supervisor.

2. "Above" is defined as exceeding the level required by the employee's supervisor.

3. "Meets" is defined as performing at a satisfactory level as required by the employee's supervisor.

4. "Needs improvement" is defined as performing below the level required by the employee's supervisor. Selection of this evaluation designation requires that the evaluator indicate improvement suggestions in the space provided for "COMMENTS" at the end of each listed job area that is being evaluated.

5. "Unsatisfactory" is defined as performing well below the level required by the employee's supervisor. Selection of this evaluation designation requires that the evaluator explain any "unsatisfactory" evaluation and, where applicable, indicate suggestions for improvement in the space provided for "COMMENTS" at the end of each listed job area that is being evaluated.

Figure 9.7a   A Trait Model Evaluation Form

KNOWLEDGE—Knowledge and understanding of job.	☐ EXCEPTIONAL
	☐ ABOVE
	☐ MEETS
COMMENTS: _____	☐ NEEDS IMPROVEMENT
_____	☐ UNSATISFACTORY

QUALITY OF WORK—The degree of accuracy, thoroughness, neatness, and timely work completion exhibited by the employee.

☐ EXCEPTIONAL
☐ ABOVE
☐ MEETS

COMMENTS: _____
_____

☐ NEEDS IMPROVEMENT
☐ UNSATISFACTORY

TEAM EFFORT/COOPERATION—The degree to which the employee works well with others (staff, students, parents, and the public).

☐ EXCEPTIONAL
☐ ABOVE
☐ MEETS

COMMENTS: _____
_____

☐ NEEDS IMPROVEMENT
☐ UNSATISFACTORY

COMMUNICATION—The degree to which the employee communicates with others (staff, students, parents, and the public).

☐ EXCEPTIONAL
☐ ABOVE
☐ MEETS

COMMENTS: _____
_____

☐ NEEDS IMPROVEMENT
☐ UNSATISFACTORY

DEPENDABILITY—The degree to which the employee applies himself or herself and the degree of supervision required to achieve results.

☐ EXCEPTIONAL
☐ ABOVE
☐ MEETS

COMMENTS: _____
_____

☐ NEEDS IMPROVEMENT
☐ UNSATISFACTORY

FOLLOWS INSTRUCTION—The degree to which the employee follows specific and/or detailed instructions.

☐ EXCEPTIONAL
☐ ABOVE
☐ MEETS

COMMENTS: _____
_____

☐ NEEDS IMPROVEMENT
☐ UNSATISFACTORY

APPEARANCE   ☐ meets
                    ☐ needs improvement

ATTENDANCE   ☐ meets
                    ☐ needs improvement

PUNCTUALITY   ☐ meets
                    ☐ needs improvement

COMMENTS: _____
_____

Figure 9.7b   A Trait Model Evaluation Form

SUMMARY:	
Signature of Evaluator	Date

TO BE COMPLETED BY EMPLOYEE—Remarks, Comments, Questions:

I have read this appraisal and understand that if I have further remarks, comments, or questions, I may contact the director of Personnel or his designee to request a meeting. My signature indicates only that I have read this evaluation and does not indicate approval or disapproval of its contents.

Signature of Employee	Date

Figure 9.7c   A Trait Model Evaluation Form

Process	*Observation*	*Comments/Data*
Standards	Students knew teacher expectations. Materials and equipment were ready. Teacher started lesson promptly.	
Anticipatory Set	Objective was stated. Objective was related to prior learning. Objective was made relevant to everyday life.	
Information Input	Adequate explanation Effective presentation strategy Modeling	
Checking for Understanding	Practice activities Learning styles addressed Reteaching	
Guided and Independent Practice	Self-quizzes Testing Homework	
Closure	Teacher summary Student summary	

Figure 9.8   Evaluating the Process of Teaching

the supervisor's word against the teacher's as to whether a given step was not part of the lesson plan. The other serious problem with this method of evaluation is that even when all the steps are present, a lesson can still be ineffective. While the likelihood of success increases with good processing, teachers who do not individualize instruction or incorporate higher-cognitive skill development in their planning may have well-executed lessons that still fall short of the mark. This shortcoming, however, can be overcome by including individualization, the development of higher-level cognitive questioning, and activities as part of the process.

The Process Model for supervision and evaluation is very legally defensible. It is based on tested research and on common sense. In addition, the courts have long held that boards of education have ultimate control over classroom methods and content.[31] Assuming the research is right, well-structured lesson plans are more likely to result in effective learning and can be required by boards of education. That being said, boards have a legal and ethical obligation, as well as a practical interest, in training administrators who will use the process model to evaluate and teachers who will be evaluated by it in the process.

The Instructional Objective Model

This method of teacher evaluation and supervision focuses on student achievement as the parameter for measuring teacher performance. The two are joined at the hip, and this model of evaluation rates teacher effectiveness in terms of student success. This method is the keystone of the accountability movement. From this do or die perspective, it becomes vital to clearly define instructional objectives, the conditions under which they are to occur, the observable behavior that is anticipated, and the means that will be used to measure objective attainment. Figure 9.9 is an example of an instructionable objective highlighting the conditions, student behavior, and means of measurement.

The idea of writing instructional objectives for students is not new. Popham and Baker,[32] Mager,[33] and McNeil[34] all advocated this supervisory approach. Proponents of this method of evaluation and supervision believe that the curriculum should be broken down into a series of instructional objectives, a virtual road map for instruction. Success is defined as meeting these objectives and is measured by continuous student improvement.

The instructional objectives approach to evaluation is growing in popularity with forty-eight of the fifty states now having policies establishing standards, assessment, report cards, and consequences for school districts.[35] Texas, for example, bases one-eighth of a teacher's yearly evaluation on the school's per-

---

CONDITION   THE INSTRUCTIONAL OBJECTIVE
[Given a demonstration] on [how to tell the difference between similes and metaphors], students

BEHAVIOR   MEASUREMENT
[will identify the similes and metaphors] in a reading selection [without error.]

Figure 9.9   An Example of an Instructional Objective

formance on state tests, and Tennessee sends "teacher-effect reports" to every teacher in grades 4–8 and to every high school math teacher.[36] However, teachers' unions remain opposed to making student achievement a part of teachers' formal evaluations, maintaining that too many uncontrollable variables have an impact on individual student learning. In Tennessee, for example, principals may not consider the teacher-effect reports in teacher evaluations, but can use them to provide advice to the teacher on professional development.

To be a fair and legally defensible way to evaluate teacher performance requires that this model have both a preconference and a postconference. The preconference is necessary in order to meet with the teacher and agree on the objective, the conditions for learning, and the observable behavior anticipated and to establish the method for measuring student achievement. The postconference will be used to review data correlating conditions and achievement.

The Performance Objective Model

The job of a teacher has many facets. Teachers have responsibilities both in and out of the classroom, and this model for evaluation and supervision focuses on the teacher's role outside of the classroom, the peripheral demands of the job that determine whether the teacher is a good employee. In this model the focus is on the teacher, not student achievement or the process of teaching, and on the quality of peripheral performance, such as punctuality, collegiality, and professionalism.

As with the Instructional Objective approach, clarity, and agreement on the definition of the performance objective are key to successful implementation. Here too a preconference with the teacher is essential in order to identify the objective, the conditions for achieving it, the observable outcome anticipated, and the way success will be measured. Performance objectives are sometimes called job targets, and while they can be remedial in nature, they need not be. This approach to evaluation can also be used as a way of formalizing professional growth plans for teachers who have no need for remediation and want to voluntarily take on new challenges. Figure 9.10 gives an example of both kinds of performance objectives, and figure 9.11 suggests a format for creating an official record of the Performance Objective Preconference.

The postconference is used to assess objective achievement and to adjust objectives and conditions as needed. In remedial situations, this method has the advantage of clearly delineating employer expectations. All cards are on the table at the preconference. Problems are identified, means for resolving problems are discussed, desired behavior is clearly described, and the time period for improvement becomes part of the measurement. The postconference is merely a time to follow up and measure progress.

A GROWTH OBJECTIVE

The teacher will select and lead a committee of five teachers in developing a school-wide discipline plan that will be accepted unanimously by the faculty.

A REMEDIATION OBJECTIVE

Given the year's calendar of scheduled faculty meetings, the teacher will be expected to abide by the contract and attend all meetings from start to finish unless officially excused or on leave.

Figure 9.10   Performance Objectives for Growth and Remediation

Teacher _____   Date _____
Grade Level/Subject Area _____   Building Administrator _____

Teachers shall be evaluated in a systematic procedure. The first step of this procedure is to establish an individual goal in the form of a job target. A job target is a quantifiable task to specifically improve professional practice. Each participant will identify and write a job target that will contain the following four components:

1. What observable accomplishments will be made?

2. What materials or resources will be required to accomplish the target?

3. What limitations exist, if any?

4. What evidence constitutes completion of the target?

I.   Job Target Statement _____
      _____

II.   Components
      A. What observable accomplishments will be made?
      _____

      B. What materials or resources will be required to accomplish the target?
      _____

      C. What limitations exist, if any? (setting, time, cost)
      _____

      D. What evidence constitutes completion of the target?
      _____

Figure 9.11   A Professional Job Target Worksheet

In summary, each of these models for the formal evaluation and supervision of teachers provides the teacher with notice of job expectations and concerns. Each requires the use of data to verify continued concern or target accomplishment, and each, if properly implemented, gives the teacher a plan for improvement. In doing so, they all place the school district in good legal standing.

INFORMAL SUPERVISION MODELS

Peer, Client, and Self-Supervision are informal ways of assessing teacher performance. These methods are designated as "informal" because they are less likely to be part of a teacher's official evaluation. The process in each of these models uses an unlicensed evaluator to assess teacher performance. As discussed in an earlier chapter, this poses problems in states where teachers collectively bargain. With peer supervision, other teachers observe and evaluate teacher performance in and out of the classroom. Client supervision entails using feedback from parents and students to evaluate client perception of teacher performance. Finally, Self-Supervision places the teacher solely in charge of the assessment process. Portfolio development is one form of Self-Supervision. While each of these approaches can provide valuable insights for the teacher, none has gained widespread acceptance as a formal method for evaluating teacher performance. Traditionally, official evaluation and supervision have been the province of trained and licensed human resource administrators. The value of feedback from untrained observers remains open to doubt, suspicion, and challenge in the face of increased demands for official accountability. That being said, informal methods of assessing performance should nevertheless be available to teachers who want additional feedback. In an earlier text, this author delineates the ways and means for implementing these "informal" approaches to supervision.[37]

SUPERVISION AND
EVALUATION OF SUPPORT PERSONNEL

There are a host of nonteaching and classified positions that play an essential role in effective school management. Media specialists, the school psychologist, the school nurse, the secretaries, custodians, aides, and sundry other individuals fall under the collective heading of support personnel, and they too require supervision and evaluation on a regular basis. There is no position in a public school above review, and most employees welcome feedback on their performance. Positive feedback will encourage continued good performance, while negative feedback can set the stage for needed notice and remediation.

Official evaluation and supervision of nonteaching personnel can actually use two of the approaches discussed for teachers. A Trait Model mirroring the employee's job description begins the process. Figure 9.12 is an example of a Trait Model for the school's custodian, noting job responsibilities, data used to assess, and measurement of achievement, while figure 9.13 lists the areas of responsibility and types of documentation that can be used to evaluate a school's principal.

Employees with unsatisfactory ratings in any area of responsibility can then work with their designated evaluator to set Performance Objectives or Job Targets addressing performance in those areas of concern. This dual approach to evaluation provides both notice and remediation.

A LEGAL PERSPECTIVE

Evaluation is an essential part of human resource management. Employees who are not evaluated on a regular basis cannot be held accountable for shortcomings in their performance. Attempts to discipline or dismiss them will fail if they have a property interest in their positions and they have received no notice of employer concerns or help in addressing those concerns. Evaluation is a means for giving employees recognition for achievement and notice of problems. It is also a springboard for structuring effective remediation.

Trait or Data Illustrating Performance	Ratings		
Keeps building clean	☐ GOOD	☐ FAIR	☐ POOR
Responds promptly to emergencies	☐ GOOD	☐ FAIR	☐ POOR
Gives timely attention to work orders	☐ GOOD	☐ FAIR	☐ POOR
Files all requested reports	☐ GOOD	☐ FAIR	☐ POOR
Complies with all regulatory mandates	☐ GOOD	☐ FAIR	☐ POOR
Gets along well with staff	☐ GOOD	☐ FAIR	☐ POOR
Gets along well with students	☐ GOOD	☐ FAIR	☐ POOR
Gets along well with administration	☐ GOOD	☐ FAIR	☐ POOR
Attendance	☐ GOOD	☐ FAIR	☐ POOR
Appearance on job.	☐ GOOD	☐ FAIR	☐ POOR
Please note that fair or poor ratings must be explained and supported by documentation.			

Figure 9.12   A Trait Model for Evaluating the School's Custodian

Area of Supervision	Trait or Data Illustrating Performance	Rating
Instruction	Students perform well on state exam	☐ GOOD ☐ FAIR ☐ POOR
	Executes innovative and effective curriculum	☐ GOOD ☐ FAIR ☐ POOR
	Evidence of individual student success	☐ GOOD ☐ FAIR ☐ POOR
Organization Administration	Promptly submits all requested reports	☐ GOOD ☐ FAIR ☐ POOR
	Complies with all district directives	☐ GOOD ☐ FAIR ☐ POOR
	Keeps good records	☐ GOOD ☐ FAIR ☐ POOR
Personnel Management	Communicates well with staff	☐ GOOD ☐ FAIR ☐ POOR
	Settles problems at the building level	☐ GOOD ☐ FAIR ☐ POOR
	Promotes low staff absenteeism	☐ GOOD ☐ FAIR ☐ POOR
Business Management	Develops appropriate and timely budgets	☐ GOOD ☐ FAIR ☐ POOR
	Maintains a clean building	☐ GOOD ☐ FAIR ☐ POOR
	Seeks grants to supplement budget	☐ GOOD ☐ FAIR ☐ POOR
Community Public Relations	Communicates well and often with public	☐ GOOD ☐ FAIR ☐ POOR
	Responds to parent and public concerns	☐ GOOD ☐ FAIR ☐ POOR
	Encourages parental involvement	☐ GOOD ☐ FAIR ☐ POOR
Program Development	Responds to identified building needs	☐ GOOD ☐ FAIR ☐ POOR
	Provides growth opportunities for staff	☐ GOOD ☐ FAIR ☐ POOR
	Shares research with staff	☐ GOOD ☐ FAIR ☐ POOR
	Presents and/or publishes in education	☐ GOOD ☐ FAIR ☐ POOR
	Addresses state directives promptly	☐ GOOD ☐ FAIR ☐ POOR
	Provides for technologic growth	☐ GOOD ☐ FAIR ☐ POOR

Figure 9.13   A Trait Model for Evaluating the School's Principal

THEORY INTO PRACTICE

1. How does your school district evaluate teachers?
2. Compare evaluation procedures in a district that collectively bargains with evaluation procedures in a district that does not collectively bargain?
3. Does your principal comply with the district's evaluation policy?
4. How often and for how long are tenured teachers observed in your district?
5. How many times in a school year are teachers formally evaluated in your district?

6. How are teachers with identified problems remediated in your district?
7. Who is responsible for evaluating and supervising support personnel in your school?
8. Review and describe the forms and procedures your school uses to evaluate secretaries, guidance counselors, and teachers' aides in terms of the models presented in this chapter.
9. Develop a job description and corresponding Trait Model Evaluation Form for the school's media specialist.
10. Develop a Trait Model Evaluation for assessing the performance of the building's assistant principal. How does it differ from that of the principal?

NOTES

1. D. Dagley, "Remediation in Teacher Termination" (paper presented at the annual meeting of the Education Law Association, Chicago, Ill., November 1999), 7.

2. *See, e.g.,* Farmer v. Kelleys Island Bd. of Educ., 594 N.E.2d 204 (Ohio Com. Pl. 1992); Snyder v. Mendon-Union Local Sch. Bd. of Educ., 661 N.E.2d 717 (Ohio 1996); Naylor v. Cardinal Local Sch. Dist. Bd. of Educ., 620 N.E.2d 725 (Ohio 1994).

3. OHIO REV. CODE ANN. § 3319.111 (Anderson 2002).

4. CAL. EDUC. CODE § 44938 (2001); ARIZ. REV. STAT. § 15-538 (2001); N.J. Stat. § 18A:6-11 (2001).

5. W. VA. CODE § 18A-2-8 (2001); MINN. STAT. § 122A.40 (9) (2001).

6. Dagley, "Remediation in Teacher Termination," 7.

7. Gilliland v. Bd. of Educ., 365 N.E.2d 322 (1977).

8. Bd. of Educ. of Argo-Summit Sch. Dist. No. 104, Cook County v. Hunt, 487 N.E.2d 24 (Ill. App. 1 Dist. 1985).

9. Hoagland v. Mount Vernon Sch. Dist. 320, 623 P.2d 1156 (Wash. 1981).

10. Pryse v. Yakima Sch. Dist. 7, 632 P.2d 60, *review denied*, 96 Wash. P.2d 1011 (1980).

11. Porter v. Pepsi-Cola Bottling Co. of Columbia, 147 S.E.2d 620, 622.

12. Pratt v. Alabama State Tenure Comm'n, 394 So. 2d 18 (Ala. Civ. App. 1980).

13. Stephens v. Alabama State Tenure Comm'n, 634 So. 2d 549 (Ala. Civ. App. 1993).

14. Gedney v. Bd. of Educ. of the Town of Groton, 703 A.2d 804 (Conn. App. 1997).

15. Rado v. Bd. of Educ., 583 A.2d 102 (1990).

16. *Rado,* 538 at 102.

17. Wells v. Madison Local Sch. Dist. Bd. of Educ., Case No. CA84-10-116 (Ohio Butler Co. App. July 15, 1985).

18. Jarvella v. Willoughby-Eastlake City Sch. Dist. Bd. of Educ. 233 N.E.2d 143 (Ohio C.P. 1967).

19. Florian v. Highland Local Sch. Dist. Bd. of Educ., 493 N.E.2d 249 (1983).

20. Altsheler v. Bd. of Educ., 476 N.Y.S.2d 282 (1984).

21. *See, e.g.,* OHIO REV. CODE ANN. § 3319.111 (Anderson 2001).

22. G. Natriello and S. M. Dornbusch, "Pitfalls in the Evaluation of Teachers by Principals," *Administrator's Notebook* 29 (1981): 1–4.

23. D. Duke and R. Stiggins, "Beyond Minimum Competence: Evaluation for Professional Development," in *The New Handbook of Teacher Evaluation,* ed. J. Millman and L. Darling-Hammond (Newbury Park, Calif.: Sage, 1990), 116–132.

24. D. T. Conley, "Critical Attributes of Effective Evaluation Systems," *Educational Leadership* 44 (1987): 60–64.

25. K. A. Acheson and M. D. Gall, *Techniques in the Clinical Supervision of Teachers,* 4th ed. (New York, N.Y.: Longman, 1997), 73–147.

26. K. Acheson, *Another Set of Eyes: Techniques for Classroom Observation* (Reston, Va.: Association for Supervision and Curriculum Development, 1987), 2 videotapes.

27. A. L. Costa and R. J. Garmston, *Cognitive Coaching: A Foundation for Renaissance Schools* (Norwood, Mass.: Christopher-Gordon Publishers, 1994), 142; B. Marczely, *Supervision in Education: A Differentiated Approach with Legal Perspectives* (Gaithersburg, Md.: Aspen Publishers, 2000), 113.

28. *See, e.g.,* Marczely, *Supervision in Education,* 35–161.

29. *The Praxis Series: Professional Assessment for Beginning Teachers* (Princeton, N.J.: Educational Testing Service, 1999).

30. M. Hunter, "Knowing, Teaching and Supervising," in *Using What We Know about Teaching,* ed. P. L. Hosford (Alexandria, Va.: Association for Supervision and Curriculum Development, 1984), 169–192.

31. *See* Ahern v. Bd. of Educ. of the Sch. Dist. of Grand Island, 456 F.2d 399 (8th Cir. 1972).

32. W. J. Popham and E. L. Baker, *Establishing Instructional Goals* (Englewood Cliffs, N.J.: Prentice Hall, 1970), 10–20.

33. R. Mager, *Preparing Instructional Objectives* (Palo Alto, Calif.: Fearn, 1962), 1–30.

34. J. D. McNeil, *Toward Accountable Teachers* (New York, N.Y.: Holt, Rinehart, and Winston, 1971), 31.

35. W. C. Bosher, "Standards-Based Education Reform" (paper presented at the Education Law Association 45th Annual Conference, Chicago, Ill., November 1999), 1.

36. A. Bradley, "Zeroing in on Teachers," *Education Week* 11 (January 1999): 46.

37. B. Marczely, *Supervision in Education,* 105–161.

Chapter Ten

Staff Development

HOW ADULTS LEARN

Once new employees are hired, oriented, and acclimated, schools like all other successful organizations have a duty to help employees grow professionally. Essentially, schools must nourish the mind and the spirit once physical needs have been addressed. Employees who continue to learn and grow in their positions are more likely to stay and perform effectively. Staff development is the process of offering employees opportunities to learn new skills and have new experiences that will enhance their personal image and professional performance.

Particularly in the field of education, human resource managers must remind themselves that adults are not children. Adults are self-directed, have experiences that form a knowledge base, and learn by solving problems.[1] Adults come to every situation with an intellectual and experiential history that is unique and cannot be ignored. Successful staff development programs are built on five premises:

1. Adults enjoy planning and conducting their own learning experiences.
2. Experiences are key to self-actualization.
3. The best learning takes place when the need to know coincides with the training.
4. Adults need opportunities to apply what they have learned.
5. Adults need some independent structured options for learning.[2]

Adults will resist change for the sake of change and programs that do not address their personal concerns. Staff development is adult education and, as such, must have purpose. Asking adults to do anything that they do not feel has at least a good chance of leading to something better is asking too much.[3]

The Need to Individualize

This is no easy task, since growth is a personal process rooted in individual experience and personal motivation. Studies confirm that, for teachers, growth and career development take place in stages.[4] Like the toss of dice, the many factors potentially affecting an individual teacher's professional growth will differ in the context of personal and professional time and circumstance. Figure 10.1 illustrates this professionally cosmic phenomenon.[5]

Staff development programs that provide different experiences for participants at different stages of their development are more apt to obtain their objectives than those in which all parties engage in common activities.[6] Parties who choose to participate in a program of staff development are more likely to find the program helpful. Therefore, it should be obvious that the day of one-size-fits-all staff development has passed. Instead, effective staff development programs offer participants a series of meaningful alternatives for reaching their personalized goals and addressing their personalized needs.

Assessing Needs

Human resource managers faced with the job of providing effective and economical staff development must both assess and narrow needs in order to prepare programs that will stimulate and satisfy a diverse population. While group programs are the most economical plan for staff development, the individual cannot be neglected in the process. Figure 10.2 is an example of a Needs Assessment Topical Survey that addresses the question of a teacher's preferred learning style as well as interests.

Feedback is an often overlooked part of the needs assessment process. Teachers want to know how the decision to offer one program over another was made. Surveys that do not report on results risk being perceived as useless facades for teacher input. Instead, narrowing available choices based on response percentages favoring each option and resubmitting surveys for additional teacher feedback to narrow the field further keeps teachers involved in the selection process and more likely to be involved in the programs ultimately offered.

Group surveys, however, should not be the exclusive impetus for staff development. There can be legal or procedural changes that require retraining, and there can be problems perceived by administrators or individual teachers that can give rise to a staff development program or an opportunity. The tendency to think of staff development only in terms of groups and majority needs undercuts what research tells about the way adults learn, that is, their need for individualization and personalized professional growth plans.

Figure 10.1   Factors Influencing Teacher Professional Development Profiles

Indicate by checking the appropriate box what you perceive to be the needs of the educational personnel in your building.

A. Building Management	Great Need	Some Need	Little or No Need
1. Providing a safe and orderly environment			
2. Providing adequate human and material resources: staffing/budget			
3. Establishing effective communication/decision-making systems			
4. Developing school building policies and mission statements			
B. Instructional Leadership	Great Need	Some Need	Little or No Need
1. Planning and developing the curriculum			
2. Becoming knowledgeable of curriculum changes			
3. Understanding mastery-learning and competency-based education			
4. Defining and writing instructional objectives			
5. Coordinating team teaching between disciplines			
C. Basic/Critical Skills	Great Need	Some Need	Little or No Need
1. Implementing reading/study skill programs			
2. Implementing math programs			
3. Implementing communication skills programs: speaking, listening, writing			
D. Assessment of Pupil Progress	Great Need	Some Need	Little or No Need
1. Implementing diagnostic/prospective educational procedures			
2. Systematizing the regular assessment of basic academic skill in the classroom			
3. Developing multiple assessment methods for teachers to assess student progress in the classroom			
4 Developing a pupil feedback, follow-up, and reporting system			

Figure 10.2a   A Needs Assessment Topical Survey

E. Instructional Evaluation and Supervision	Great Need	Some Need	Little or No Need
1. Developing formal classroom observation and evaluation procedures			
2. Developing informal classroom observation procedures			
3 Implementing effective supervision of instruction			
4. Providing effective staff development			
F. School–Community Relations	Great Need	Some Need	Little or No Need
1. Involving parents and the community in the academic achievement of students			
2. Communicating effectively with parents about student academic achievement			
3. Promoting home–school collaboration in planning assignments for student academic success			
4. Promoting business–industry cooperation to increase student career awareness			
G. Personal Growth and Development	Great Need	Some Need	Little or No Need
1. Developing time management strategies for principals and teachers			
2. Developing stress management techniques for principals and teachers			
3. Providing opportunities for career growth and development			

H. Teaching/Learning Model

Check beside the mode(s) that best describe the most effective instructional experience for you.

____ Theory = Lecture, visual/auditory aids

____ Instruction = Question and answer, discussion, illustrations or examples

____ Modeling = Portrayal of behavior being taught by videotape or role-playing

____ Enactment = Activity compels trainer to perform the behaviors being taught from the theory; Simulation

Please write below other areas of need that may not have been identified above. If you see the need for your building or district to adopt a specific goal, please identify that also.

Figure 10.2b   A Needs Assessment Topical Survey

CHARACTERISTICS OF EFFECTIVE STAFF DEVELOPMENT

Every school district offers some form of staff development, but not every school district has effective staff development. Figure 10.3 is a guidance for creating effective staff development provided by the National Staff Development Council.[7]

Teacher involvement in staff development should occur during planning as well as implementation. Needs assessments are a starting point for teacher

1. **Involvement in planning**

   Staff development activities tend to be more effective when participants have taken part in identifying the objectives and planning the activities.

2. **Time for planning**

   Whether the staff development activities are mandated or participation is voluntary, participants need time away from their regular teaching for administrative responsibilities in order to plan the program.

3. **Involvement of principals**

   Staff development activities in which principals as active participants are more effective. Active involvement means that principals need to participate in most if not all of the activities in which their teachers are involved.

4. **District administrative support**

   For staff development activities to be effective, district-level support needs to be active and visible.

5. **Expectations**

   Participants should know what is expected of them during the activities, as well as what they will be asked to do when the experience is over.

6. **Opportunities for sharing**

   Staff development activities in which participants share and provide assistance to one another are more apt to attain their objectives than activities in which participants work alone.

7. **Continuity**

   Staff development activities that are thematic and linked to school and/or district goals are more effective in producing significant, long-lasting results than a series of one-shot activities on a variety of topics.

8. **Follow-up**

   Staff development is more successful if follow-up activities are part of the program's design.

9. **Opportunity for practice**

   Staff development activities that include demonstrations and practice with feedback are more likely to accomplish their objectives than those activities that expect participants to store up ideas and skills for use at a future time.

10. **Active involvement**

    Successful staff development activities are those that provide participants with a chance to be actively involved. Participants are more likely to apply what they have learned when they have "hands-on" experiences with materials, actively participate in exercises that will later be used with students, and are involved in small group discussions.

11. **Opportunity for choice**

    When participants have chose to be involved in a program, there is a far greater likelihood that the experience will be helpful. A meaningful series of alternative activities should also be

Figure 10.3a   Characteristics of Effective Staff Development Activities

offered within a staff development program.

12. Building on strengths

People like to be recognized as valued, competent, liked, and needed. Staff development activities that view each participant as a resource are usually more favorably received by participants.

13. Content

Successful staff development activities are often geared toward a relatively narrow grade-level range and address a specific topic or a specific set of skills. They help participants develop a plan that is ready for immediate use or a set of instructional materials that translate the ideas presented into practice.

14. Presenter

Successful presenters approach a subject from the participants' points of view. The presenter's expertise is important, as is his or her ability to convey genuine enthusiasm for the subject.

15. Individualization

Staff development programs that provide different experiences for participants who are at different stages of their development are more apt to obtain their objectives than those in which all participants engage in common activities.

16. Number of participants

Some presentations are as effective with 100 participants as they are with 10.

However, for staff development activities requiring personal contact, informality, and an exchange of ideas, seven to ten participants appears to be optimal. There are exceptions based on the skill of the presenter, the organization of the activity, and the nature of the topic.

17. The learning environment

As a general rule, successful staff development activities occur within a low-threat, comfortable setting in which there is a degree of "psychological safety." Openness to learning is enhanced when peers can share problems and solutions.

18. The physical facility

Accessibility of supporting materials, appearance of the facility, room temperature, lighting, auditory and visual distractions, and many other physical factors have subtle but sometimes profound effects on the success of a staff development activity.

19. Time of day and season

Staff development activities that take place at the end of a school day are often less successful than those offered when participants are fresh. Furthermore, staff development activities are less likely to be successful when they are scheduled at times of the year when seasonal activities (e.g., parent conferences, holiday celebrations) occur.

Figure 10.3b   Characteristics of Effective Staff Development Activities

participation in planning successful programs, but teachers should also be involved in the actual selection of the speakers, formats, and environments for program components. Top-down control of staff development is unlikely to be successful because administrators are too far removed from the classroom, are rarely privy to what teachers really want or need, and are too busy to give the task the time it requires. Remember, staff development is adult education, and adults, unlike students, learn best when they are directly involved in planning their learning experiences. Adults also learn best when they have choices. Thus, good staff development programs should provide options with respect to speakers, formats, activities, expectations, and goals.

VARIED APPROACHES TO STAFF DEVELOPMENT

Although staff development is presently equated with topical lectures to large groups, there are indeed other ways to provide for professional growth for teachers. Figure 10.4 summarizes eight separate models for encouraging teacher growth.[8] A brief discussion of the critical elements and goals of each approach follows:

Classroom-Centered Staff Development

Classroom-centered staff development has the goal of making the teacher a better teacher. Professional growth objectives center on the classroom and instruction. For teachers experiencing difficulty in the classroom, this method of professional growth should be tailored to the teachers' specific needs identified through observation and data collection. This model assumes that teaching can be objectively observed, analyzed, and evaluated and that improvement can result from feedback on performance.[9] That improvement equates with professional growth.

While this method of staff development is obviously good for new teachers or teachers exhibiting problems with classroom performance, it can also benefit veteran teachers, with or without identified concerns. Veterans will benefit by observing colleagues, gathering data, preparing feedback, and discussing the common experience,[10] and by being observed and engaging in a discussion of the data collected during that observation. Teachers who participate in this model should be trained in clinical supervision techniques, that is, in data collection, objective analysis, and conferencing.

Unlike administrative observations, these collegial observations and exchanges should have nothing to do with official teacher evaluation. These observations and exchanges are a professional growth option and, as such, attach no official consequences to teacher performance. They exist as pure learning experiences. Teachers are unlikely to move from one developmental level to another without feedback on their performance from some external source.[11] This staff development model is structured to provide the unconditional and non-threatening feedback required for true growth. Executed properly, the model fosters internal evaluation, the highest order of thinking, and the ultimate professional growth goal.

Model	Focus	Teacher Type	Method
Classroom-Centered	Improvement of Teaching	Teacher with Problems Teacher Seeking Self-Improvement	Clinical Supervision of Teaching
Training	Acquiring New Skills	Teacher in Need of New Skills	Scheduled Training by Skilled Expert
Research-Centered	Testing Theory in Practice	Meticulous Researcher/Writer	Gathering Data to Prove or Disprove Theory
Merit Recognition	Recognizing Successful Practice	Competitive Achiever	Recognition for Documented Exceptional Performance
School Improvement	Solving Building Problems	Problem-Solving Team Players	The School Committee with Specific Goals and Objectives
Internal Career Ladder	Responsibilities beyond Classroom	Teacher in Need of Challenge Outside of Classroom	Recognition for Performance of Tasks Other Than Teaching
External Career Ladder	Responsibilities beyond School and/or District	Veteran Teacher with Proven Ability. Capable of Representing District in External Projects	Recognition for Performance Representing District in Publication, Exchange, Presentation
Self-Directed	Whatever Teacher Deems Necessary to Professional Growth	Intelligent, Creative Self-Starter with Proven Achievement	Teacher Proposes; Administration Provides Resources and Support

Figure 10.4   Eight Models for Personalized Staff Development

Training for New or Improved Performance

Training is what most educators usually equate with staff development. One or more speakers, experts in their fields, who purport to be able to impart new skills to their audiences, present the classic workshop. Selection of workshop leaders is central to making training an effective professional growth experience. Ideally, there should be elements of comparison and evaluation in selecting presenters. That is, selection should be made from a field of likely candidates versed in the topic. This approach gives those planning the workshop an opportunity to research and compare not only presenters but also aspects of the topic they may have missed but should include in a training session.

There is a method for selecting presenters, and that method is based on the three Rs of training program planning: Research, References, and Remuneration. First and foremost, what qualifies the speaker as an expert on the selected topic? To see if the presenter has in-depth expertise, look for educational qualifications and achievements such as published books, articles, awards, and media exposure.[12] Selection committees would be wise to review published research records of prospective speakers in order to validate expertise and to better understand the topic and the viewpoint of the speaker. Second, those selecting presenters should ask for and check the speaker's references. The question of past performance and customer satisfaction is very important. Even when references are positive, not every speaker is right for every audience. If selectors have an opportunity to see a presenter in action, they should. If not, feedback from those who have is essential. Fiscal responsibility requires that those in charge of making these decisions make them based on information gathered from reliable sources.

The selection process should also include a request for a summary of the presenter's program, perhaps an audition tape, an agenda, or a sample of handouts that will allow the committee to make their own comparisons among prospective presenters. Both style and substance will be factors in determining the potential success of a training session. Finally, selection committees must have a clear understanding of what price they will pay for a given presenter's services and what that price includes. Is airfare and lodging an issue? Will the speaker require any additional equipment, and who will be responsible for duplicating materials for distribution? Does the presentation price include any follow-up visits or consultations? Contracts should reflect the specific performance agreed on by the presenter and the district, including provisions for cancellations in the event of unforeseen emergencies or catastrophes on either the speaker or District's part.

Time, place, and environmental management must also be considered in structuring effective training. Since training usually involves large group instruction, training should be scheduled in comfortable facilities at convenient times and the speaker and workshop participants should feel welcomed and supported in their efforts. Effective training programs pay attention to these vital details that can make or break the best of presentations.

Finally, program structure should be clearly delineated before a contract is signed. Ideally, training translates theory into practice, and effective training programs have been found to share the following elements:

1. presentation of theory,
2. modeling or demonstration,

3. practice under simulated conditions,
4. structured and open-ended feedback,
5. coaching for application.[13]

Therefore, those planning a training program must work with the presenter to see that all elements are present.

As part of fiscal accountability, evaluation of program effectiveness should also be part of this model. There are two prongs to this evaluation. First, was the presentation itself worthwhile and well received? Second, did the presentation have its intended effect? Districts have the right to presume that the time and money they invest in training will have the desired effect. Program evaluation provides an official record of success or failure. Teacher surveys and interviews will measure the immediate response to training, but the true measure of training effectiveness will be determined by whether or not teachers use what they have learned and use it effectively.

Site-Based Research

Real teachers in real classrooms have made significant research findings.[14] Another more personalized approach to staff development that capitalizes on this history is site-based research. This model encourages classroom teachers to become on-site researchers exploring the effectiveness of what they do. Such action research is a search for answers to questions relevant to educators' immediate interests, with the primary goal of putting the findings immediately into practice.[15] Improved instruction, more reflective learners, professional growth, and collegial sharing—all can result from involving teachers in classroom research.[16]

In this model, a teacher's professional growth is tied to the teacher's efforts to develop and test educational theory in the classroom laboratory. The adult learner identifies a problem to be solved and then proceeds to design a research plan for solving it. The teacher becomes an educational researcher in search of the most effective teaching strategies. Action research is a change process encouraging risk taking and raising the status of the educator from skilled technician to scholar practitioner.[17]

Administrative support for this model of staff development begins with simple encouragement and interest. Administrators who share research findings they themselves find interesting set the stage for teacher involvement in this staff development model. Additionally, on-site researchers should be given a forum for discussing and disseminating their findings. In-house newsletters or journals devoted to the discussion of educational research, as well as planned meetings for sharing information, give teachers the recognition and encouragement their efforts as researchers deserve.

School Improvement Projects

For more gregarious educators, participation on school improvement committees can be yet another opportunity for professional growth. Once again the element of problem solving comes into play. School improvement committees essentially focus on identified school concerns and work together to address concerns and to solve problems. The quality of school improvement initiatives is enhanced when teacher professional growth and school improvement are integrated.[18] Thus, both the school and the teacher will benefit from this approach to professional growth.

Teachers involved in school improvement initiatives grow socially, intellectually, and professionally. Socially, they have the opportunity to lead or contribute to the project and to learn from the group experience. This is a particularly effective way to socialize teachers new to a school or district. Intellectually, they are challenged to analyze problems, to identify the factors that must be addressed in solving those problems, and to develop a solution in light of these factors. School improvement committees that successfully rise to the occasion are rewarded with the satisfaction of making a true professional contribution.

Career Ladders: Internal and External

Career ladders are yet another method for encouraging professional growth among teachers. Career ladders are opportunities for growth outside of the classroom. Teachers who opt to participate in career ladder programs are recognized and rewarded for doing more than they are required to do by contract. Teachers who pursue this option take on responsibilities for roles and projects that have no direct connection to their teaching assignments, but do make a contribution to the educational community. Both teachers and the general public have been found to favor the development of career ladder plans with extra pay for extra duties.[19] However, even when pay for performance is not possible, career ladder participants are rewarded by their sense of autonomy and by the recognition such positions often carry.

While not every teacher may want to leave the classroom for growth opportunities, those who do can act as administrative assistants, teacher mentors, grant writers, curriculum writers, and public relations liaisons, to name just a few career ladder options. This model gives teachers the opportunity to meet new challenges on a very personal level. Internal career ladders allow them to link their personal growth to positive contributions in their schools. On the other hand, external career ladders will give interested teachers the opportunity to perform outside of the school itself. External options can include role exchanges, university teaching, textbook writing, development of marketable education materials, and opportunities to create and present staff development programs in other districts.

This model can rescue teachers facing midlife career crises, that is, teachers who suddenly find themselves bored and unmotivated by their job descriptions. Education, as it presently exists, gives teachers relatively few options for overcoming career stagnation. Perhaps that is why growing numbers of teachers seek administrative or counseling certification, and they are then lost forever to the classroom. Internal and external career ladders can give teachers new incentives that do not necessarily require them to leave the classroom.

Merit Pay and Professional Growth

Teaching is a profession with relatively few extrinsic rewards. Teachers move routinely through the steps of a predetermined pay scale based on the degrees and graduate credits they earn for academic work and their years of experience as teachers. Aside from the occasional negotiated stipend or pay for performance under a supplementary contract, teachers have no opportunities for additional extrinsic rewards. However, recently the concept of merit pay, that is, an extrinsic, monetary reward for exemplary performance has come to the fore. Merit pay is appropriate where it is clearly observable that one employee is more productive than another and that other employees know, or can be told, what they must do to receive a merit increase in pay.[20] Merit pay plans that act as a stimulus or incentive for better teaching become a professional growth option.

Self-Directed Plans for Professional Growth

As educators, we know that no two individuals learn and grow in exactly the same way. All individuals differ in the ways they perceive and process information and the modes of learning that are most effective for them,[21] and only the individual has a real handle on what works best. Applying this bit of researched wisdom to staff development for teachers leads to the conclusion that probably the best professional growth plans are those teachers develop for themselves.

This final model for professional development does not limit the teacher to choosing projects directly related to classroom or professional performance, although both are viable options. Instead, teachers are free to involve themselves in enrichment projects that may have only a tangential effect on classroom or professional performance. This plan recognizes that incorporating opportunities for individuals to pursue diverse interests will make them better professionals in the long run. Most other professions operate from this perspective. Other professions allow their members to personalize professional growth plans that are totally self-directed and that sometimes seem unrelated to their immediate professional responsibilities.

Teachers who seek additional certification in new areas or who wish to travel in the interest of professional growth are engaged in self-directed staff development. For example, a math teacher who chooses to learn a new foreign language is involved in professional growth, although the teacher may never choose to teach the language. This model is based on the premise that there are many ways to stimulate personal growth and development, and traditional approaches that are always connected to the classroom and administratively directed or monitored may not, in the final analysis, be as effective as a model that leaves both direction and monitoring to the teacher.

A Statewide Model for Staff Development

This differentiated and personalized approach to staff development has actually been adopted in Ohio. Through the development of Individual Professional Development Plans, educators have far greater flexibility in selecting the types of professional development activities that are meaningful to them.[22] As opposed to traditional staff development systems that recognized only formal course work or workshops as legitimate professional development experiences, Ohio's new plan allows a far greater range of professional development options. For example, figure 10.5 illustrates some of the activities that can be incorporated into an Individual Professional Development Plan.[23]

While Ohio's new format represents a significant change, Individual Professional Development Plans must still be based on the needs of the educator, the students, the school, and the school district, with each professional development activity that is completed being clearly related to the teacher's area of licensure and/or classroom teaching.[24] Local Professional Development Committees consisting of three classroom teachers, one principal, and one other district employee appointed by the superintendent are responsible for reviewing course work and other proposed or completed professional activities to determine if they meet the requirements needed for renewing certificates and licenses (figure 10.6).[25]

Ohio's new approach to staff development for teachers has made great strides in returning responsibility for professional growth to teachers.

STAFF DEVELOPMENT FOR CLASSIFIED STAFF

Every school employee should be provided with opportunities to grow professionally. There is something new to be learned in every area of responsibility, and effective human resource managers must develop plans for classified staff as well as teachers. Figure 10.7 gives examples of training for secretaries, custodians, educational assistants, and cafeteria staff. In addition to these job-related programs, employee groups would also benefit from human resource presentations dealing with such relevant topics as employee health plans, retirement programs, workplace laws, and sexual harassment.

Through the creation of Individual Professional Development Plans, educators will have far greater flexibility in selecting the types of professional development activities that are meaningful to them. Where the old system recognized only formal course work or workshops approved for Continuing Education Units (CEUs), the new structure will allow a far greater range of professional development activities. For example, the following could be incorporated into an Individual Professional Development Plan and be approved by the Local Professional Development Committee.

- Curricular projects

- Research, action research, inquiry

- Serving as a mentor teacher

- Peer coaching

- Student-teacher supervision

- Professional writing/publication

- School–community partnership initiatives

- Teacher-initiated projects

- Visitations to schools

- Preparing and giving presentations at workshops and conferences

- Reflective/analytical portfolios such as those completed for National Board Certification

- Teacher networks

- Coaching, shadowing, externships

Along with increased flexibility in the types of professional development activities that are accepted, there is also an increased emphasis on the "relevance" of the professional development activity. Individual Professional Development Plans must be based on the needs of the educator, the students, the school, and the school district. Each professional development activity that is completed must be clearly related to the area of licensure and/or classroom teaching.

Figure 10.5   Individual Professional Development Plan Options

Name _____

Date Submitted _____   Date Completed _____

1. If course work was taken or a workshop was attended, please attach an official transcript, or certificate of completion, or letter from presenter verifying attendance and completion of assignments.

Attachments Necessary

2. If equivalent activity was completed, please provide some kind of appropriate documentation that verifies participation and completion of the activity.

_____   Log of hours

_____   Copy of product created

_____   Written report

_____   Other

Attachments Necessary

Signed _____   Date _____

In the judgment of the Local Professional Development Committee (LPDC), the activity is completed and verified

and is worth ___   ☐ PDUs   ☐ CEUs   ☐ Semester credits

LPDC Chairperson _____   Date _____

Figure 10.6   Verification of Professional Development Plan Completion

Position	Program
Cafeteria Workers	Nutritious Menu Planning Safety in Food Preparation Budgeting
Custodians	Safety on the Job Disposing of Harmful Chemicals OSHA Standards
Educational Assistants	Techniques for Working with Special Education Students Behavior Management Tutoring Techniques
Secretaries	Office Etiquette Using New Equipment and Computer Programs Record keeping and Confidentiality

Figure 10.7   Suggested Programs for Classified Staff

Just as no school employee is exempt from supervision and evaluation, so no school employee should be denied the opportunity for professional growth. Often human resource managers forget just how important the classified staff are to the functioning of schools. Classified employees who have no professional growth opportunities, like unsupervised teachers, come to feel neglected and out of touch with district expectations.

A LEGAL PERSPECTIVE

Boards of education are legally authorized and encouraged to provide staff development programs for their employees. Boards have statutory authority to use district funds to cover any reasonable and necessary expense entailed. They are authorized to enter into cooperative agreements to establish and operate staff development programs for teaching, nonteaching, and classified staff. However, this authority carries with it a collateral legal responsibility to be sure the funds expended are not misappropriated or wasted. Training should be targeted to needs and used by those trained. Merit pay should be selectively awarded based on legally defensible criteria. Career ladder positions should be defined and assigned on the basis of nondiscriminatory criteria. Finally, in states that sanction collective bargaining, all staff development efforts, as terms and conditions of employment, should be duly negotiated.

THEORY INTO PRACTICE

1. Describe the last staff development program in which you participated. Was it effective? Why or why not?
2. What aspect of your classroom performance do you feel needs improvement?
3. Read about and test an instructional improvement theory.
4. Take a position, pro or con, on the concept of merit pay, and defend that position.
5. Develop an internal career ladder position for your school.
6. Develop an external career ladder position you would like to fill.
7. What professional training needs do you have?
8. Develop a school improvement project for your school that could serve as a staff development opportunity.
9. How does your district determine its staff development program?
10. How does your district evaluate its staff development programs?

NOTES

1. M. Knowles, *Using Learning Contracts: Practical Approaches to Individualizing and Structuring Learning* (San Francisco, Calif.: Jossey-Bass, 1986).

2. D. C. Orlich, *Staff Development: Enhancing Human Potential* (Boston, Mass.: Allyn & Bacon, 1989).

3. B. Raebeck, "The School as a Humane Business," *Phi Delta Kappan* 75, no.10 (1994): 761–765.

4. L. Ingvarson and P. Greenway, *Portrayals of Teacher Development* (Washington, D.C.: ERIC Document Reproduction Service) No. ED 200 600.

5. B. Marczely, *Personalizing Professional Growth* (Thousand Oaks, Calif.: Corwin Press, 1996), 4.

6. National Staff Development Council, *Workshop Handout* (April 1991), 5.

7. National Staff Development Council, *Characteristics of Effective Staff Development Activities* (April 1991), 5.

8. Marczely, *Personalizing Professional Growth: Staff*, viii.

9. D. Sparks and S. F. Loucks-Horsley, *Five Models of Staff Development* (Oxford, Ohio: National Staff Development Council, 1990).

10. D. Sparks and S. F. Loucks-Horsley, *Five Models of Staff Development* (Oxford, Ohio: National Staff Development Council, 1990).

11. L. Thies-Sprinthall and N. A. Sprinthall, "Experienced Teachers: Agents for Revitalization and Renewal as Mentors and Teacher Educators," *Journal of Education,* 169 (1987): 65–69.

12. T. Brady, "Workshops, Seminars, and Conferences: Not All Alike," in *Bound to Make You Succeed* (Chicago, Ill.: The Dartnell Corporation, 1992), 1.

13. B. Joyce and B. Showers, *Student Achievement through Staff Development* (New York, N.Y.: Longman, 1995), 112.

14. R. Gable and V. Rogers, "Taking the Terror out of Research," *Phi Delta Kappan* 68 (1987): 690–695.

15. J. A. McKay, "Professional Development through Action Research," *Journal of Staff Development* 13, no. 1 (1992): 18–21.

16. R. W. Johnson, "Where Can Teacher Research Lead? One Teacher's Daydream," *Educational Leadership* 51, no. 2 (1993): 66–68.

17. J. A. McKay, "Professional Development through Action Research," *Journal of Staff Development* 13, no. 1 (1992): 18–21.

18. E. F. Iwanicki, "Teacher Evaluation for School Improvement," in *The New Handbook of Teacher Evaluation*, ed. J. Millman and L. Darling-Hammond (Newbury Park, Calif.: Sage Publications, 1990), 158–171.

19. J. C. Parker, *Career Ladder/Master Teacher Programs: Implications for Principals* (Reston, Va.: National Association of Secondary Principals, 1985).

20. S. Keith and R. H. Girling, *Education, Management, and Participation* (Boston, Mass.: Allyn & Bacon, 1991).

21. R. Dunn and K. Dunn, *Teaching Students through Their Individual Learning Styles: A Practical Approach* (Reston, Va.: Reston Publishing, 1978).

22. Ohio Department of Education, *Transforming Professional Development in Ohio: A Resource Guide for Establishing Local Professional Development Committees* (Columbus, Ohio: Ohio Department of Education, March 1998), 5.

23. Ohio Department of Education, *Transforming Professional Development in Ohio,* 5.

24. Ohio Department of Education, *Transforming Professional Development in Ohio,* 6.

25. Ohio Rev. Code Ann. § 3319.22 (Anderson 2001).

Chapter Eleven

Record Keeping and Reporting

Two major functions of human resource management are recording and reporting. As the preceding chapters have shown, data collection is at the core of almost every human resource activity. Effective human resource managers routinely gather, organize, and analyze data so that they have experiential reasons for the decisions and recommendations they make, and therefore they can evaluate the effectiveness of policies and procedures that are in place. Human resource management is a paper chase. However, legal issues regarding the collection, maintenance, and dissemination of human resource data are central to effective human resource management.

EMPLOYEE PRIVACY

Resumes, transcripts, applications, references, evaluations, requests for leave, medical reports, and attendance reports are but a few of the kinds of personal information routinely collected and warehoused by human resource managers. This data is central to studying and supporting policy and employment decisions. Nevertheless, these routine records obviously can make the collator and reader privy to some very personal employee information. Therefore, the question of how much or how little privacy an employee is entitled to as a matter of law and contract becomes inextricably linked to how this data, once acquired, is managed.

In 1974 Congress passed the federal Privacy Act ensuring the accuracy of information the federal government collects about individuals and protecting personal information from unauthorized disclosure.[1] The states have their own privacy acts mirroring the procedures and intent of the federal Privacy Act. The seeming protection of personal privacy promised by these state and federal laws, however, is offset by the prescriptions of the federal Freedom of

Information Act and similar public records laws adopted by state governments. The Freedom of Information Act is designed to assure an informed citizenry by allowing citizens to request information regarding governmental activities. Citizens get information regarding governmental activities by requesting public records pertaining to those activities. Thus, these two types of federal and state legislation create a tension between the individual's right to privacy and the public's right to know. Human resource management provides a frequent forum for the ongoing struggle between these conflicting interests.

WHAT IS A PUBLIC RECORD?

A public record is any record kept by a government agency. Since school districts are state governmental agencies, the data they routinely gather in the course of human resource management are all public records subject to disclosure under the Freedom of Information Act or state public records acts. There are some exceptions to the types of documentation open to citizen review. Medical records, such as physical or psychiatric exams, are generally exempt from disclosure, as are documents involving attorney/client privilege or doctor/patient privilege. Private notes shared with no one or purely personal communications are also not considered public records and are exempt from disclosure. Most other records, however, are open to disclosure on request.

As a general rule, right of access to public records is restricted only if access can be shown to endanger the safety of the record or if access would unreasonably interfere with the operation of the agency having custody of the record. Collective bargaining agreements sometimes place restrictions on access to teacher records, but these restrictions are usually procedural and seldom overcome the right to ultimate record disclosure. For example, contracts may prescribe that teachers be notified when their records are requested, that they give permission for record release, or that they have the right to review their records and contest content. These procedural rights, however, have done little to thwart the ultimate release of public records not specifically exempted by federal or state law.[2] The courts have repeatedly ruled that any doubt as to the appropriateness of disclosure should be decided in favor of public disclosure.[3]

In particular, the courts have ruled that personnel files are subject to open records laws unless specifically exempted by law.[4] Public record laws and the court decisions favoring disclosure seek to give members of the public information they need to address legitimate public concerns.[5] For example, a Texas court recognized that the public's interest in evaluating teacher competence outweighed a teacher's right to keep her college transcript private.[6] Settlement agreements made between school boards and teachers or administrators are also subject to disclosure as a legitimate public concern. Settlement agreements are essentially contracts made by a public agency and must be treated as public records, even if they do contain confidentiality clauses. For example, a separation agreement made between a board of education and a teacher accused of sexual misconduct was ruled a public document open to disclosure, even though it contained a confidentiality clause.[7] The court found the nondisclosure clause contrary to public policy and unenforceable.[8] Similarly, a settlement agreement with a district administrator containing a confidentiality clause was ruled a public record open to disclosure as a matter of legitimate public concern.[9] Note that the Family Educational Rights and Privacy Act that shields student records from public review does not protect teachers' records. This law applies only to students and their educational records, not to the personnel records of school employees.[10] Teachers are public employees, so the public has a legitimate concern about the qualifications for the positions they hold and the caliber of their past and present performance.

MEASURES FOR COMPLIANCE

Most public records acts, patterned after the federal Freedom of Information Act, require that public records be made available on request. The person making the request cannot be required to establish a proper purpose or, for that matter, any purpose for a records request.[11] Therefore, the first step in complying with public records laws is to acknowledge and accept the requestor's right to the information they are seeking. A recent study undertaken by the Citizens League and the Society of Professional Journalists in Ohio found that one in three police departments did not supply any information, and more than half the time requestors were asked why they wanted to see the records before they viewed them, a clear violation of Ohio's open records law, while the Cleveland School Board simply refused to supply any information.[12] These are clear violations of Ohio's Public Records Act, but they are indicative of a national problem that can only lead to unnecessary litigation and public distrust.

Public records open to disclosure include microfilm, computer disks, and videotapes, as well as written records. Also note that the person requesting access to such public records has the right to ask for copies or to make copies of the requested records, and, in either case, they may be charged a reasonable duplication fee. However, requests for information are not considered requests for public records. Most public records laws do not sanction random fishing expeditions. The requestor must ask for specific documents already in existence. State agencies, including school districts, are not required to create documents in response to requests for information or to answer "blanket" requests for undifferentiated volumes of information. In the first instance, the public document requested simply does not exist, and in the second instance, filling the request would place an undue burden on the agency and interfere with its normal operations. State agencies are also under no obligation to decipher or interpret the documents they produce on request. The agency's sole obligation is to provide the requested record.

In view of their legislated duty to turn over existing public documents on request, it behooves school districts to be sure that the information in personnel files is accurate and relevant to job performance. Irrelevant or retaliatory documents have no place in employee files and become the basis for libel charges. Probably the best way to monitor the maintenance of accurate and relevant personnel files is to appoint an administrator to oversee personnel records. This human resource manager would be responsible for adopting rules and procedures for operating a record system that accords with law and contract. The system should ensure that only necessary, accurate, and job-related information is included in personnel files and that there is only one "official" personnel file in the district. Often collective bargaining agreements place similar restrictions on personnel file management.

One of the best ways to ensure personnel file integrity is to encourage employees to review their personnel files on a regular basis. Collective bargaining agreements may actually contain clauses requiring employee notification when items are added to the employees' files. Some contracts even go so far as to require an employee signature on the document indicating formal notice and agreement with the entry. Employee agreement, however, should never become an official prerequisite for including a relevant piece of information in an employee's personnel file. Employees who object to items or notations made in their files can be given the opportunity to request the removal of the objectionable material, and if that request is denied, they can require inclusion of an addendum giving the employee's response to the disputed entry.

Regular review of personnel files assigns shared responsibility for accuracy and relevancy. Human resource managers should investigate the accuracy of disputed material in an employee's file and delete it if it proves inaccurate or inappropriate. On the other hand, human resource record managers must not cave in to demands that relevant personnel documents that address identified problems be removed, simply because an employee takes issue with their presence in a file. Personnel files should be, above all else, accurate public records that preserve the integrity of the supervision process.

Employees should, as a common courtesy, have the right to know that access to their files has been requested by a third party. At the same time, they must understand, however, that disclosure cannot be denied by the school district, except in the limited circumstances discussed earlier. Figures 11.1 and 11.2 attempt to summarize some of the categories of personnel information that are exempt from disclosure and those that are open to disclosure as public records.

Note that lists, of grades and similar evaluative material, with student names expunged from the record to protect student privacy, can be requested as a public record documenting teacher performance. Thus, concerned members of the public who want to assess a teacher's fairness or discriminatory bias in the classroom can, for example, use such lists.

PENALTIES FOR NONCOMPLIANCE

In mirroring the federal Freedom of Information Act, state courts may assess state agencies for reasonable attorney fees and other litigation costs reasonably incurred in any case in which a complainant has substantially prevailed.[13] Congress [and state legislatures] realized that too often insurmountable barriers presented by court costs and attorney fees to the average person requesting information under the Freedom of Information Act [or states' public records acts] enabled the federal government [and state agencies] to escape compliance with the law.[14] Therefore, statutory allowance for attorney fees and litigation costs has been provided to encourage individuals to seek judicial relief for the

Applications	Curricula
Transcripts	Proficiency Test Results
References	Parent Complaints
Interview Rating Forms	Student Complaints
Teacher Contracts	Grievance Forms
Salary Agreements	Settlement Agreements
Attendance Records	Dismissal Letters
Annual Evaluations	Lesson Plans
Observation Records	Directory Information
Leave Requests	Grade Lists [with student names omitted]
Seniority Lists	Discipline Referrals [with student names omitted]
Board Minutes	

Figure 11.1   Personnel Records Open to Disclosure

Medical Records	Personal, Unshared Notes
Physical Exams	Material Protected by Attorney/Client Privilege
Psychiatric Exams	Material Protected by Doctor/Patient Privilege
Social Security Numbers	

Figure 11.2   Personnel Records Exempt from Disclosure

purpose of vindicating national [and state] policy.[15] Similar provisions for the payment of plaintiff attorney fees and litigation costs are found in many states' public record acts.

In order to be eligible for reasonable attorney fees and other litigation costs, a plaintiff must have "substantially prevailed" in securing public record disclosure. It is left to the courts to determine whether the complainant has substantially prevailed. This requirement can be met where only some portions of requested materials are ordered released, while other withholding is sustained by the court.[16] Even where no documents are released, a plaintiff may be deemed to have substantially prevailed if the suit brought by the plaintiff forced an agency to comply with the law.[17] Probably the greater costs incurred in disclosure litigation stem from the loss of public trust that is frequently a consequence of such actions. Negative press leaves the taxpaying public with the perception that the school district has something to hide.

THE REPORTING FUNCTION

This text has dealt with myriad federal and state laws and regulations affecting human resource management. Most of these laws have posting requirements, specifically ordering district officials to disseminate information regarding employee rights in each building in the district. Failure to post laws where employees are likely to see them can actually cause a district to be fined. However, simple posting is never enough to have laws and regulations function as they were intended. Reporting should be more than ad hoc display on a bulletin board. Effective human resource management has an ongoing educational component. Human resource administrators have a duty to know and understand legislation affecting any and all aspects of human resource management and a responsibility for explaining these laws and their implications to employees. Contract explication should also be part of what human resource administrators routinely do. Unnecessary litigation can be virtually eliminated if employees understand both their rights and their responsibilities under law and contract.

There are several effective approaches for addressing the educational demands of effective human resource management:

1. Development and dissemination of a newsletter devoted to human resource management issues.
2. Development of a series of targeted workshops addressing specific groups and legal issues, such as sexual harassment, family and medical leave, and retirement.

3. Regular meetings with union leadership to monitor and discuss contract issues, such as cumbersome contract language, giving rise to grievances
4. Regular meetings with district administrators to discuss the effect of law and contract on their respective working environments
5. Workshops for all employees regarding specific local policies and procedures connected to rights and responsibilities accorded by law and by contract, that is, the paper trail

A PERSONNEL NEWSLETTER

The job of human resource management should not be a paper chase conducted behind closed doors. Effective human resource management is founded on meaningful contact and exchange of information with the human resources being managed. Figure 11.3 illustrates a general format for a personnel newsletter.

Human resource managers are the link between legislated theory and administrative practice. Their role is, for the most part, ministerial. That is, they must read, report, and apply legislated and contractual prescriptions to employee behavior in the school setting. However, nothing is ever that cut and dry in the field of educational administration. Therefore, creating ways to present, discuss, and study the effect of law and contract gives the human resource administrator opportunities for the personal contact that will, in the final analysis, determine the human resource manager's own effectiveness.

LAW EXPLICATION	A PERSONNEL CALENDAR
e.g., What are a teacher's rights and responsibilities under the Family and Medical Leave Act?	Dates for submitting: Tenure Requests Retirement Notices Leave Requests Evaluations
FORM FOCUS	**CONTRACT CLAUSE EXPLICATION**
e.g., A copy of the form teachers should use to request family and medical leave.	*e.g.,* What does it mean when the contract says a teacher returning from leave will be placed in the same or an equivalent position within the teacher's area of specialization?

Figure 11.3   A Personnel Newsletter Format

A LEGAL PERSPECTIVE

Record keeping and reporting are the two sides of the information management system. Neither can exist nor be effective without the other. Teachers, for example, must have notice regarding what their public record may include, and they must also know how that information will be maintained and disseminated. In states that collectively bargain, record keeping and reporting are terms and conditions of employment subject to negotiations. In districts that do not collectively bargain, record keeping and reporting are aspects of employment protected by a variety of federal and state laws addressing individual privacy and the public's right to know. In summary, record keeping and reporting are probably subject to law and contract prescriptions more than any other aspect of human resource management.

THEORY INTO PRACTICE

1. Review your state's Privacy Act and determine the extent to which the law protects teacher records from public disclosure.
2. Review your state's Public Records Act and determine the extent to which it favors public disclosure.
3. What are some of the documents and materials defined as public records in your state?
4. Interview your district's human resource administrator regarding the frequency of requests for public disclosure of the schools records pertaining to human resource management.
5. As an experiment, request a public record from your own, or a neighboring school district, and comment on the district's willingness to comply with your request. Were you asked to give a reason for your request?
6. Conduct an inspection throughout your district regarding the posting of federal and state laws affecting human resource management, specifically, Title VII, Title IX, the Americans with Disabilities Act, and the Family and Medical Leave Act, and report on the extent of district compliance with posting requirements.
7. Interview a random cadre of teachers in your district to determine their familiarity with the rights accorded them by Title VII, Title IX, the Americans with Disabilities Act, and the Family and Medical Leave Act.

8. If you are in a district that collectively bargains, how does the contract protect teacher interests in the record-keeping process?

9. If you are in a district that does not collectively bargain, how are official teacher records developed, monitored for accuracy, accessed, and disseminated?

10. What programs does your district provide to familiarize teachers with their rights and responsibilities under law and contract?

NOTES

1. 5 U.S.C. § 552a, Pub. L. No. 93-579 (1974).

2. *See, e.g.,* State *ex rel.* Dispatch Printing Co. v. Wells, 481 N.E.2d 632 (Ohio 1985).

3. *See, e.g.,* Brouillet v. Cowles Publ'g Co., 791 P.2d 526 (Wash. 1990); Minneapolis Fed'n of Teachers, AFL-CIO, Local 59 v. Minneapolis Pub. Schs., Special Sch. Dist., 512 N.W.2d 107 (Minn. Ct. App. 1994); Wooster Republican Printing Co. v. City of Wooster, 383 N.E.2d 124 (Ohio 1978).

4. Hovet v. Hebron Pub. Sch. Dist., 419 N.W.2d 189 (N.D. 1988).

5. *Brouillet,* 791 P.2d at 526.

6. Klein Independent Sch. Dist. v. Mattox, 830 F.2d 576 (5th Cir. 1987), *cert. denied,* 485 U.S. 1008 (1988); *Hovet,* 419 N.W.2d at 189.

7. Bowman v. Parma Bd. of Educ., 542 N.E.2d 663 (Ohio App. 1988).

8. *Bowman,* 542 N.E.2d at 663.

9. State *ex rel.* Sun Newspapers v. Westlake Bd. of Educ., 601 N.E.2d 173 (Ohio App. 1991).

10. Klein Independent Sch. Dist. v. Mattox, 830 F.2d 576 (5th Cir. 1987), *cert. denied,* 485 U.S. 1008 (1988).

11. *Freedom of Information Act Compilation and Analysis,* House Committee on Government Operations, 90th Cong., 2d Sess. 7 (1968).

12. T. Breckenridge, "Public Records aren't Made Public," *The Plain Dealer* 27 (March 2001), sec. 2B.

13. 5 U.S.C. § 552(a)(4)(E).

14. Cuneo v. Rumsfeld, 553 F.2d 1360, 1363–64 (D.C. Cir. 1977).

15. Northcross v. Bd. of Educ. of the Memphis City Schs., 412 U.S. 427 (1973).

16. *See, e.g.,* Cook v. Watt, 597 F. Supp. 552, 555 (D. Alaska 1984).

17. Halperin v. Department of State, 565 F.2d 699, 706 n.11 (D.C. Cir. 1977).

Index

adversarial bargaining, 49–53. *See also* collective bargaining process

advertising the job, 121–22. *See also* recruitment

advisory arbitration, 62. *See also* alternative dispute resolution

affirmative action, 82–84, 122–33, 130. *See also* recruitment; Title VII of the Civil Rights Act of 1964

affirmative defenses, 86–88. *See also* Title IX of the Education Amendments of 1972

Age Discrimination in Employment Act, 81. *See also* Title VII of the Civil Rights Act of 1964

agency shop, 26. *See also* collective bargaining

alternative dispute resolution, 59–63; rights arbitration, 70–75. *See also* advisory arbitration; arbitration; binding arbitration; fact-finding; interest arbitration; last best offer binding arbitration; mediation

Americans with Disabilities Act, 90–93; disparate impact, 93; Equal Employment Opportunity Commission (EEOC), 93; medical exams, 91; qualified disabled individual, 91; reasonable accommodation, 91–92; remedies, 92, 94; retaliation, 93; right to sue letter, 94. *See also* disability; drug testing; substantially limiting impairment; undue hardship

Another Set of Eyes, 187. *See also* supervision

application process, 123; forms, 127–29

arbitration, 62. *See also* alternative dispute resolution

arrests, 141. *See also* reference checking

bargaining unit, 23–24. *See also* collective bargaining

binding arbitration, 63. *See also* alternative dispute resolution

bona fide occupational qualification, 118–19. *See also* planning function

certification/licensure, 131–33; citizenship, 132; disparate impact, 131; emergency licensure, 133; license revocation, 133; licenses, 133; requirements, 131–32. *See also* loyalty oaths; National Teachers Exam

Civil Rights Act of 1991, 80–81. *See also* Title VII of the Civil Rights Act of 1964

COBRA, 100

collaborative bargaining, 49–53. *See also* collective bargaining process

About the Authors

Bernadette Marczely completed her doctoral work in educational administration at Columbia University and served as a public school teacher, principal, and district administrator before assuming her current position as a professor in the College of Education at Cleveland State University. At present, she is the director of Cleveland State's graduate program in educational supervision, a program designed to prepare and license future public school administrators.

In addition, Marczely received a law degree from Cleveland Marshall College of Law and is a licensed Ohio attorney with a practice limited to employment and labor arbitration. As an active member of the American Arbitration Association, she has been asked to render decisions on a wide variety of workplace issues in both the public and private sector.

Marczely's research centers on employment and labor law and on the application of employment and labor law to actual workplace practice. She has published extensively in these areas, particularly concerning the effect of recent court decisions interpreting existing law on the public school environment and administrative practice. This text is based on that research and is designed to familiarize future school administrators with current legal mandates affecting school management.

David W. Marczely completed his doctoral work in meteorology at the Pennsylvania State University and his law degree at Cleveland Marshall College of Law. David Marczely is an environmental scientist and a licensed Ohio attorney with a background in both education and business. Before coming to Ohio, Marczely was a professor at Southern Connecticut State University in the Department of Earth Science and taught both Meteorology and Earth Science.

Since receiving his law degree, Marczely has worked as an environmental compliance officer with the Environmental Design Group. This position has given Marczely the opportunity to combine both his scientific and legal interests. In addition, he is an adjunct professor at Cleveland Marshall College of Law, teaching environmental and administrative law.

Marczely is the current chair of the Northern Ohio Chapter of the Air and Waste Management Association and is its former newsletter editor. He has also published several articles dealing with environmental issues and coauthored several employment and labor law publications.